THE ULTIMATE MIXED MARTIAL ARTS TRAINING GUIDE

TECHNIQUES FOR FITNESS, SELF DEFENSE & COMPETITION

CHAD SEIBERT

BETTERWAY SPORTS
Cincinnati, Ohio

 Published by Betterway Sports, an imprint of F+W Media, Inc., 4700 East Galbraith Road, Cincinnati, Ohio 45236. (800) 289-0963. First edition.

For more fine books from F+W Media, visit www.fwmedia.com.

13 12 11 10 09   5 4 3 2 1

Distributed in Canada by Fraser Direct
100 Armstrong Avenue
Georgetown, Ontario, Canada L7G 5S4
Tel: (905) 877-4411

Distributed in the U.K. and Europe by
David & Charles
Brunel House, Newton Abbot, Devon, TQ12 4PU, England
Tel: (+44) 1626-323200, Fax: (+44) 1626-323319
E-mail: postmaster@davidandcharles.co.uk

Distributed in Australia by Capricorn Link
P.O. Box 704, Windsor, NSW 2756 Australia
Tel: (02) 4577-3555

Library of Congress Cataloging-in-Publication Data

Plyler, Danny.
The ultimate mixed martial arts training guide : techniques for fitness, self-defense, and competition / Danny Plyler and Chad Seibert.
p. cm.
Includes bibliographical references and index.
ISBN 978-1-55870-883-9 (pbk. : alk. paper)
1. Martial arts--Training. I. Seibert, Chad. II. Title.
GV1102.7.T7P57 2009
796.815--dc22   2009018748

Edited by *Kelly Nickell*
Designed by *Terri Woesner*
Photography by *Ric Deliantoni*
Production coordinated by *Mark Griffin*

Dedication

To Mom, Dad, and L: Simple words will never be able to express how much I love you and how honored I am to have your presence in my life. God gave me the best family in the entire world, and you are the inspiration for all that I do. I will be forever grateful for your support, encouragement, and strength. Every day you motivate me to be a better human being and to go after my goals with a warrior's spirit.
I love you.

Chad Seibert

This book is dedicated to my Lord and savior, Jesus Christ. Your love is my true strength. My wife, Beth, without your love, support, and understanding this would not have been possible. You are my hero! My mother, Carol, the sacrifices you made to ensure we had a home, evening meals together, and clothing was amazing. There is no doubt where I get my fight from!

Danny Plyler

table OF CONTENTS

13 Weight Cutting for the Warrior ... 264

14 And Now, Standing in This Corner ... 275

1 ★★★

THE HISTORY OF MIXED MARTIAL ARTS

For thousands of years, the thrill of seeing two athletes engaged in martial competition has garnered our attention as human beings. Spectators and audiences love to see two competitors fiercely vying for supremacy, each trying to win the match and achieve victory. We become fascinated by the personal stories of the fighters, cheering them on as they test their strength, endurance, and skills against an adversary.

Today, we're witnessing the evolution of the combative arts. Singular arts have been combined and transformed into the newest and fastest growing sport in the world: mixed martial arts, or MMA. The quickest and easiest way sum up this electrifying sport is that it is an integration of Olympic boxing, Olympic wrestling, Olympic judo, Muay Thai kickboxing and Brazilian Jiu-jitsu. Fighters go all out for anywhere from fifteen to twenty-five grueling minutes of hand-to-hand combat, pushing their minds and bodies to the limit.

The top fighters in mixed martial arts are some of the most highly conditioned athletes in the world. In addition to having supreme anaerobic endurance, they also have incredible strength, flexibility, and speed. The MMA warriors at the top of the sport have developed incredibly advanced skill sets and techniques in each of the prominent combative arts. They are highly intelligent competitors who develop in-depth tactics and strategies to overcome their opponents.

Perhaps even more important than their amazing stamina or arsenal of techniques is the fact that these individuals have developed a level of mental toughness that few possess. Let's face it, how many people will voluntarily face significant bodily harm by going toe to toe against another highly trained and conditioned fighter? Call them crazy, but these Type A athletes thrive on the competition of stepping into a cage and putting their skills to the test against another warrior. And that is exactly what these men and women are: warriors.

The story of how mixed martial arts has evolved into the most up-and-coming sport of modern times is filled with excitement, challenges, disappointments, and victories. Not surprisingly, many of its participants' stories mirror the journey of the sport itself. Just like the path of the warrior, the sport has traveled a long and tough road to reach its current level of success. Perhaps that is one reason why so many fans and fighters alike enjoy the sport. And true to a warrior's creed, the proponents of mixed martial arts have no intention of stopping to rest, as the world of MMA continues to grow and develop every day.

The history of what we know today as mixed martial arts is a fascinating journey that takes us from the beaches of Brazil to the streets of Las Vegas. It is the story of how an idea can transition from a spectacle that draws enormous political criticism to the fastest growing sport in the world in under fifteen years. But like most stories, it started a long, long time ago in a place far, far away.

MMA: OLD SCHOOL STYLE

In ancient times, martial competitions were training events to test the skills of warriors in preparation for battle. Perhaps the first known equivalent of a modern day mixed martial art event was held as a part of the Olympic games in ancient Greece. The event combined elements of boxing and wrestling and formed the fundamental base for the art referred to as pankration. From the limited information we have about those early Olympic contests, there were very few rules, no time limits, and no weight classes.

The matches were often very brutal, and it wasn't uncommon for fighters to suffer severe and sometimes permanent injuries as a result of competing. Many bouts ended by one contender knocking the opponent unconscious or by joint locks that caused a fighter to submit and surrender the match. A referee was present only to enforce rules that prevented biting, eye gouging, and groin shots. These ancient Olympic pankration contests were practiced for approximately one thousand years, from 648 B.C.E. to 404 A.D., when they were abolished along with the gladiator events at the Roman Coliseum.

From Japan to Brazil

Many people are intrigued to discover that the popular term *jiu-jitsu* originally comes from the warrior art *jujutsu* that was practiced by the Japanese samurai. Although the deadly parts of this martial art were eliminated when the samurai were disbanded, jujutsu continued to expand to include a wide variety of specialty areas including some early ground-fighting techniques. At the turn of the twentieth century, an entirely new art emerged in Japan called Kodokan Judo. Founded by a man named Jigoro Kano, judo set out to merge the throwing, grappling, and striking techniques of various jujutsu styles.

In the early 1900s, a successful Japanese businessman and martial arts practitioner named Mitsuyo Maeda immigrated to Brazil. Maeda was a top student of Jigoro Kano and had made a name for himself as he traveled around the world perfecting his judo and jujutsu and taking on challenge matches to test his skills.

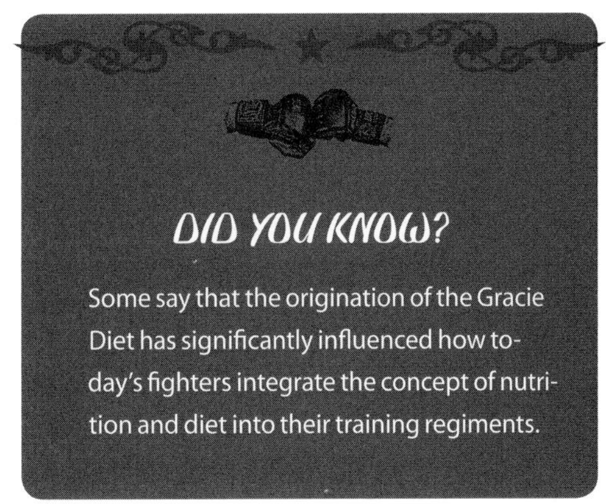

DID YOU KNOW?

Some say that the origination of the Gracie Diet has significantly influenced how today's fighters integrate the concept of nutrition and diet into their training regiments.

Around 1917, Mitsuyo Maeda married and moved to a Brazilian town known as Belém. A politician named Gastão Gracie helped him get settled, and in exchange, Maeda agreed to teach his son Carlos the art of jujutsu. In the early 1920s the Gracie family moved to Rio de Janeiro, and Carlos opened his first martial arts school around 1925. He began teaching his friends and younger brothers, including his youngest brother, Helio. Helio was a sick and frail child, and Carlos, a doctor, began formulating a nutritional regimen that would later become known as the Gracie Diet. In the following months, Helio's health improved, and he later became a noted instructor alongside his brothers. Over the decades, the Gracie family expanded upon Maeda's teachings, creating Brazilian Jiu-jitsu and pioneering a new art they refer to as Gracie Jiu-jitsu.

As the Gracie family was developing their art of jiu-jitsu, a new format of martial arts competition was becoming popular in Brazil. What became known as vale tudo entered into Brazilian mainstream culture in the late 1950s. *Vale tudo* is a Portuguese term that can be translated as "everything is allowed" and refers to the minimal rules set in place for the events. These early no-holds-barred tournaments typically pitted one style of martial arts against another, with each fighter attempting to prove his art's supremacy. Although the competitions were open to any art, the three most common styles were capoeira, luta livre, and Brazilian Jiu-jitsu.

Vale tudo came to prominence with a television showed called *Ring Heroes*, which featured members of the Gracie family, including Helio Gracie, as some of the hosts, matchmakers, and producers. Due to the violent nature of the competitions, controversy around the show eventually caused it to be cancelled, and by the mid-1960s, vale tudo returned to more of a sub-culture phenomenon. Although it effectively went underground, it continued to gain support, and the early success of vale tudo inspired the Gracie family to further advance their style of Brazilian Jiu-jitsu.

From Brazil to America

A second generation of Gracies, some of the sons of Helio and Carlos, eventually immigrated to the United States during the 1970s. When they arrived, the Gracie family brought their unique art to America and began teaching Brazilian Jiu-jitsu. To expand interest in their art, they opened schools and issued open challenges to other martial artists, inviting them to test their skills against Brazilian Jiu-jitsu. This became known as the Gracie Challenge, and eventually a videotape series, called *Gracies in Action*—which featured some of these matches—was created.

It was at this point that Rorion Gracie, Helio's oldest son, met up with a man named Art Davie. Davie was a former advertising executive living in California who had become interested in Brazilian Jiu-jitsu while doing some research for a marketing project. Eventually, he became a student of Rorion's, and along the way, he met another Gracie student, John Milius, a well-known screenwriter and filmmaker. Following the success of the Gracie videotape series, Rorion, Davie, and Milius hatched the idea to take the franchise to the next level and bring the concept of the Gracie Challenge to the TV screen.

The three entrepreneurs put together a business plan to organize a vale tudo-style tournament where fighters from various martial arts would compete against one another for a cash prize and the notoriety of being proclaimed the best hand-to-hand fighter in the world. After raising capital from investors, Rorion Gracie and Art Davie founded WOW Promotions in late 1992, and along with John Milius, the trio set about securing a contract with a pay-per-view producer for the venue. After HBO and Showtime passed on the proposal, WOW Promotions found a willing partner in May 1993 when they sealed a deal with Semaphore Entertainment Group (SEG). The name for the event was chosen and the

Ultimate Fighting Championship (UFC) was born.

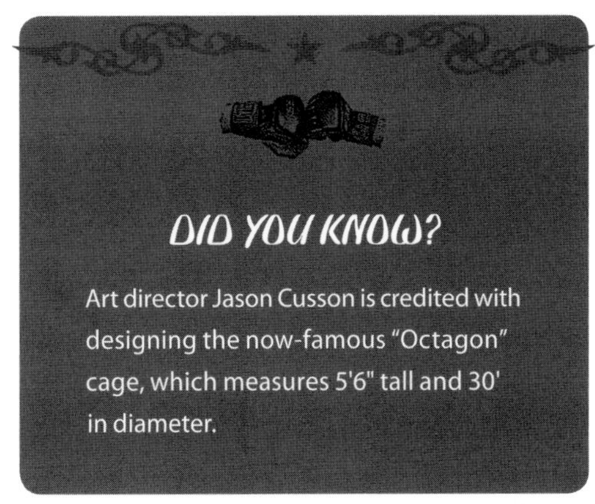

DID YOU KNOW?

Art director Jason Cusson is credited with designing the now-famous "Octagon" cage, which measures 5'6" tall and 30' in diameter.

THE PATH TO THE FIRST UFC

To select a location, it was decided that the best alternative would be a state where there was no boxing commission to interfere with the event regulations. Colorado was selected, and Denver became the host city for the venue. SEG fronted approximately $400,000 to produce the event, and in June 1993, Art Davie began searching to find fighters to fill the card. Although this was thought to be an easy task, acquiring fighters turned out to be more challenging than originally anticipated. Many protested on grounds that such an event would betray the ideals of honor and respect that traditional martial arts were founded upon. Others believed their styles were too deadly to enter the competition.

There were to be eight fighters total, and at least one was already accounted for to showcase the style of Brazilian Jiu-jitsu. Originally, it was thought that Rickson, the brother of Rorion, would represent the Gracie family name in the Ultimate Fighting Championship. Rickson was known as one of the family's best fighters, having won numerous jiu-jitsu tournaments and vale tudo matches in Brazil. However, a falling out between Rorion and Rickson led to the younger Royce Gracie being chosen as the fighter to enter the contest. Although Rickson wasn't happy about being sidelined, he chose to help ramp up Royce's training in preparation for the tournament.

After advertising in martial arts magazines and networking with old contacts, Art Davie was eventually able to secure the seven remaining fighters needed to complete the card. As was intended, the field of competitors was very diverse. Scheduled for the tournament were top-ranked kickboxer Patrick Smith, Hawaiian sumo wrestler Teila Tuli, pancrase fighter Ken Shamrock, well-known boxer Arthur Jimmerson, Dutch savate fighter Gerard Gordeau, kickboxer Kevin Rosier, and kempo stylist Zane Frazier.

There were also some logistical hurdles to overcome with the pay-per-view distribution, since it was a live event and no one was quite sure how long the fights would actually last. Rorion also had to find commentators, and well-known kickboxing champions Bill Wallace and Kathy Long were chosen along with the famous NFL football player Jim Brown. Two referees were secured from the Jiu-Jitsu Federation to manage the action once the fights got underway.

The day before the event, the fighters, coaches, and reporters gathered in a Denver hotel conference room to discuss the format and rules. Most of the fighters were under the impression that there were no rules, but were informed that biting, eye-gouging, and groin strikes were prohibited. The event would be an elimination style tournament with the winner of each match advancing to the next round. As a result, the fighters would need endurance as well as their skills to capture the championship. Combatants could win by knockout, causing their opponent to tap out, or the opponent's corner throwing in the towel. Although there were to be five rounds of five minutes, no judges were acquired because no one thought the fights would last that long.

On November 12, 1993 the first Ultimate Fighting Championship was held at the Michnicols Sports Arena in Denver, Colorado. No one, including the commentators, knew what to expect. How would a boxer fair against Brazilian Jiu-jitsu? Would a sumo wrestler defeat a savate fighter? Could top-ranked kickboxer Pat Smith take the championship with his technique and speed? Would the muscular Ken Shamrock dominate the tournament with his strength and agility? As pay-per-viewers tuned in, what was about to happen was anyone's guess, but it would certainly change the martial arts forever.

THE ULTIMATE FIGHTING CHAMPIONSHIP BEGINS

The first fight of the evening was the sumo wrestler Teila Tuli vs. the savate fighter Gerard Gordeau. Tuli charged across the ring, but after a flurry of punches and a hard round kick to his head from Gordeau, the referee intervened and stopped the match. Bloodied and missing several teeth, Tuli had lost in less than thirty seconds. The next match was equally devastating as Kevin Rosier faced off against Zane Frazier. After a rough bout, Rosier suffered a broken jaw, and after the fight, Frazier was admitted to the hospital for a severe asthma attack.

In the third match, Royce Gracie took down boxer Arthur Jimmerson, who tapped out quickly after just a couple of strikes. Unlike the competitors in the first two matches, Royce and Jimmerson left the ring more or less unharmed. Royce went on to challenge the heavily favored Ken Shamrock in a semifinal match—after Shamrock gained a win with an ankle lock over Pat Smith. Despite a forty-pound weight disadvantage,

Royce secured a takedown and submitted Shamrock with a choke in just under sixty seconds.

Gracie now became the crowd favorite, and the crowd was on its feet as Royce came out for the finals. Gerard Gordeau, despite suffering a broken hand and a couple of Tuli's teeth still embedded in his foot, had beaten Kevin Rosier with a series of punches and elbows and had also advanced to the finals. The match lasted only two minutes, as Royce executed another takedown, got to Gordeau's back, choked him out, and became the first Ultimate Fighting Champion.

An Unexpected Star Is Born

When the UFC started, very few people thought the mild-mannered Royce would have a chance against the bigger, stronger, and faster opponents on the card. It was a classic David vs. Goliath story, and the best part was that it was completely real. In less than four minutes of competition inside the Octagon, Royce Gracie had defeated three opponents in front of a stadium full of spectators and almost 90,000 pay-per-viewers. If his impressive victories didn't win people over, his humility after winning certainly did.

After taking the championship and being asked about his plans for the $50,000 prize, a calm Royce said, "I'm not here for the money; I'm here for the honor of my family." It was clear that even though some believed that this event would damage the reputation of martial arts, Royce and the Gracie family were very serious about the qualities of honor and respect.

In another display of his modesty, when the interviewer asked Royce about his future plans, he simply replied, "There are no plans. I'm just Royce." But SEG and WOW Productions definitely had future plans. The show was a tremendous success, and almost overnight, Gracie Jiu-jitsu was in huge demand. People wanted to see more of Royce, and the UFC spawned a renewed interest in martial arts. Everyone wanted to learn the techniques of Brazilian Jiu-jitsu. A second Ultimate Fighting Championship was scheduled for just four months later.

UFC II, held on March 11, 1994, featured an expanded card of sixteen fighters from over ten different martial arts styles. This time Art Davie had no problem filling the card, as he received almost 250 applications. Kickboxer Pat Smith returned, although the popular Ken Shamrock was not able to compete due to a broken hand.

There were other changes as well, including the complete elimination of rounds and the addition of the now famous UFC referee "Big" John McCarthy. Some of the calls made by the referees in the first Ultimate Fighting Championship sparked controversy, and Rorion felt that

McCarthy's 6'4", 250-pound frame and law enforcement experience made him an excellent replacement choice.

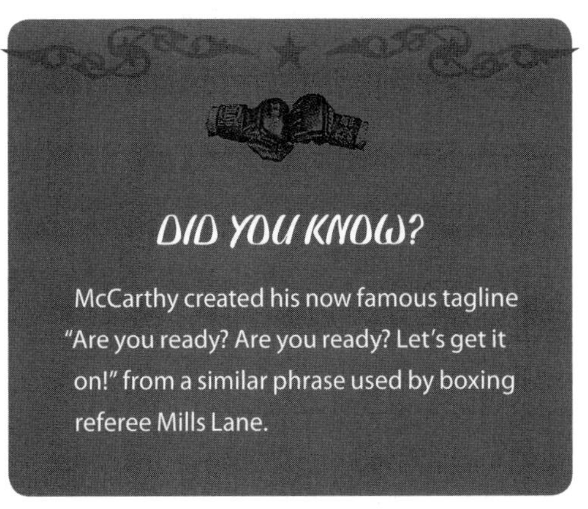

McCarthy created his now famous tagline "Are you ready? Are you ready? Let's get it on!" from a similar phrase used by boxing referee Mills Lane.

Although the first show was a success, other alterations beginning in UFC II would eventually lead to heavy criticism from the media. The tagline for the event became "There Are No Rules," and a press release that stated, "Each match will run until there is a designated winner, by means of knockout, surrender, doctor's intervention, or death." It was that last part that critics in the press used over and over again to emphasize the violent aspects of the event. Another overhyped marketing ploy was the statement that the event was "banned in forty-nine states." But the publicity worked, and more than 125,000 viewers tuned in for the second Ultimate Fighting Championship.

There were several interesting bouts, but all eyes were on Royce Gracie to see if he could continue his winning streak and retain his title. Royce tapped out Japanese karate contender Minoki Ichihara with a combination arm bar and choke for his first victory of the competition. Next, he faced kung fu stylist Jason Delucia, defeating Delucia by arm bar. In an anticipated matchup, Royce's third bout was against another jiu-jitsu practitioner, Remco Pardoel. Pardoel was over one hundred pounds heavier than Gracie, but fell victim to a gi choke in less than two minutes.

Kickboxer Pat Smith had returned with a vengeance and made his way through the tournament to face Royce in the finals. In typical Gracie fashion, Royce took the kickboxer down and then started laying on some punches. Smith's corner threw in the towel, and Royce was again named the Ultimate Fighting Champion. The Gracie family hoisted him in the air, with Royce beaming a smile and holding his $60,000 check. With his second tournament win, Royce proved once and for all that Brazilian Jiu-jitsu was here to stay.

The Saga Continues

In preparation for UFC III, to be held in North Carolina on September 9, 1994, SEG centered its marketing on the two favored contenders: Royce Gracie and Ken Shamrock. This set the stage for an epic battle between the two warriors, which unfortunately failed to materialize. Royce, after winning a grueling match against Kimo Leopoldo, forfeited his next fight against Canadian Harold Howard. It was later discovered that Royce was suffering from hypoglycemia and was severely dehydrated. Shamrock won his first and second bouts, but after finding out that he wouldn't face Gracie in the finals, he decided to call it quits. An alternate, Steve Jennum, walked into the ring completely fresh and beat out Howard to win the tournament.

Just three months later, UFC IV was held in Tulsa, Oklahoma on December 16, 1994. Royce was back and swept the tournament, defeating Dan Severn in the finals. Severn, a wrestler with more than seventy amateur records, returned in UFC V to claim the championship. He also ushered in a new era for the Ultimate Fighting Championship, one where wrestlers would dominate the competition.

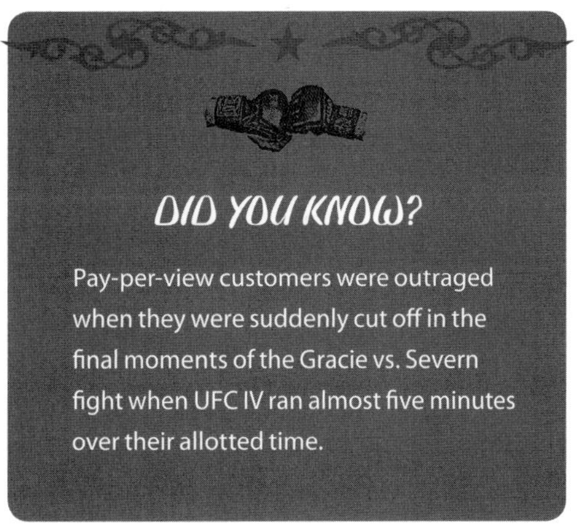

DID YOU KNOW?

Pay-per-view customers were outraged when they were suddenly cut off in the final moments of the Gracie vs. Severn fight when UFC IV ran almost five minutes over their allotted time.

In addition to the tournament style, UFC V featured the event's first super-fight: Gracie vs. Shamrock. Their match was heavily marketed, but proved somewhat disappointing to viewers as the match became a thirty-minute stalemate with neither fighter pressing the action. A five-minute overtime period yielded a strong punch from Shamrock, but ended in a draw since there were no judges. Nonetheless, the event was the most successful to date, with over 286,000 people watching on pay-per-view.

THE UFC CHANGES HANDS AND FACES NEW CHALLENGES

Despite the success, WOW Productions and SEG were having serious disagreements when it came to the future of the Ultimate Fighting Championship. Rorion didn't like the idea of time limits, which became a necessity to stay within pay-per-view time frames. He was also against a proposed introduction of judges and additional rule changes. Art Davie and Rorion were also having their own personal differences, and just twelve days after UFC V, SEG bought out WOW Productions to become the sole owner of the UFC. SEG president Bob Meyrowitz hired Davie as the matchmaker for the Ultimate Fighting Championship, and Royce Gracie, with Rorion out of the picture, stepped down from competition.

Political pressure also increased against the UFC. Arizona's Senator John McCain called it "human cockfighting" and pressured broadcasters to pull the events. McCain also sent a letter to state governors trying to persuade them to stop the tournaments from being hosted in their states. State athletic commissions also joined the mounting public crusade against the UFC. Even the president of the American Medical Association released a statement denouncing the contests.

SEG countered the rising accusations by stating that the Ultimate Fighting Championship was actually safer than most major sports, including boxing. Although it might seem like bare-knuckle fighters would inflict more damage than professional boxers with gloves, the UFC argued that the opposite was true. A fighter had to consider the limited number of headshots he could deliver before the small bones in his hands would break. A boxer had hand wraps, tape, and heavy gloves that protected the fists and allowed him to deliver an estimated five hundred head shots in a twelve-round bout. Boxers were also given a standing eight count if they were knocked down and the match could continue, which contributed to a significant number of concussions.

In addition, boxers took all the punishment to only two targets, the head and the body. In the UFC, fighters had numerous ways to win, including a multitude of submissions. Although occasionally some injuries did occur as a result of submissions, they were no more serious than bone or joint injuries that happen in football or soccer. SEG also countered with testimonials from the ringside doctors and cut men who attended to the fighters. They attested to the minimal injuries sustained during fights and supported the claim that the UFC was a reasonably safe tournament.

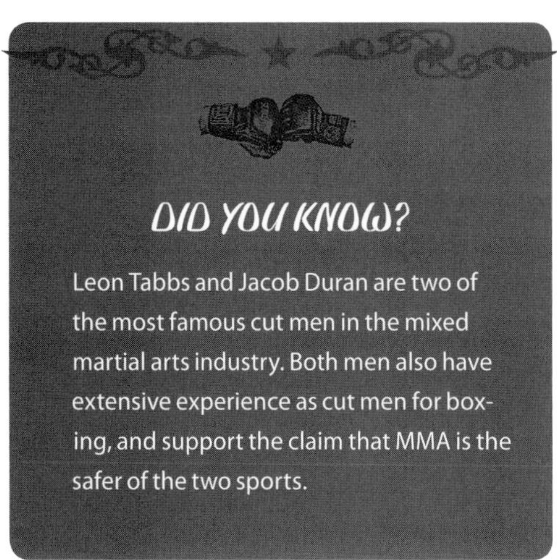

DID YOU KNOW?

Leon Tabbs and Jacob Duran are two of the most famous cut men in the mixed martial arts industry. Both men also have extensive experience as cut men for boxing, and support the claim that MMA is the safer of the two sports.

While SEG was busy trying to persuade politicians and the media about the relative safety of the UFC events, its marketing department had a completely different angle. The advertising hyped the "no rules" slogans and played on the raw appeal of seeing two fighters battle it out inside of a cage. Unfortunately, this approach gave the media even more ammunition to hammer the events and would continue to plague SEG plans for expansion.

New Trends in Ultimate Fighting

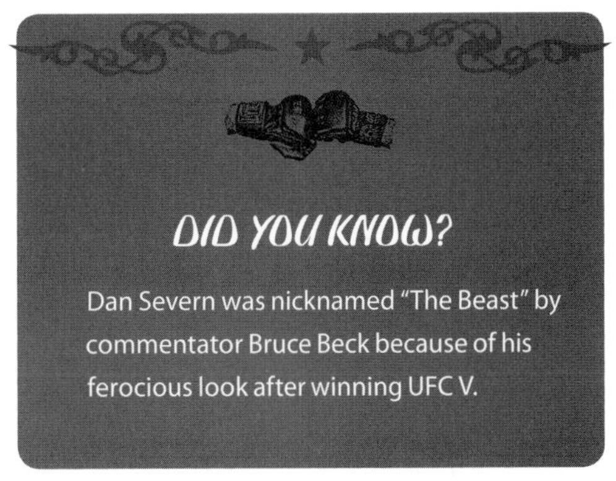

DID YOU KNOW?

Dan Severn was nicknamed "The Beast" by commentator Bruce Beck because of his ferocious look after winning UFC V.

Up until UFC IV, Royce Gracie and Brazilian Jiu-jitsu had dominated the competition. As fighters and other martial artists were scrambling to learn Gracie Jiu-jitsu, a fascinating trend began to emerge. Everyone began to add jiu-jitsu to his own style, and the door to mixed martial arts started to open.

Although he lost in the UFC IV finals to Royce Gracie, Dan Severn elevated the skill level of the Ultimate Fighting Championship. In their hard-fought match, Severn dominated Royce with his wrestling skills for fifteen minutes until the patient Royce was able to secure a triangle choke and get Severn to tap out. Although Gracie won and the crowd went wild, it was clear that Severn's wrestling ability was phenomenal.

When Royce skipped the tournament matches in UFC V to fight Ken Shamrock in the super fight, the door was open for a new fighter to take the lead. On April 7, 1995, Severn returned to the Octagon and swept the tournament by mixing his exceptional wrestling skills with effective striking. By winning the UFC, Severn proved that wrestling was an important element of fighting.

As Royce left the UFC after it was sold to SEG, Severn became one of its new rising stars along with Ken Shamrock. The two new stars battled each other in the UFC VI super fight, where Shamrock secured a victory by a guillotine choke in two minutes and fifteen seconds. Despite his super fight losses to Gracie and Shamrock, Severn set the stage for the evolution of the next wave of competitors.

Alongside Severn and Shamrock, another unlikely star emerged: UFC bad boy David "Tank" Abbott. Abbott was a classic street fighter with heavy-handed punches that devastated his opponents. His aggressive, in-your-face style and persona would create a cult-like following within the UFC. With Abbott racking up several victories, it was clear that effective striking was also coming into the fold, as the skill sets of fighters continued to expand.

In UFC VIII, a new fighter stepped into the Octagon for the first time and successfully mixed great striking ability with excellent wrestling ability. Don Frye had wrestled under Dan Severn and also held a successful winning record in professional boxing. The 6'1" Arizona native looked like a muscular Tom Selleck and weighed in at just over two hundred pounds. Frye was able to defend his opponents' takedowns and punish them with hard, accurate punches, winning him the Ultimate Fighting Championship. Frye won his single matchup in UFC IX and returned for UFC X, where he made it to the finals to face Mark Coleman.

Mark Coleman was an NCAA Ohio State wrestling champ and also competed on the U.S. Olympic wrestling team in 1992. Although Coleman didn't have any professional boxing experience, he was able to trade punches with Frye and the bout went an exhausting eleven minutes. Coleman emerged victorious and clinched the UFC X title after a second doctor stoppage ended the match. Mixing wrestling techniques and superior striking skills became the new recipe for success in the UFC.

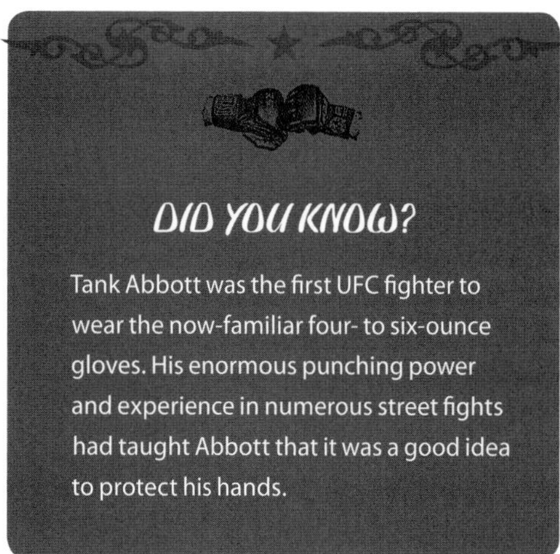

DID YOU KNOW?

Tank Abbott was the first UFC fighter to wear the now-familiar four- to six-ounce gloves. His enormous punching power and experience in numerous street fights had taught Abbott that it was a good idea to protect his hands.

Tough Times for the UFC

Unfortunately, the SEG had its hands full trying to keep the UFC afloat. Competition to the UFC had entered the picture with the World Combat Championship, which was held just one month after UFC VII in October 1995. The event was held in front of a sellout crowd in Salem, North Carolina, and featured a grand prize of $120,000. Topping the fight card was Renzo Gracie, a cousin of Royce, who won the elimination tournament and all three of his matches in less than nine minutes of total competition time. The event was successful, but financing proved to be an obstacle to create any additional shows.

Battlecade Extreme Fighting was also in the mix, holding its debut event in New York on November 18, 1995. Just thirty-six hours before the first match was set to begin, mounting political pressure caused the entire event to be moved to North Carolina. The Battlecade fight card featured a strong Gracie Jiu-jitsu contingent, with Ralph Gracie, Carlson Gracie Jr., and Gracie Jiu-jitsu students Mario Sperry and Marcus Silveira. Although the Extreme Fighting shows featured excellent fighters and great matches, political and media opposition limited the success of the first two Battlecade events.

If rising competition wasn't enough, a change in leadership at TCI Cable caused the UFC to be dropped from the company's cable network.

Time Warner Cable quickly followed suit, and since both companies jointly held majority ownership in Viewer's Choice, the largest pay-per-view distributor, the decision was also made to drop the UFC from its lineup. This effectively meant that the UFC lost a majority of its biggest income stream, and distribution was now limited to less than 10 percent of its original pay-per-view reach. SEG had to target the much smaller satellite TV audience instead, which brought in only a minimal amount of revenue.

Although its cable reach was dwindling, SEG ended up with a lucky break when it came to competition in North America. Due to its lower viewership numbers, Battlecade was losing even more pay-per-view distribution, and the company folded a couple of weeks after the fourth Extreme Fighting show in April 1997. Some of the fighters from Extreme Fighting then migrated over to the UFC, including Battlecade champion kickboxer Maurice Smith and wrestler Kevin Jackson.

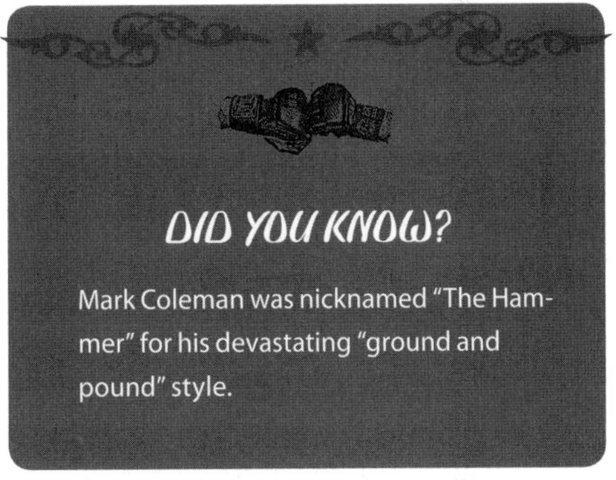

Changing Things Up

To help assuage the criticism of the tournaments, SEG decided to institute a few more rules. Head butts and groin shots became illegal, and all fighters were now required to wear four- to six-ounce gloves. They also changed things up within the event by shifting to four-man tournaments with lightweight and heavyweight divisions in UFC XII. In May 1997, SEG added a middleweight division at UFC XIII. A couple of future stars emerged from the latter tournament in the form of wrestlers Randy Couture and Tito Ortiz.

UFC XIV produced one of the greatest battles inside the Octagon that fans had seen to date. Extreme Fighting champion and kickboxer Maurice Smith fought UFC champion and wrestler Mark Coleman on July 27, 1997. The classic matchup of striker vs. grappler had fans standing on their feet. Coleman secured a quick takedown and rained down punches, but Smith defended well and forced his opponent to exhaust energy. The fight returned to the feet after nine minutes on the ground, and Smith delivered some effective strikes.

Coleman secured another takedown and the match stayed on the ground until the end of the fifteen-minute regulation period. The fight continued and went into double overtime with an exhausted Coleman losing to

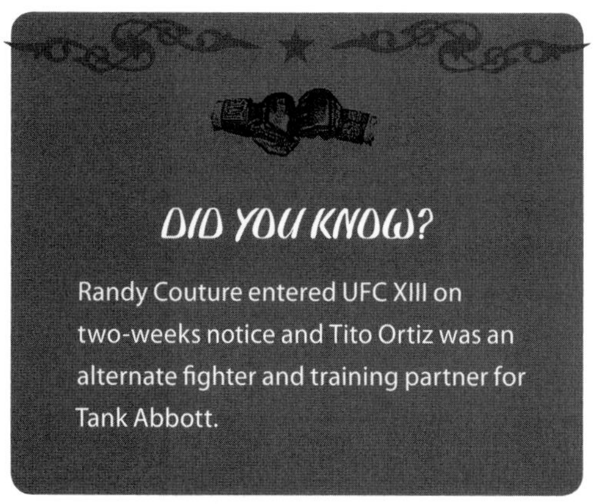

DID YOU KNOW?

Randy Couture entered UFC XIII on two-weeks notice and Tito Ortiz was an alternate fighter and training partner for Tank Abbott.

a well-conditioned Smith by unanimous decision. Maurice Smith was named the UFC Heavyweight Champion and had demonstrated that a good striker could still perform well inside the Octagon.

Five months later, in December 1997, the Ultimate Fighting Championship traveled to Japan in an attempt to broaden its base. Dubbed "Ultimate Japan," the event would feature the first ever middleweight championship match. Although a few UFC fighters were ready to battle the Extreme Fighting champion Kevin Jackson for the title, deciding who would get the shot wasn't easy. Guy Mezger and Jerry Bohlander were successful UFC competitors and both protégés of Ken Shamrock and his Lion's Den school. Ken's non-biological brother, Frank Shamrock, was also in the running after successfully winning the King of Pancrase title.

Frank won out against his fellow Lion's Den competitors and got the slot against Kevin Jackson in a highly anticipated championship match. Jackson charged across the cage with a flurry of punches and took Shamrock down to the ground. Shamrock, from the guard position, immediately trapped one of Jackson's arms and locked it in an arm bar that forced Jackson to tap. Frank Shamrock had just submitted a world-class wrestler and Extreme Fighting Champion in only sixteen seconds! The newly crowned UFC middleweight champion would become one of the most likable fighters in the Ultimate Fighting Championship and one of its most notable fighters.

Heavyweight champion Maurice Smith defended his title against up-and-comer Randy Couture in a very technical match. Couture secured a takedown early in the fight, but spent the entire fifteen-minute regulation time period in Smith's guard. Two overtime periods gave Smith a chance to land some leg kicks and earned Couture another takedown, although neither would be able to finish the other. The match, and the heavyweight title, went to Couture by decision. Couture subsequently left the UFC and relinquished his title to pursue other interests, although he returned in UFC XXVIII and went on to become one of the sport's most famous figures.

In March 1998, UFC XVI introduced a lightweight division, and newcomer Pat Miletich became the lightweight champion. Miletich successfully defended his title and later created a training camp called Miletich Fighting Systems that became one of the most prominent training systems in MMA. Frank Shamrock also successfully defended his middleweight title in UFC XVI, XVII, and Ultimate Brazil.

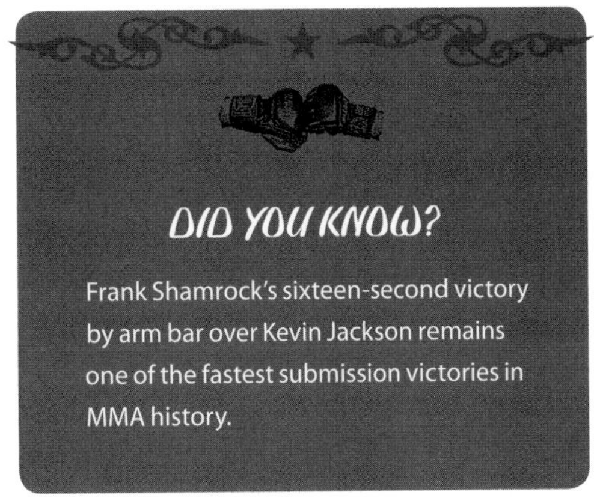

DID YOU KNOW?

Frank Shamrock's sixteen-second victory by arm bar over Kevin Jackson remains one of the fastest submission victories in MMA history.

UFC XVII was the second to last event to have a tournament-style format, as SEG started to transition to single matchups. It featured the first appearance of future MMA stars Chuck Liddell, Dan Henderson, and Carlos Newton. Tito Ortiz was also working his way up the ranks and started to develop a following with an aggressive fighting style and brash attitude that reminded fans of his training partner, Tank Abbott. With wins against Lion's Den fighters Jerry Bohlander and Guy Mezger, the "Huntington Beach Bad Boy" was the next in line to fight Frank Shamrock for the middleweight title.

A significant UFC rule change occurred in July 1999. SEG, in an effort to get on the good side of state athletic commissions, introduced five-minute rounds into the competition. Preliminary bouts would be two rounds, main event fights would be three rounds, and championship matches would be five rounds. There would be a one-minute rest period in between rounds. SEG invited the Nevada State Athletic Commission to observe UFC XXI, hoping to persuade them to sanction the sport. Eventually, SEG decided against pushing for a vote in Nevada because it didn't feel it had majority support to pass the bill.

When Ortiz and Shamrock collided on September 24, 1999 in UFC XXII, Ortiz pressed the action against Shamrock, getting a takedown and landing solid punches in the first round. The second and third rounds were similar, and Ortiz seemed to be controlling the fight. Near the end of the fourth round, however, Shamrock turned the tide with a barrage of strikes that stunned Ortiz and gave Shamrock the win. Shamrock later left the UFC, but Ortiz had cemented a loyal fan base and continued to grow in popularity.

Changing of the Guard

Despite changes, the UFC was continuing to lose money and on the verge of bankruptcy. During 1999, the events became less frequent, relying on gate sales to generate the majority of the income. SEG stopped releasing the videos of the events after UFC XXII, which took out another part of the franchise's revenue stream.

In April 2000, the California State Athletic Commission created a set of rules to govern mixed martial arts events. Due to budget restrictions at the time, the rules were not able to receive a formal commission vote in California. Another opportunity surfaced when Larry Hazard, commissioner for the New Jersey Athletic Commission, stepped up to test an MMA event under those rules. The test was successful and New Jersey adopted the Unified Rules of Mixed Martial Arts in the fall of 2000. UFC XXVIII, held in November at the Taj Mahal Casino, was the first Ultimate Fighting Championship to be sanctioned by the New Jersey State Athletic Commission. This was a major milestone and set the stage for the future of the sport.

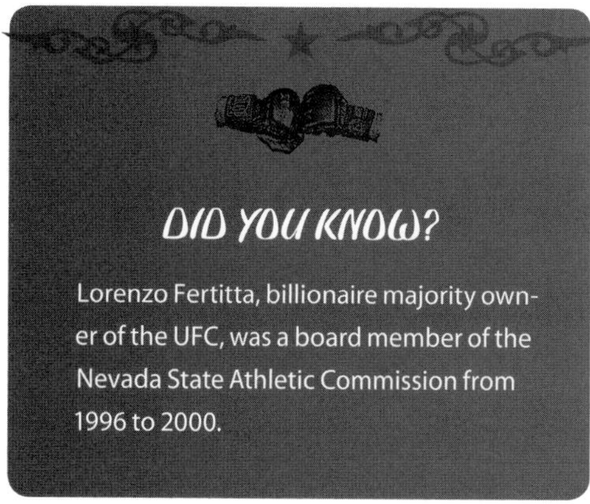

DID YOU KNOW?

Lorenzo Fertitta, billionaire majority owner of the UFC, was a board member of the Nevada State Athletic Commission from 1996 to 2000.

In late 2000, rumors surfaced that SEG President Robert Meyrowitz wanted to sell the UFC. Word eventually reached Dana White, who was managing Tito Ortiz, Chuck Liddell, and several other UFC fighters. As he was attempting to negotiate his fighter contracts, White learned that the UFC was nearly bankrupt and might be open to a sale. An entrepreneur, former amateur boxer, and gym owner, Dana White saw potential in the fledgling company. The street-smart manager decided to contact one of his longtime friends, Lorenzo Fertitta, to see about putting together an offer to buy the UFC from SEG.

Fertitta was co-owner of Station Casinos Inc., one of the largest casino companies in the country. His father had founded the successful business and eventually retired and handed over operations to his sons Lorenzo and Frank (III). Together, the Fertitta brothers expanded the casino holdings, taking the company public and turning it into a billion-dollar company.

Fertitta had gone to high school with White, and the two reconnected at a friend's wedding after White moved to Las Vegas. While running aerobics classes at a few Vegas gyms, White began to train Fertitta, and the two started to work out together. They also shared a common passion for boxing. As a result of this interest in fighting, Fertitta joined White at UFC events. After seeing the live fights, Fertitta was hooked and started taking Brazilian Jiu-jitsu lessons from one of the UFC fighters.

White approached Lorenzo and his brother Frank about the opportunity. All three shared a vision for where they could take the company, including changing the focus and marketing of the events. They evaluated the strategies needed to make the brand successful and decided that purchasing the UFC could turn out to be a very profitable business investment. The three friends formed Zuffa, LLC and approached Meyrowitz at SEG with an offer to buy the UFC. Out of cash and out of options, Meyrowitz sold the company to Zuffa for approximately $2 million in January 2001.

The Fertitta brothers, their hands full with Station Casinos, appointed White as Zuffa's president to run the day-to-day operations for the UFC. For the first time, the Ultimate Fighting Championship had everything it needed: access to significant capital, important connections, and a talented leader at the helm. Success didn't happen overnight, though, and the Zuffa trio knew they would benefit most by taking a long-term, strategic approach to developing the UFC. Several changes needed to be made, and White set out to relaunch the brand, starting only a month later with UFC 30.

A New Look for MMA

Held on February 23, 2001, at the Taj Mahal Casino in Atlantic City, UFC 30 was a breath of fresh air for fans in attendance. When Lorenzo Fertitta first started attending UFC events, he found that there was little to no merchandise available for purchase. "I couldn't even get a t-shirt," he later said in an interview. Zuffa wanted to capitalize on this missed revenue stream and had full-color programs, posters, and t-shirts for sale. To create a better event experience, UFC 30 featured the ambiance of a rock concert, complete with a laser light show. To add to the excitement that night, Tito Ortiz won the championship main event by knocking out Evan Tanner in the first round.

Another event was held at the Taj Mahal Casino, where future lightweight champion B.J. Penn made his debut, before moving to the larger Meadowlands venue for UFC 32. Although Zuffa lost more than $2 million on the event, they were able to pack the arena with the largest attendance to date through billboard advertising. They also invited key business and media connections, which helped to secure a pay-per-view distribution deal with In Demand cable. Dana White was also working on getting the UFC sanctioned by the Nevada State Athletic Commission so that some of the events could move to Las Vegas.

The Zuffa team knew that getting sanctioned by state athletic commissions was the key to getting a wider pay-per-view distribution. Working under the new rules for mixed martial arts, the UFC adopted the now standard weight divisions: lightweights were at 155 pounds, welterweight at 170 pounds, middleweight at 185 pounds, and light heavyweight at 205 pounds. By working closely and cooperatively with the state athletic commissions, the UFC started to regain respect among some politicians and legislators. Even Senator John McCain, who had previously led the charge against the events, began to change his viewpoint about MMA.

On the marketing side, Zuffa's strategy was to use targeted advertising in men's magazines like *Playboy*, *Maxim*, and *Stuff* to increase demand. The advertising began to reflect a new direction, dropping the "no rules" slogans and shying away from the brutal side of the events. Instead, ads focused on labeling MMA the *sport* of the future. It was precisely this decision that helped White exponentially grow the UFC brand. This new approach helped Zuffa move toward the goal of making each show bigger and better.

DID YOU KNOW?

When the first modern mixed martial arts event was held in the United States, the format closely mirrored the format of the ancient Olympic games: no time limits, no weight classes, and limited rules.

Newly sanctioned under the Nevada State Athletic Commission, UFC 33 was held on September 23, 2001, at the Mandalay Bay Casino in Las Vegas. The prestigious venue added respectability, and, for the first time in years, the event was available on pay-per-view. Although Zuffa hoped the event would put the Ultimate Fighting Championship back on the map, the recent terrorist attacks on the Pentagon and World Trade Center contributed to low buy rates.

In addition, the matches went over the allotted time limit and viewers didn't get to see the end of the match. Fans were also disappointed by the number of matches that stalled on the ground and went to a judge's decision. Later, a rule was implemented allowing the referee to stand fighters back up if they weren't pressing the action on the ground. In the next half dozen shows, the UFC moved around to various locations, including venues in Connecticut, Louisiana, Las Vegas, and even London. Unfortunately, pay-per-view buys remained low, and at one point, Zuffa was $44 million in the red.

Climbing to the Top

Zuffa got a boost in June 2002, when Fox Sports Net's *The Best Damn Sports Show Period* wanted to air a complete match. The event was held at a smaller venue at the Bellagio hotel in Las Vegas but was broadcast to more than 50 million homes in the United States. It was the first ever MMA match on cable TV. The mainstream exposure helped broaden the reach of the UFC and inspired the future goal of putting mixed martial arts on free cable.

Five months later, in November 2002, the MGM Grand in Las Vegas hosted UFC 40: Vendetta. It was the largest MMA event in the United States to date, with more than 13,000 fans in attendance. The main event pitted Tito Ortiz against longtime rival Ken Shamrock. Ortiz secured the victory after a dominating three rounds of pummeling Shamrock with elbow strikes.

As the UFC started to regain its popularity, White molded the new brand image of MMA. The portrayal of the events was no longer about two guys beating on each other inside a cage. It was of two highly trained and well-conditioned athletes competing against one another in an extreme sport. Hyping MMA as "the fastest growing sport in the world" and making the focus about the individual athletes helped the UFC widen its base of support.

DID YOU KNOW?

Some say that the origination of the Gracie Diet has significantly influenced how today's fighters integrate the concept of nutrition and diet into their training regiments.

Zuffa required fighters to participate in autograph sessions for fans as well as pre- and post-event press conferences. This further helped promote the image of a sport and maximized the exposure of the fighters. Websites catering to the MMA crowd also began growing at an incredible pace and helped to connect fans to the latest MMA news. In promotional advertising, Zuffa showcased interviews with fighters to help fans connect with their personal stories. The incredible talent and fitness conditioning of the fighters was also touted, and for the first time, many of the athletes started receiving the recognition they deserved.

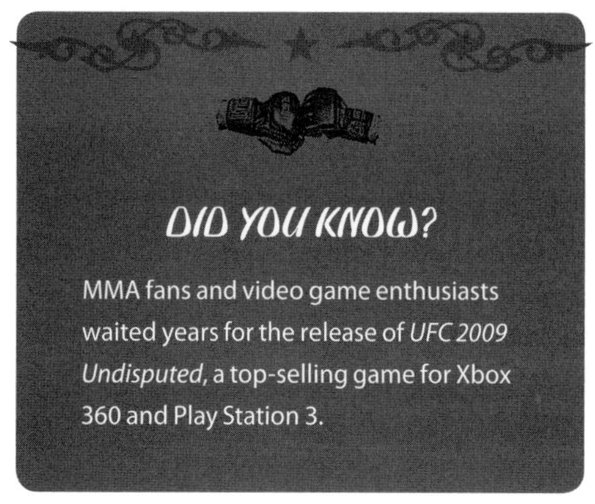

DID YOU KNOW?

MMA fans and video game enthusiasts waited years for the release of *UFC 2009 Undisputed,* a top-selling game for Xbox 360 and Play Station 3.

This also proved a useful strategy as Joe Silva, vice president of talent relations, sought to develop the UFC's top athletes into sports stars by putting together great matches. As the sport continued to evolve, the talent level increased, and fighters like Chuck Liddell and Matt Hughes rose to prominence. Zuffa focused on building action-packed events centered on great headliners and notable up-and-coming fighters.

As UFC 45: Revolution marked the tenth anniversary of the Ultimate Fighting Championship, White and the Fertitta brothers were gaining ground. Attendance was consistently more than 10,000 people, and events regularly began to gross more than $1 million in gate sales. Pay-per-view buys also began to increase, hovering around 100,000 per show.

To further increase their profit margins, Zuffa partnered with a video distribution company and began putting the UFC events back out on DVD shortly after they were held. The UFC had also entered the lucrative video game market with *UFC: Throwdown*, *UFC: Tapout* (1 & 2), and *UFC: Sudden Impact* on the major game consoles like Xbox, Gamecube, and Play Station 2.

In April 2004, UFC 47: It's On! became one of the most memorable fight cards, with a long-awaited light-heavyweight bout between Tito Ortiz and Chuck Liddell. The Iceman knocked Ortiz out in the second round and went on to face Randy Couture for the light-heavyweight title a year later.

Learning from their Fox Sports Net experience and wanting to put their product on free cable, the Zuffa team met reality-show producer Craig Piligian through their business relationship with United Talent Agency. Piligian had approached Lorenzo and Frank Fertitta about his *American Casino* show on Discovery Channel, and the group started talking about the UFC. Zuffa had knocked on a lot of doors, including MTV, CBS, ABC, ESPN, Spike, and USA, attempting to get on cable television.

Every single one had turned them down, but Craig Piligian suggested a new approach: Zuffa would front the money for the show and finance it on their own. It could then go directly to sponsors to sell advertising to cover its expenses. It was a radical idea and Dana White and Lorenzo Fertitta went to the phones, calling back the stations that had previously turned them down. Spike TV agreed and *The Ultimate Fighter* reality television show was born.

Zuffa was betting heavily on the success of the program and went to great lengths to ensure it had a well-thought-out plan for the show. The focus was on a group of fighters together in a house, showcasing their training as they competed against one another, with the winner receiving a six-figure UFC contract. For the show's format, fighters were broken down into two weight classes, with eight light heavyweights and eight middleweights. There were two teams, each coached by a top UFC fighter. Chuck Liddell and Randy Couture were selected as the coaches because the reality series also helped to promote their upcoming fight at UFC 52.

The Zuffa team was on edge though because competing shows by Oscar De La Hoya and Mark Burnett's *The Contender* made companies nervous about committing to advertising on *The Ultimate Fighter.* As a result, Zuffa was unable to secure any sponsors or even sell any commercials to help cover the costs of financing the program. At the end of filming production, they had almost $10 million invested and had to spend almost another $3 million to buy their own billboard, radio, and TV advertising to hype the release of the show.

The first episode aired on January 18, 2005, and *The Ultimate Fighter* received excellent ratings. The series increased in popularity and viewership with each show, leading up to the live event finals on April 9, 2005, at the Cox Pavilion in Las Vegas. It was the first live UFC broadcast on non-pay-per-view television and featured an exceptional main fight card. The middleweight final was between Diego Sanchez and Kenny Florian; Sanchez picked up the win by TKO and secured a contract. The light-heavyweight final between Stephan Bonner and Forrest Griffin turned out to be one of the top fights in UFC history, as the two warriors battled it out for three rounds. Fans were on their feet as the judges' decision was awarded to Griffin. White declared that "there was no loser in this fight" and also awarded Stephan Bonner a contract.

The final fight of the evening was up-and-comer Rich Franklin vs. Ken Shamrock. Franklin knocked out Shamrock and went on to become one of MMA's most notable fighters, winning the middleweight championship just two months later. *The Ultimate Fighter* finale broadcast was a phenomenal success, receiving record ratings on Spike TV. As a result, the UFC secured a multi-year contract with Spike for the show.

The ratings for the live finale were incredible, and the show became a huge success. Zuffa's plan had worked, and the investment in the show paid off as UFC 52: Liddell vs. Couture 2 became the highest-grossing

Ultimate Fighting Championship ever just one week later. UFC 52 pulled more than 14,000 fans into the MGM Grand casino, generating more than $2.5 million in ticket sales. Liddell knocked out Couture two minutes into the first round to become the new light-heavyweight champion.

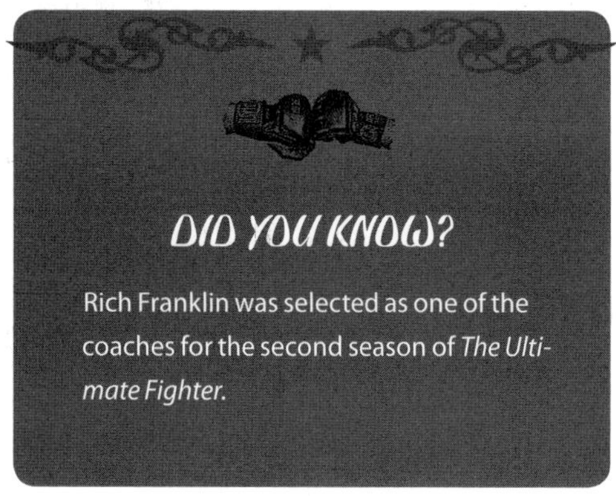

DID YOU KNOW?

Rich Franklin was selected as one of the coaches for the second season of *The Ultimate Fighter.*

The pay-per-view buy rate was almost 300,000, nearly tripling recent events. The Ultimate Fighting Championship had finally hit the jackpot, and Zuffa was rumored to have broken even in late 2005. Season two of *The Ultimate Fighter* went into production and welterweight champion Matt Hughes was selected as the second coach. The season aired from August through November 2005, and the season finale received record ratings.

In 2006, Zuffa expanded its success with Spike TV by creating the *UFC All Access* show. This program, hosted by UFC Octagon Girl Rachelle Leah, took viewers behind the scenes and into the lives of the top fighters as they prepared for major upcoming matches. Usually aired the same week as a UFC pay-per-view event, this program further promoted the UFC to Spike's viewers.

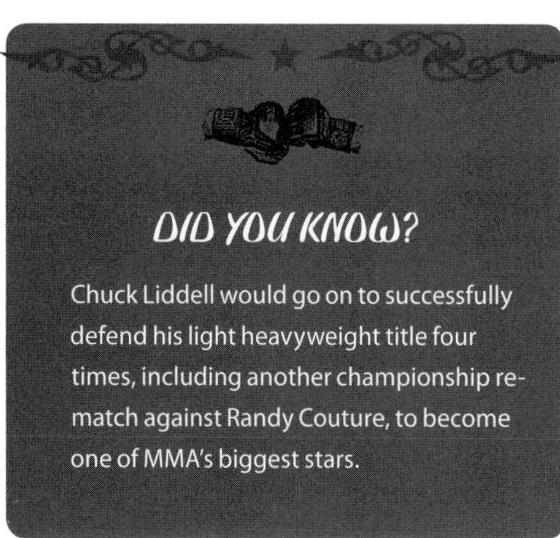

DID YOU KNOW?

Chuck Liddell would go on to successfully defend his light heavyweight title four times, including another championship rematch against Randy Couture, to become one of MMA's biggest stars.

To offer more UFC products to consumers, Zuffa signed a licensing agreement with Century Martial Arts in early 2006. Century Martial Arts, the world's largest martial art supply company, worked with the UFC to create a line of MMA products. This move cemented MMA in the traditional martial arts arena, as many school owners received requests for MMA gear and classes.

In August 2006, the UFC signed Mickey's Fine Malt Liquor and Brewing Company as a sponsor. Three months later, in November 2006, Zuffa secured a deal with Fox Sports en Español to broadcast six UFC events on the top-rated Spanish-language cable network. Zuffa purchased the WEC:

World Extreme Cagefighting promotion from Scott Adams and Reed Harris in December.

The WEC promotion featured excellent talent at lighter weight classes, so the decision was made to drop the heavyweight and super heavyweight divisions. WEC kept its bantam (135 pounds) and featherweight (145 pounds) divisions, and events began to air on the Versus Sports Channel in June 2007.

MIXED MARTIAL ARTS: PRESENT DAY

The year 2007 was an incredible one for the world of mixed martial arts. Zuffa started the year by announcing a multi-year deal with THQ, a major video game developer, to create video games for the UFC. Fans had been clamoring for a new game since 2004, and the move was a welcome one among avid video gamers.

The next announcement from Zuffa was one so big that it would have seemed impossible just a few years earlier. In March 2007, the UFC announced that it was purchasing its major international competitor, PRIDE Fighting Championships, in a buyout that was rumored to be close to $70 million. Owned by Dream Stage Entertainment, PRIDE had been the predominant mixed martial arts promotion in Japan. It had held some of the largest MMA events in the world, with crowds exceeding 60,000 people. After the buyout, some of PRIDE's most talented fighters moved to the UFC, including Anderson Silva, Dan Henderson, Quinton Jackson, Wanderlei Silva, and Antonio Rodrigo Nogueira.

May 2007 was a big month for the Ultimate Fighting Championship. Light-heavyweight champion Chuck Liddell was the first MMA fighter ever to be featured on the cover of *ESPN The Magazine*. Subsequently, ESPNEWS broadcast the weigh-ins for UFC 71: Liddell vs. Jackson, marking the first time a major national sports television network featured live event coverage of weigh-ins. Last, but certainly not least, Zuffa hired former CNN Director of Partnerships and Sponsors Michael Pine as its vice president of ad sales and sponsorships. Pine's

DID YOU KNOW?

On September 8, 2007, UFC 75: Jackson vs. Henderson was aired on Spike TV and became the most watched mixed martial arts broadcast in North America to date, with 4.7 million viewers.

new role was to focus on securing large sponsors to help drive the UFC brand name.

In October, Zuffa announced a brand new online UFC fantasy game. The game, which coincides with live events, allows fans to predict the winning fighters, the type of victory, and the time and round the match ends. This interactive feature helped to drive additional traffic to the UFC website and engage fans in a new and innovative way. Yahoo! Sports also took note of the growing online fan base and added a separate web channel for MMA. Zuffa also secured a huge $100 million deal with Spike TV to continue to air UFC programming. The three-year deal included twelve live UFC Fight Nights, thirty-nine episodes of *UFC Unleashed*, and seasons nine through twelve of *The Ultimate Fighter*.

Endeavoring to continue to provide innovative ways to connect fans to the sport of mixed martial arts, Zuffa partnered with Saffron Digital to release UFC Mobile in December. Users could now download wallpaper, ring tones, video, and updates on their mobile phones. The Ultimate Fighting Championship ended the year with a bang on December 29, 2007. UFC 79: Nemesis featured Matt Hughes against Georges St-Pierre and Chuck Liddell vs. Wanderlei Silva in an action-packed event. The show pulled in an estimated $5 million in tickets sales and close to 700,000 pay-per-view buys.

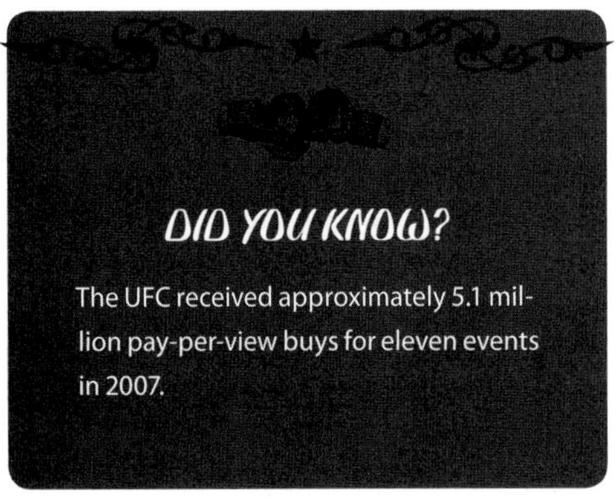

DID YOU KNOW?

The UFC received approximately 5.1 million pay-per-view buys for eleven events in 2007.

If 2007 was big, 2008 was even bigger. Michael Pine had been busy since coming on board, and the year started with Zuffa announcing a major sponsorship deal with Harley-Davidson motorcycles. In February 2008, Anheuser-Busch and Bud Light announced three-year sponsorship deals with the UFC. With these two powerhouse sponsors, the UFC had proven its staying power as a major established sports franchise.

Zuffa also signed a deal with Yahoo! Sports to become the online distributor for UFC live pay-per-view events. The move helped to develop its global distribution and allowed anyone with an Internet connection to see live video streaming of the Ultimate Fighting Championship. In June, a huge announcement was made, as Lorenzo Fertitta stepped down from Station Casinos to join the UFC full time. Taking on internationally related tasks, the business maverick put all his energy and focus into helping the UFC to become a billion-dollar enterprise.

In July, the UFC signed a multi-year deal with sponsor Bio-Engineered Supplements and Nutrition (BSN), naming the world leader in sports nutrition products as the UFC's official supplement provider. To further extend its reach, Zuffa signed a two-year pay-per-view agreement in October with satellite broadcaster WOWOW to telecast the UFC in Japan. They also inked a three-year deal with Globosat in December 2008 to distribute the UFC in Brazil.

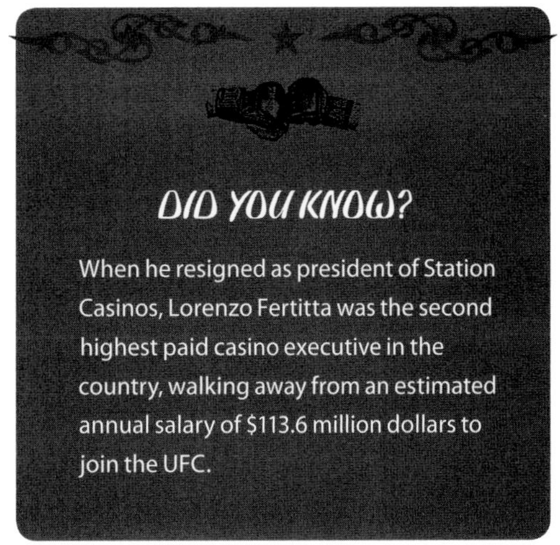

The year was also a defining one in terms of competition between MMA organizations. As a result of the UFC's success, two new competitors had attempted to enter the MMA marketplace. Fox Sports Net made a television deal with the International Fight League in 2007, showcasing a team format for their programming. Another promotion, EliteXC, began in late 2006 and secured an agreement with Showtime and later CBS to broadcast events. Due to financial troubles, however, both promotions closed down in 2008, further paving the way for the UFC to become the undisputed champion of MMA events with more than 90 percent market share.

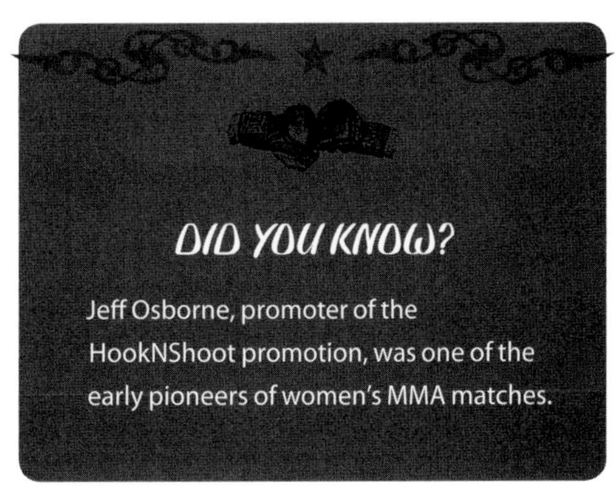

Women Enter the Ring

Another first in the MMA world came with the announcement of the first women's MMA bout to be nationally televised in the United States. On February 10, 2007, the promotion EliteXC broadcast their first event on Showtime, which featured a prelim match between Gina Carano and Julie Kedzi. Despite a heavily anticipated main card match between Frank Shamrock and Renzo Gracie, the prelim Carano and Kedzie bout was rated the best fight of the night.

Although women's MMA matches have been taking place at smaller shows for years, the EliteXC bout between Carano and Kedzie helped put

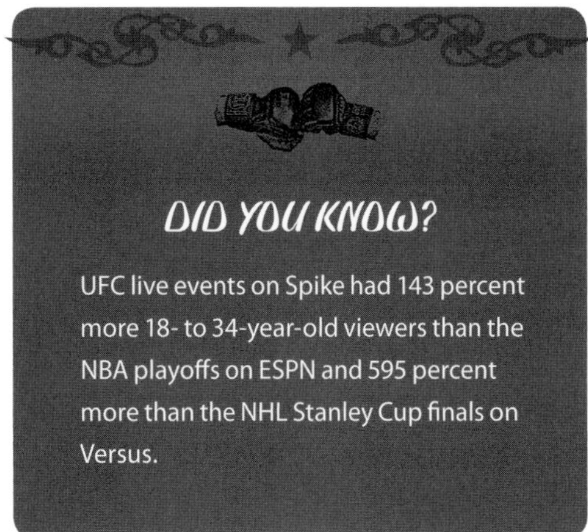

women's MMA on the map in front of a national audience. Women's MMA is still in its infancy, but it has both an increasing number of talented female fighters and a growing fan base.

THE FUTURE OF MMA

Today, the sport of mixed martial arts is experiencing exponential growth and moving more into the mainstream. From local area events to the big stage of the Ultimate Fighting Championship, the MMA fan base is growing at an incredible pace. With official sanctioning by state athletic boards in thirty-seven states, MMA has emerged from the dark days of no-holds-barred spectacles. The regulation improvements and increasing public support have attracted top-level global corporate sponsors and helped establish MMA as an expanding industry in the sports world.

Zuffa, LLC and the UFC, with Dana White and billionaire Lorenzo Fertitta at the helm, are focused on taking the sport global. The company made over $200 million in pay-per-view revenue alone in 2006, positioning the UFC to eclipse both boxing and professional wrestling pay-per-view buys in the near future. As a company, it is estimated that the UFC is worth a billion dollars, which is approaching the value of the publicly traded World Wrestling Entertainment (WWE).

On television, the UFC and Spike TV have worked together developing programs that have become some of the most popular shows in sports programming. *The Ultimate Fighter* show averages almost two million viewers, and live UFC events average more male viewers in the 18- to 34-year-old demographic than many basketball, football, baseball, hockey, and NASCAR events. Teaming up with the Versus Network, the WEC is also expanding its viewership and climbing the ratings ladder.

Seen as the premier MMA event, the Ultimate Fighting Championship has over two hundred fighters on its roster and is seen in over 170 countries. Live events consistently sell more than 10,000 tickets and 500,000 pay-per-view buys. Celebrities like Jay-Z, Mandy Moore, Paris Hilton, Dwayne "The Rock" Johnson, Criss Angel, and Pink are regulars at live UFC events.

The number of MMA products available to loyal fans has exploded. MMA t-shirts and other apparel are sold in many major department stores, and the Tapout clothing company made more than $22 million in sales in 2007. There are more than 100 UFC DVDs on the market. MMA video games are becoming increasingly popular, and the newest release from THQ might become a top-selling game in 2009. For younger fans, there are trading cards, and some of the top fighters even have action figures.

The fan base continues to grow online as well, with UFC.com reportedly receiving 4.5 million unique visitors per month. Some of the top visited MMA websites include: Sherdog.com, MMAWeekly.com, and MixedMartialArts.com. On these and other sites, users can download an enormous amount of content, including fights on demand.

With all of these factors contributing to its fast-paced growth, MMA is quickly becoming one of the premier sports in the world.

2 ★★★

MMA: THE SPORT OF WARRIORS

If horse racing is the "Sport of Kings," then MMA is the Sport of Warriors. Mixed martial arts has exploded over the past few years to become the fastest-growing sport in the world. Drawing an ever-increasing number of fans viewing events on both cable TV and pay-per-view, its audience continues to become more mainstream. Now that you understand the background and history of this fast-paced sport, it's time to get familiar with the specific details of competition.

After adopting the Mixed Martial Arts Unified Rules of Conduct, MMA events had a formula to follow that would help them to get recognized and sanctioned by state athletic commissions. Using this approved format gave the sport credibility and signaled that the UFC was serious about cooperating with athletic regulating bodies. The New Jersey and Nevada State Athletic Commissions were among the first to approve these rules, and today MMA events are sanctioned in thirty-seven states.

REQUIRED FIGHT GEAR

First, let's take a look at what a combat athlete needs to compete in this sport. A fighter needs four pieces of equipment to step into the cage:

1. MMA gloves and hand wraps
2. Mouthpiece
3. Groin protection
4. MMA shorts/kickboxing trunks

Hand wraps are used to protect the small bones in the hand and wrist. MMA gloves are four to six ounces and are half the weight of typical boxing gloves. The lighter weight, although easier to inflict damage, is actually safer for the fighters. This is because a single knockout causes less harm to the head than repeated strikes over a long period of

Hand Wraps

Fight Gloves

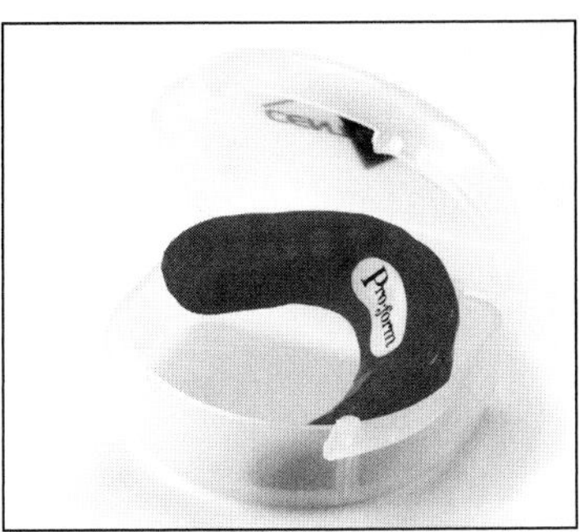

Mouthpiece

MMA Shorts

time. MMA gloves are also different from boxing gloves because they have finger separations to help the fighter to grapple effectively.

To make sure they retain their teeth and their ability to have children, fighters are also required to wear a mouthpiece and a groin protector.

Lastly, competitors need to wear MMA shorts or kickboxing trunks. Shirts, gi tops, and shoes are no longer allowed under the Unified Rules.

RULES

Speaking of the Unified Rules, there are a number of illegal moves, often called fouls, in MMA. At the top of the list, fighters are strictly prohibited from intentionally head butting, eye gouging, or biting their opponents. Striking to the groin, fish hooking, and hair pulling are also fouls. To prevent major trauma to the body, striking to the spine, back of the head, and throat are also illegal. Some other illegal moves include:

- applying small joint locks, including fingers, wrists, and toes
- clawing, pinching, or twisting the flesh or grabbing the clavicle
- throwing an opponent out of the ring or cage
- slamming an opponent on his neck or head
- holding the ropes or fence
- striking downward with the point of the elbow
- holding on to an opponent's gloves or fight shorts

As the action goes to the ground, the following moves are also considered fouls:

- kneeing or kicking the head of a grounded opponent
- stomping an opponent who is on the ground
- kicking an opponent in the kidney with the heel (a move from the guard made popular by Royce Gracie in the early UFC events)

Lastly, unsportsmanlike conduct is strictly prohibited. This includes using abusive language and spitting at an opponent or referee. Flagrantly disregarding the instructions of the referee and interference by the corner are also examples of unsportsmanlike conduct. Attacking an opponent who is under the care of the referee, or after the bell sounds the end of the round or match, is not tolerated and is completely illegal.

Interestingly enough, there is also a rule for timidity. This means that a fighter who avoids contact with an opponent, lacks aggression, or intentionally fakes an injury will be charged with a foul.

THE REFEREE'S ROLE

The referee in a MMA event has numerous responsibilities. The first is the care and condition of the fighters. Although MMA is an extreme sport, the referee has to stay focused on the action at all times to help prevent serious injury to the competitors. If a fighter appears to be losing consciousness or can no longer intelligently defend himself, the ref has the duty to intervene and stop the match. The referee can also ask the ringside physician to examine an injured fighter to determine the athlete's ability to continue the bout.

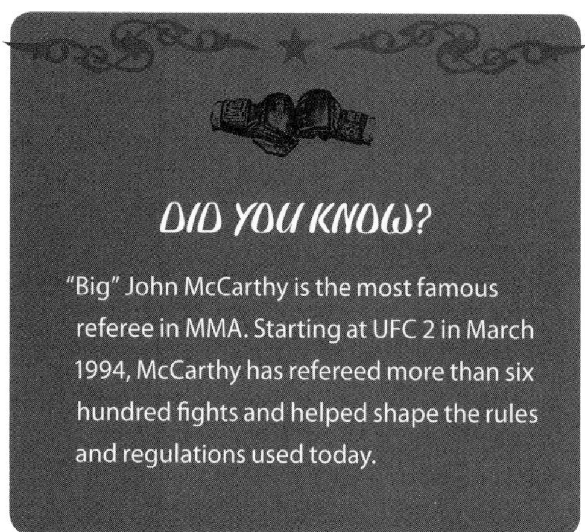

DID YOU KNOW?

"Big" John McCarthy is the most famous referee in MMA. Starting at UFC 2 in March 1994, McCarthy has refereed more than six hundred fights and helped shape the rules and regulations used today.

Another major responsibility of the referee is to ensure that both athletes uphold good sportsmanship and strictly adhere to the rules. A minor infraction may cause the ref to momentarily stop the action to give a warning to a fighter. Repeated infractions or a major foul can cause the referee to issue the judges to charge a competitor with a foul and deduct points from the fighter's score.

It can also lead to a fighter's disqualification if the situation merits. For instance, if a fighter is injured and unable to continue as the result of an intentional foul, the instigating fighter is disqualified. In this case, the injured fighter would be declared the winner of the fight. Occasionally, a fighter becomes injured due to an accidental illegal technique. If a competitor commits an unintentional foul and the opposing fighter is unable to continue, the bout may be ruled a "no contest." An example of this would be a fighter accidentally getting poked in the eye and being incapable of finishing the match due to the injury.

To keep the action moving, a referee also has to ensure that the fighters are continuously striving to win the match. When a fight has stalled against the fence or on the ground, the ref can intervene. If there is a lull in the match, where neither competitor is pressing the fight, the referee can restart a match on the feet.

WAYS TO WIN

What makes MMA so exciting is the numerous ways to win a match. During a fight, the bout can end standing or on the ground in the following ways:

- Knockout
- Tap out (submission)
- Referee stoppage
- Doctor stoppage

Competitors can seek to knock out their opponents in various ways. The first is by strikes to the head. In boxing, fighters can only punch to the head, but in MMA fighters can also knee, elbow, and kick to the head. A body shot that incapacitates a fighter could also be considered a knockout if it renders the fighter unable to defend himself. A knockout may come from a single well-placed shot or a series of strikes. These added techniques greatly increase the opportunity for a combat athlete to score a knockout victory.

MMA athletes can also force their opponents into submission, otherwise known as causing the opponent to tap out. A fighter can tap out physically or verbally. A physical tap out occurs when a fighter who is in danger signals defeat by quickly tapping on his opponent's body or the mat three times in a row. This often happens during submission chokes, where a competitor cannot verbally tap out.

If a competitor is unable to physically tap, he may submit by verbally telling the referee to stop the fight. A verbal tap out is typically seen when a fighter pins his opponents' body and simultaneously secures a joint lock. This allows a referee to stop a match if a fighter is in a disadvantaged position, but doesn't have the ability to physically tap out. If a fighter taps out, his opponent must immediately release the submission hold and separate from the losing fighter. This allows the referee to rapidly separate the fighters and ensure the defeated competitor's safety.

The referee also has the ability to stop the fight if a fighter:

- suffers unconsciousness due to a submission hold
- is unable to intelligently defend repeated strikes that could lead to excessive injury
- has received significant injuries that could significantly endanger his well-being

The final way a fight can end is by doctor stoppage. If a fighter receives considerable damage, the referee can call a time out to have the fight physician evaluate a fighter's condition. This typically takes place when a fighter has a large cut, especially on the head or face. The corner's cutman will try to stop the bleeding as the physician checks the wound. If the cut is significant, the doctor can advise the referee that a fighter is unfit to continue. The referee has the final decision, however, as to whether or not the match should continue.

ROUNDS

Under the Unified Rules, fights have specific round and time limits. Non-championship fights are three rounds and championship fights are five rounds. There is a one-minute rest period in between rounds, and each round lasts five minutes in duration. Thus, if a fight goes the distance, non-championship fights can last up to fifteen minutes and championship fights can last up to twenty-five minutes.

It is interesting to note that these round and time limits are different from boxing. In boxing, rounds are three minutes with up to ten rounds for a championship fight. MMA makes up for fewer rounds by increasing the time in each round. This means that MMA fighters need superior conditioning because they fight longer and have fewer rest periods.

DID YOU KNOW?

Matt Hughes verbally submitted to Georges St-Pierre in UFC 79: Nemesis. St-Pierre had Hughes in an arm bar, but Hughes's other hand was pinned and unable to signal a tap out.

DECISIONS

If a match goes the specified number of rounds without a winner, the decision goes to the judges to award a winner. Typically, there are three judges who score the fight. Judges use a ten-point scoring system, with the winner getting ten points and the loser of the round receiving nine or less points. If a judge feels the round was a draw, both competitors are awarded ten points.

There are four decisions that can be reached by the judges:

1. Unanimous decision
2. Split decision
3. Majority decision
4. Draw

If all three judges score the match in favor of only one fighter, a unanimous decision is awarded. If two judges score the match for one fighter, but the third judge scores it for the second fighter, then the contest is ruled a split decision. A majority decision occurs when two judges score the bout for one fighter, but the third judge scores the match a draw. Although it is an uncommon occurrence, a fight could be scored as a draw if one judge votes for fighter A, the second judge votes for fighter B, and the third judge scores it a draw.

WEIGHT CLASSES

Under the Unified Rules, there are several weight classes for MMA competitors. The establishment of weight classes, beginning with the New Jersey State Athletic Commission, has helped MMA events become more sport oriented. Under these regulations, fighters compete against one another at a comparable weight. This results in better fights and has improved the image of the sport.

Currently, in the UFC there are five separate weight classes:

- Heavyweight: Minimum of 205 pounds up to a maximum of 265 pounds
- Light Heavyweight: Minimum of 185 pounds up to a maximum of 205 pounds
- Middleweight: Minimum of 170 pounds up to a maximum of 185 pounds
- Welterweight: Minimum of 155 pounds up to a maximum of 170 pounds
- Lightweight: Minimum of 145 pounds up to a maximum of 155 pounds

In the WEC, there are also five separate weight classes:

- Welterweight: Minimum of 155 pounds up to a maximum of 170 pounds

- Lightweight: Minimum of 145 pounds up to a maximum of 155 pounds
- Featherweight: Minimum of 135 pounds up to a maximum of 145 pounds
- Bantamweight: Minimum of 125 pounds up to a maximum of 135 pounds
- Flyweight: Minimum of 115 pounds up to a maximum of 125 pounds

Similar to boxing and wrestling, MMA fighters will often "cut" weight prior to the weigh-in for the event. This means that there can sometimes be a significant difference between what a fighter weighs in at and how much they actually weigh at the time of the match.

Most weigh-ins take place no longer than twenty-four hours prior to the event, which allows athletes to sharply drop their weight to meet the requirements for their division and then replenish immediately following the weigh-in. This process will be covered in more depth in chapter thirteen: Weight Cutting for the Warrior.

DID YOU KNOW?

The only highly recognized weight division not currently utilized by the UFC or the WEC is the super heavyweight division for fighters over 265 pounds.

TRAINING GEAR

Training in the sport of MMA isn't for everyone. It takes a tremendous amount of hard work and dedication to become successful. Nearly all of the most talented combat athletes have professional trainers and coaches and are members of MMA team training centers and professional gyms. Although these elements are important at the high end of the sport, they aren't necessities to begin training in mixed martial arts.

The good news is that many of today's top fighters started off with just the bare essentials for their training. Several current champions began with just the basic gear and a garage or basement as a place to train. What follows is some of the common training equipment that MMA athletes use as they are preparing for competition.

Cardio Equipment

Most combat athletes will have a number of pieces of equipment to increase their cardio endurance. One of the primary pieces in a fighter's training bag is a good jump rope. A couple sets of sparring gear are also important because sparring tends to be one of the best all-around exercises a fighter can do to improve his conditioning. A speed bag, heavy bag, and striking pads are also invaluable.

There are numerous exercises that can be done with just a handful of pieces of equipment, and many fighters will integrate "stations" of exercises into their cardio program. Athletes will do one particular exercise for a given period of time and then immediately move on to the next exercise in the series. This gets a competitor's heart rate up and keeps it there as he trains in various tasks. Having a stopwatch and a heart monitor for these exercises can help a fighter track and evaluate his cardio conditioning.

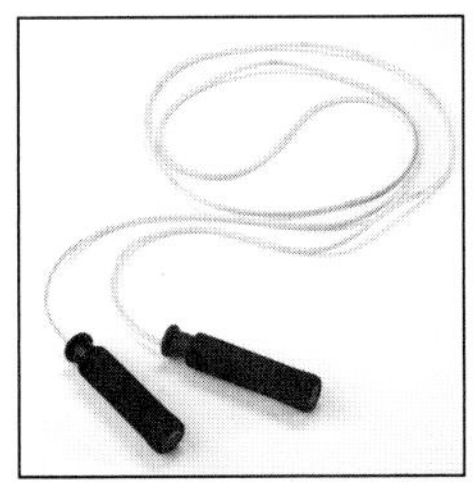

Jump Rope

Speed Bag

Heavy Bag

Kicking Shield

Striking Pads

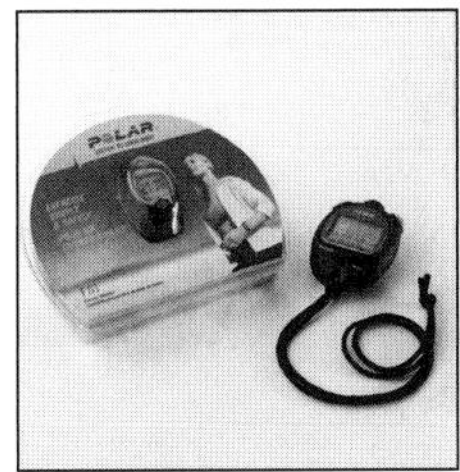

Heart Monitor and Stopwatch

Strength Equipment

To help build strength, MMA athletes will utilize both traditional and more unconventional techniques and equipment. The majority of fighters will integrate a weight lifting program into their training routine, so having access to a free weight set is very important. Most gyms offer reasonable monthly rates, so many fighters choose to become members of a fitness center rather than purchase their own weights.

Fighters will also employ resistance tools, like elastic bands, to build muscle strength. Other commonly used fitness items include plyometric boxes and physioballs. If there isn't a good gym close by, or if the fighter wants to incorporate unique strength conditioning exercises into his training, the combat athlete will often acquire other equipment to help build power. This can include items like a medicine ball, weight pulling sled, and even giant tractor tires.

Free Weights

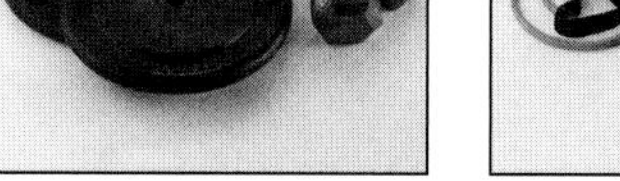
Elastic Resistance Bands

Physioball

Medicine Balls

Sparring Gear

Sparring Gear

MMA Gear

Combat athletes training in MMA will often have at least a couple sets of sparring gear. This generally includes heavier boxing gloves, shin pads, foot protection, and headgear. Sparring is an important part of an MMA warrior's training. It helps a fighter to get comfortable with being hit, as well as providing an opportunity to apply his skills in practice rounds.

WARRIOR ATHLETES

Knowing the rules, fight formats, and weight classes is just the first step in understanding this incredible sport. Now that you have learned the basics of MMA competition, it is time to take the next step and discover how these fighters become some of the most highly trained and conditioned athletes in the world.

3 ★★★

WARRIOR PREPARATIONS

Not only is mixed martial arts the fastest growing sport in the world, the fighters that compete are some of the most well-conditioned athletes in the world. Within the Unified Rules for the sport, championship matches last for five five-minute rounds. That means that a fighter has to train hard enough to develop the stamina needed to last up to twenty-five minutes of combat against an equally skilled opponent.

The training of MMA is some of the most grueling on the planet. The mental focus needed to compete requires a high degree of intelligence and discipline. Success in this sport, as with any endeavor in life, requires thorough preparation. Training includes many different elements, from physical and mental training to health and nutrition.

To prepare for battle, the athletes of MMA take all of their training seriously. In many ways, undertaking the journey of MMA is undertaking the path of the warrior. It is also a way to discover more about yourself, understanding your strengths and weaknesses, both physically and psychologically. As a result, fighters learn to face their fears and accomplish their goals to become the best athletes they can. It all starts with understanding the multitude of aspects of this incredible sport.

MENTAL TRAINING

High-level athletes in any sport will tell you that the mental game is one of the most important aspects of their success. MMA is no different, and competitors face some of the same challenges when it comes to staying focused and developing strong mental conditioning. Mastering their own minds is a constant battle for all athletes, but mental discipline is especially complex in the world of MMA. Make no mistake about it; fighters face a whole host of psychological hurdles because of their chosen profession.

Fear plays a crucial role for an MMA fighter. First and foremost, a fighter has to overcome the fear associated with getting into a cage against another opponent. This alone begins to separate out the warriors from the wannabes. Anyone who has ever competed in a live match will tell you that it is one thing to talk about competing and another thing to actually get in the ring and fight. Most successful MMA athletes who have actually been there and done it will remark that it feels natural to them and that they thrive on the excitement of testing their skills.

Next, an athlete has to overcome the innate fear of being hit, choked, or forced to submit. This is where physical training comes into play. Coaches and training partners push competitors outside of their comfort zones, forcing them to face and overcome these fears. Using physical conditioning drills, fighters can push themselves mentally to a new level, where they continue through any fear they are experiencing.

In any physical sport, continuing to compete through pain is a part of the process. In the world of MMA, pain is the name of the game. After overcoming their personal fears, MMA warriors seek to develop their mental resolve to a razor-sharp edge. One of the reasons that physical training in this sport is so intense is because it helps to build the attributes of determination and perseverance. In an actual match, fighters expect to experience the pain of being punched or kicked. Therefore, they train rigorously to continue through pain and focus on achieving their objective.

This increased determination actually helps fighters to evolve to the next phase of their mental training. One of the critical mental components of MMA is the ability to stay calm and centered. If you ask mixed martial artists who have actually fought in matches, they'll tell you that the process is an emotional roller coaster. There is a high level of anticipation before the match, the nerve-wracking process of stepping into the cage, followed by the adrenaline dump as the bell rings. After the match, there is a surge of emotions—from the elation of winning to the disappointment of losing. By cultivating an ability to remain calm, fighters can seize more opportunities and improve their chances during the match.

If fighters can learn the psychological keys of overcoming their fears, developing a strong sense of determination, and finding a way to stay calm, they'll probably find themselves improving on the next important mental skill: creativity. Being able to think on your feet and adapt is one of a mixed martial artist's most valuable attributes. A fighter has to learn a myriad of techniques, but how they are integrated successfully in an actual match involves a great deal of creativity and spontaneity. Whether it is executing a unique combination of techniques, or finding an unusual escape from a submission attempt, the MMA warrior often has to be very creative to achieve victory.

Many top athletes take that creativity to the next level with what is called *visual motor rehearsal*. Think of this as a type of self-visualization meditation. Fighters close their eyes and visualize the entire match in their minds. Going over every possible scenario and observing themselves throughout the fight helps them to see possible opportunities that may not have occurred during their physical training. This process may give them insights and ideas to improve their training regimen. It also helps to increase the fighters' confidence, as they visualize themselves winning the bout, their hand held high in victory.

Overall, the mental side of MMA involves a number of different aspects. From learning how to overcome fear to utilizing creativity and creating a training strategy, a fighter has to develop a strong mind to gain success in this sport. But the mental game is just one attribute of what makes the MMA warrior unique.

PHYSICAL TRAINING

After all the personal mental development, it is time to move on to creating a physical training strategy. In this stage, with the help of their coaches and training partners, fighters will develop a training regimen and strategy. Each training schedule and strategy is custom designed to the individual needs of the fighter. For instance, an athlete may have excellent physical conditioning, but lack ground-fighting techniques. In this case, his training regiment would focus on developing the submission and escaping skills of jiu-jitsu and the fundamental movements of wrestling. Another fighter may have excellent jiu-jitsu skills but is missing the standup skills necessary to be a well-rounded fighter. Here, the fighter would seek to develop his boxing and Muay Thai kickboxing abilities to improve his standup game.

The physical training of a mixed martial artist is second to none, combining a high level of anaerobic performance with incredible strength training. MMA warriors have to be fast, strong, and have incredible endurance. In addition, flexibility is an often-overlooked component of their physical training regiment. When it comes to wrestling and jiu-jitsu, it pays to have a flexible body, which can help fighters escape from submissions or positions of disadvantage.

Cardiovascular Fitness

Cardiovascular fitness is a crucial element of MMA training. Fighters have to develop the endurance to push their bodies for up to twenty-five minutes of competition. Anyone who has ever done any type of martial art can share how quickly the body can become exhausted by continuously striking a heavy bag or grappling with a training partner. Most

MMA athletes break down their cardiovascular exercise regiments into two major components: aerobic and anaerobic training.

Most people are familiar with aerobic fitness, which includes exercises performed at moderate levels of intensity for longer periods of time. In aerobic training, exercise improves the oxygen consumption of the body, and an athlete's heart rate increases about 70 to 90 percent above his normal resting heart rate. While some fighters incorporate aerobic exercises into their fitness routines, most choose to focus on developing anaerobic conditioning.

Anaerobic exercise focuses on short bursts of intense exertion, which increases the heart rate above the aerobic level. In anaerobic exercise, the body is oxygen deprived and uses other metabolic processes to generate energy. Mixed martial arts is mainly an anaerobic sport because fighters are pushing their bodies to the limit, going all out for a five-minute round. If the bout continues to the next round, the competitors get a one-minute rest and then go all out for another five minutes.

In order to maximize their workouts and get their bodies accustomed to functioning in this manner, many fighters design their workouts around five-minute exercises. Think of it as a five-minute sprint, followed by a one-minute rest. In fact, sprinting, not distance running, is a typical component of a mixed martial artist's exercise regimen. Think about it. If you look at an Olympic sprinter's body, it is strong, muscular, and powerful. This is because strength and power are a result of anaerobic conditioning.

Weightlifting and Resistance Training

To develop the muscle groups necessary for combat, the MMA warrior uses some unconventional methods to build strength and power. In addition to a more normal weightlifting routine and resistance training, most athletes utilize a series of strongman exercises to boost their conditioning. These unique exercises work the fighter's entire body, forcing him to focus his power while having to maintain balance. Some examples are weight sled pulling, heavy- or sand-bag flips, sledgehammer swings, and flipping giant tractor tires.

Gaining upper-body muscle strength is vital for combat athletes. Having the power to take down or slam an opponent is a valuable asset in competition. So is having the strength to defend takedown attempts or utilize wrestling skills to gain a position of advantage. Making sure they have the arm strength to deliver powerful punches is also a key element for MMA warriors.

Fighters work regularly to strengthen their core muscle group, especially the abdominal muscles. These muscles are critical to helping the fighter move quickly and generate power for their strikes. Well-conditioned abdominal muscles are also important on the ground, helping the fighter to battle for a superior position.

Mixed martial artists also focus on building their leg strength. The more powerful the leg muscles are, the more the fighter can blast his opponent with devastating kicks. Of course, the combat athlete knows his opponent might also employ thigh kicks, so developing the legs is just as much a defensive tactic. Additionally, having powerful legs means that the fighter will have the speed to initiate takedowns and put his foe on the ground.

Flexibility Training

Another component of physical training in MMA is flexibility training. It may seem surprising, but many of today's top fighters regularly take yoga classes to help keep their bodies limber. Anytime a match goes to the ground, flexibility can be an important advantage. Having flexible hips and legs gives a competitor a better opportunity to defend his opponents' attempts to gain a superior position. It can also keep a fighter out of a submission and in some cases can even be used offensively to secure a submission and force a tap out.

THE FIVE COMBATIVE DISCIPLINES OF MMA

When the UFC first began, most viewers thought that striking would obviously be the way the fights would end. When Brazilian Jiu-jitsu proved to be so successful, competitors started to study ground fighting and then mix it with the striking arts. At the time, this was a revolutionary concept in the martial arts world. This integration of disciplines would lead the way to the evolution of MMA as we know it today.

There are five main disciplines that encompass the skills utilized in MMA competitions. To add credibility and identify the peak fitness conditioning of its athletes, MMA is often referred to as a combination of Olympic boxing, Olympic wrestling, and Olympic judo. Add in the leg kicks and knee strikes of Muay Thai kickboxing and the ground-fighting submissions of Brazilian Jiu-jitsu, and you have the five major combative arts of MMA.

1. **Olympic boxing.** Boxing skills are incredibly valuable to combat athletes for a number of different reasons. First, understanding how to execute proper punches can immensely improve

a fighter's standup game. Learning targeting, accuracy, and defensive applications also helps a fighter to expand his skill set. Some of the footwork and evasion techniques of boxing can dramatically increase a fighter's ability to avoid being hit.

2. **Greco-Roman wrestling.** Many of today's top fighters have a background in amateur freestyle or Greco-Roman wrestling. One of the oldest forms of grappling in the world, wrestling plays an important part in MMA. Controlling an opponent's body movement, defending takedowns and throws, and securing a superior position when the action lands on the mat are some of the key attributes of wrestling. These skills translate well into the world of MMA and provide a solid base for a fighter's grappling abilities.

3. **Olympic judo.** Judo is an art that focuses on how to use an opponent's weight against him. Mixed martial artists use this discipline to learn how to alter their opponent's balance and execute throws and takedowns. By understanding the components of balance, a fighter can determine how best to maneuver when he gets in a clinch. If a fight goes to a judge's decision, takedowns count for points and can put a fighter over the top. In some cases, a well-executed throw or slam can end the fight by knocking the opponent unconscious.

4. **Muay Thai kickboxing.** Muay Thai kickboxing brings a powerful arsenal of devastating kicks and vicious knees to the MMA athlete. Many fighters implement this style's low-leg roundhouse or thigh kick, which can be incredibly painful and set up additional striking techniques. Sometimes, if a fighter sees his opponent drop his hands, a quick Muay Thai head kick can finish the fight. This discipline is also famous for its "Muay Thai clinch" in which a fighter locks his hands around his opponent's neck to control his upper body. Depending on the situation, the fighter may use short powerful elbow strikes to his opponent's head or pull his neck down to deliver a series of knees.

5. **Brazilian Jiu-jitsu.** Last, but certainly not least, Brazilian Jiu-jitsu adds its wide array of submission techniques to round out a fighter's skill sets. First taking prominence with the Gracie family in the early UFCs, the techniques contained within this art include ankle locks, arm bars, leg locks, shoulder locks, and chokes. This

incredibly technical art also has the defensive elements of counters and escapes to add to a combat athlete's repertoire.

To become successful in MMA, a competitor needs to study the key components of all five major disciplines. Most fighters have had previous training in one or two particular disciplines, but seek to expand their skill sets within each separate art. As they increase their abilities and become more well-rounded fighters, combat athletes gain more options and therefore have more opportunities for victory.

HEALTH AND NUTRITION

Although they may go through extremely rigorous and painful training, taking care of their physical bodies is one of MMA fighters' top priorities. It usually comes as a shock to many people unfamiliar with the sport, but combat athletes closely monitor the food they eat and take regular nutritional supplements. To compete in MMA, fighters needs to keep their bodies in peak physical condition. This means being smart about injury prevention as well as keeping their bodies as healthy as possible during the build up to a fight.

Nutrition is an important aspect of a fighter's training regimen. The combat athlete knows that what he puts into his body contributes greatly to its performance. Because of the rigorous training schedule, every fighter wants to supply his body with the fuel it will need to operate at its best. To illustrate this, think of the physical body as a car. A combat athlete has a high-performance sports car, and in order to make it run smoothly, it needs premium fuel.

To operate efficiently, the majority of fighters greatly increase their caloric intake during training. Some competitors consume 5,000 calories a day or more to keep up with the intense workouts. In order to keep their bodies functioning at high levels throughout the day, fighters usually eat meals more frequently. Typically spread out every few hours, these meals give the body the chance to consistently replenish its fuel supply.

When it comes to food, every fighter is different. Some athletes have strict dietary restrictions on the types of foods they eat, while others don't. Most competitors base their meals around protein and complex carbohydrates, although some also include small amounts of simple carbs and even Omega-3 or non-saturated fat. As high-performance athletes, MMA warriors also center their diets on organic, whole-food sources instead of processed foods.

Sports and nutritional supplements are also an important part of a fighter's health strategy. After a strenuous workout, an athlete's energy reserves are depleted and need to be replenished. Supplements come in liquid or powder packs, which are typically combined with a juice or shake. Many fighters consume a post-workout nutritional shake to help their body recover quickly from training. This usually is a non-fat, protein, and simple carbohydrate shake, which rapidly replenishes muscle-glycogen reserves to help repair muscles. A number of combat athletes also take a regular multivitamin to ensure their body is getting a complete range of vitamins and minerals.

MMA warriors know that they are assuming a high level of risk when they begin training in this sport. Some injuries are accidents, or the result of competing, but coaches help their fighters to take as many precautions as possible to reduce their risk during workouts. First, combat athletes work with their coaches to assess their individual risk for potential injuries. This includes taking past injuries into account as well as assessing under-trained muscle groups.

Some of the most common injuries in MMA are shoulder and knee dislocations, along with ankle, knee, and wrist sprains. Fighters also have to be aware of preventing groin, back, and neck strains, which can put them out of commission for weeks. During their training, coaches will constantly monitor their fighters' performance and help them to be aware of their entire bodies. Increasing an athlete's range of motion and joint stability raises his body awareness level, which is a critical component to avoiding injury.

When a fighter strains or sprains part of his body during training, most athletes follow the R-I-C-E formula. This stands for *rest, ice, compression*, and *elevation*. The first goal is to reduce inflammation, particularly with a joint injury. By applying ice for no more than twenty minutes every hour and elevating the injured area, a fighter can significantly decrease swelling. Some athletes also incorporate an ice massage of the affected area to help relax the muscle groups surrounding the injury.

By adding compression, typically in the form of an elastic bandage wrap for intervals of two to four hours, a combat athlete can help to stabilize the affected area. When the swelling has been reduced and the surrounding muscles are relaxed, fighters often begin to gently stretch and slowly move the joint through its range of motion. In combination with the R-I-C-E formula, this strategy has proven successful to help MMA athletes recover from injuries. Of course, if the situation warrants medical attention, fighters always seek the advice of a physician to determine the extent of an injury.

Care and maintenance of the body is also important to a competitor's long-term objectives. Successful fighters know they have to work very hard over a long period of time to achieve their goals, especially if they are seeking to win a championship title or belt. For that reason, many combat athletes have regular chiropractic adjustments to help keep their skeletal system in proper alignment. Another often-used practice is to have regular sports massages to release tension in over-worked muscles and relax the physical body.

ARE YOU READY?

As you can see, there is a tremendous amount of preparation that goes into developing the combat athlete. An MMA warrior has to have a strong mindset to overcome fear and adversity, while maintaining a steadfast and focused determination in the pursuit of success. The mixed martial artist has to push his body faster and harder than the average athlete, striving for flexibility, anaerobic endurance, and building enormous strength.

As a martial artist, the MMA warrior needs to develop advanced skill sets in each of the major combative disciplines used in the sport. Learning the punching skills of boxing and the devastating kicks and knees of Muay Thai, and implementing judo techniques to use an opponent's leverage are all a part of acquiring a great standup game. When the action heads towards the mat, the combat athlete needs to be well versed in the positioning strategies of wrestling and the joint locks and chokes of Brazilian Jiu-jitsu. Understanding how to integrate these disciplines is the key to becoming a well-rounded fighter.

To be in top physical condition, an athlete also needs a health and nutrition strategy. Creating a specifically formulated, high calorie diet is crucial to keeping the body performing at peak levels. Adding supplements, identifying injury prevention methods, and maintaining the body through additional practices is all a part of an MMA warrior's wellness plan.

Now that you understand these components, it's time to discover the journey of the MMA warrior and what separates the combat athlete from everyone else.

4 ★★★

INSIDE THE WARRIOR'S MIND

Somewhere along the way, chances are good that you've met a warrior. They stand out in a crowd. You can usually recognize them by their presence and the way they carry themselves. Extremely confident in themselves and their abilities, warriors love a challenge. Born with a competitive spirit, they thrive on working towards a goal with a focused determination. When presented with a difficult situation or obstacle, they find a way to accomplish their missions when most people just give up. Warriors never give up. It's not in their nature.

The persona of the warrior is different than most: They exude a sense of calm, especially in stressful situations, and have an inner strength that goes way beyond the normal person. That inner strength emanates from the knowledge that while they may temporarily lose or have a setback, they can never be defeated. This is the spirit of the warrior.

PURPOSE

While there are several aspects to a warrior's mindset, it all begins with this: purpose. To be successful and reach the top, combat athletes must have a clearly defined purpose. This means that warriors need to establish their goals. Once identified, these goals become the catalyst for an athlete's performance objectives.

If you are just beginning your journey into this incredible sport, you probably have some basic goals you want to achieve. Your goals may be physical ones, including losing weight, building strength and cardiovascular endurance, improving your flexibility, and overall health and nutrition. Or they may be training related, such as taking your standup game to the next level, improving your takedown defenses, or learning to escape a particular submission.

Every aspect of your training should have a goal attached to it. Some examples are:

- **Time goals:** Accomplishing a specific task in a specific amount of time. Examples: Running three miles in twenty-one minutes, grappling for five minutes without getting submitted, fifteen minutes of continuous bag or pad work, etc.

- **Endurance goals:** Continually improving your workload. Examples: Doing five sets of push-ups vs. your last week best of four, increasing your maximum bench press by ten pounds, grappling for four rounds instead of three, etc.

Any successful mixed martial artist will tell you that one of the most important things you can do with these goals is to write them down and track your progress. Overlooking this simple step is one of the main reasons so many people fail to accomplish their New Year's resolutions every year. Anyone can say he is going to do something. Only by putting those desires down on paper and creating an action plan to achieve those goals can you expect success.

As you advance in your training, your goals will probably change as well. For those individuals who decide to compete in this sport, it may be the desire to experience what it is actually like to step into the cage and fight. Amateur fighters also often feel a compelling need to test their skills against an opponent. Fighters who advance to a professional level often develop a single focused goal: to become the champion and best pound-for-pound fighter in their weight class.

No matter what your goals are, understanding what motivates you to succeed as an athlete is critical to victory. Some individuals are motivated by a negative outcome. For instance, some MMA warriors propel themselves forward in their training because they can't stand the thought of failing. Losing isn't an option for certain fighters, and they push themselves relentlessly in training to avoid an unsuccessful outcome.

Other fighters have something to prove, either to themselves, to their families, or to an authority figure. Perhaps someone told them they weren't good enough, fast enough, or strong enough to compete in this sport. Sometimes the opposite is true, and combat athletes are strongly motivated by a desire not to let someone down. On some level, all warriors simply want to prove to themselves that they can achieve their dreams. They want to be the best they can possibly be, and this inner desire fuels their ambition to win.

This inner sense of purpose is the foundation of a warrior's mental game. A fighter's goals become the outward manifestation of their inward intentions. At one point or another, every athlete has to ask himself why he is putting himself through hell to chase after his aspirations. When someone's suffered a loss or had a setback in training, it is easy to fall back into negative thinking. When this happens, a warrior returns to his roots and restores his focus towards his ultimate purpose.

Understanding the core purpose that lies behind their outward goals is what reveals fighters' true natures. Their purpose becomes their rock and provides the warriors with the inner strength to take action. All the other attributes of a combat athlete's mental game build on this particular principle.

FOCUS

During training, it can sometimes be easy to lose focus or otherwise become distracted. An athlete can have a wandering attention span for any number of reasons. It can happen if training drills become mundane and repetitive or when a fighter has a number of personal thoughts weighing on his mind. Any good coach will tell you that if an athlete's mental game isn't 100 percent, it can greatly affect his performance.

In the highly competitive sport of mixed martial arts, it is pivotal to cultivate a laser-like mental focus. Once inside the cage, becoming distracted even for a second can lead to defeat. To avoid this outcome, fighters must diligently train their minds to focus intently on their current actions. During training, it is imperative that combat athletes strive for a high level of attention to detail. Keeping this peak level of concentration helps an athlete to notice more details during an actual fight. Having a high degree of mental focus could be the difference between capitalizing on an opportunity and missing it entirely.

Given the demanding training that mixed martial artists go through, it is no surprise that physical pain and exhaustion can factor into a fighter's loss of concentration. When this happens to you, stay focused on the positive side of the present moment. If your mind jumps ahead to how much more you have to do, it will make it that much more enticing to quit. But quitting is not in the warrior's vocabulary, so you need to train your mind to refocus on accomplishing your goal.

One of the best ways to do this is to focus on your breathing every time you become frustrated or feel like giving up. The more you become aware of your breathing, the easier it will be to regulate it. The importance of proper breathing cannot be overstated and will be addressed in greater depth in later chapters. For now, it is important to know that by calming your breathing, you can help to center your mind.

By bringing your attention back to your breathing, you start to clear your head and eliminate distracting thoughts. Once your mind is clear, it becomes easier to reorient yourself on completing your goals. There is nothing more satisfying than achieving a goal that you've set for yourself, and staying focused will lead to success.

For the MMA warrior, developing focus takes both dedication and discipline. It also takes an understanding of how emotions play into a fighter's mental game. In almost every major sport, competitors try to psyche out their opponents in what becomes a form of mental chess.

MMA is no different, and combat athletes often endeavor to intimidate or provoke an opponent to throw him off his game plan. The instigating fighter hopes that by upsetting his rival, the opponent will lose focus and abandon whatever strategy he had created. By doing this, the instigating fighter attempts to gain a tactical advantage by causing his adversary to get angry and distracted.

The best fighters in MMA keep their cool both outside and inside the cage. This includes keeping their emotions in check as the fight prepares to get underway. There is an incredible emotional and adrenaline dump that happens to a fighter just before a match. Staying mentally calm helps an athlete see more openings and opportunities and maximizes the chances of victory. By taking a few moments for some deep breathing exercises, a fighter can harness his focus and be on top of his mental game.

DISCIPLINE

Discipline is another indispensable component of the warrior mindset. In order to accomplish their objectives, fighters need to have the self-discipline to tackle all of the challenges they face during their training. To achieve results, combat athletes must apply their enhanced mental focus to a winning structure. Setting up a training program and formalizing a workout plan help create the environment a fighter needs to develop his skills and find success.

Self-discipline is required in just about every area of a mixed martial artist's life. From keeping consistent with a workout schedule to studying the combative arts to maintaining a healthy diet plan, discipline is an essential part of an MMA competitor's mental game. It is also one of the most difficult aspects of the mental side of this sport. Gathering the willpower to continue training when your mind and body are exhausted isn't an easy task.

Athletes understand this, which is why having training partners and coaches to help them stay on track is such powerful tool. For the most part, it is easier to let yourself down than to let other people down. The mere presence of a coach can dramatically increase a fighter's output in training by creating a sense of accountability. Being held accountable motivates an athlete to perform and to do the hard work necessary to achieve his objectives.

A warrior knows that in order to successfully reach a long-term goal, he has to accomplish smaller ones along the path to victory. This means that during training, a combat athlete sets measurable and attainable goals. Small triumphs help to increase a fighter's self-esteem and improve his overall discipline. The more empowered a warrior feels, the easier it is to use heightened focus and added discipline to stay on track during training.

CONFIDENCE

Perhaps one of a fighter's biggest assets is his confidence. Having unparalleled faith in yourself and your abilities is a key to winning, both in this sport and in life. A warrior knows that to do the seemingly impossible takes a great deal of self-assurance and personal belief. Mixed martial artists, like many athletes, have a great deal of confidence in themselves. Let's face it; it takes guts to step into a cage against an equally skilled opponent who wants to knock you unconscious. Some might say it's the ultimate test of confidence.

But this trait can be a dual-edged sword, and sometimes a fighter can become over-confident. When combat athletes get too cocky, they tend to get complacent and think that they are unstoppable. A fighter who develops a gigantic ego will inevitably slack off on his training and usually underestimate his opponent. This is typically when the walls come tumbling down, and a conceited fighter gets beat because he cut corners in training and lost focus.

A warrior knows how to effectively wield this duel-edged sword by developing a high level of confidence without becoming egotistic. It can be a fine line, but ultimately the combat athlete knows that this balance affects his performance inside the cage. Therefore, an MMA athlete works diligently to build supreme confidence in his skills and abilities.

The best way to improve self-confidence is through good old-fashioned hard work. This is why a warrior trains so rigorously to refine his techniques and enhance his conditioning. The more a fighter trains, the more confidence he builds in himself. This translates into a winning attitude that gives a warrior the momentum to push beyond his comfort zone. By keeping a positive and optimistic mindset, combat athletes can break through any self-imposed barriers and produce the outcome they desire.

SELF-EVALUATION

The way that a fighter tempers his increased confidence is through constant self-evaluation. To become the best in any sport, an athlete needs to constantly assess his performance. This is another prominent part of a warrior's mental game. Becoming the best is about consistently tracking your progress and examining the results. For a fighter, this sometimes means changing up the training curriculum.

For example, a combat athlete may find that he has surpassed the skills of his sparring partners and is no longer learning new techniques. Through measuring his performance, the MMA practitioner may come to realize that he is underperforming in a specific combative art. To remedy this inconsistency, a fighter may choose to increase his practice time in that discipline to boost his skills. From time to time, a fighter may also realize that a particular coach has taken the competitor as far as he can and it is time for a change.

To be the most capable athlete possible, a smart MMA warrior learns from both successes and failures. Some of the best fighters in the world watch videotape of themselves to spot holes and expose weaknesses in their own fight games. Filming training segments, workouts, and sparring sessions and reviewing the footage can be an invaluable tool to locating areas that need improvement.

After a fight, many combat athletes watch the match to identify their mistakes. Watching themselves in action also helps a mixed martial artist to see where he could have capitalized on a missed opportunity. If examined properly, this will assist in redesigning a training program to help the fighter spot the openings he overlooked during the bout.

How was his mental game? His physical conditioning and endurance? His application of techniques and use of overall strategy? Knowing the answers to these questions provides the warrior with the self-knowledge necessary to maximize training time. It also shows that the MMA athlete has the ability to select positive training habits and eliminate unproductive ones. In this way, the warrior is always seeking to improve his game through self-evaluation.

RESOLVE

When you are trying to improve yourself in any aspect of life, you must connect with this aspect of the warrior. Whether you are endeavoring to improve your jiu-jitsu skills or take your cardio endurance to the next level, you'll need a specific mindset to accomplish your goals. An iron will is perhaps one of the most critical factors of a fighter's mental game. The resolve to push through any pain or obstacle is what constitutes the warrior mentality.

Let's get realistic; there will be numerous times when you will be frustrated in your training. You may be unable to execute a particular technique, or you may be physically exhausted but have three more sets to complete your workout. Your training partner may submit you time and time again during training matches, or your boxing coach may seem to be pummeling you for his own enjoyment. The bottom line is the same: The combat athlete never, ever gives up. The ability to overcome anything that is thrown his way, either in training or in life, is what defines the warrior.

When your training gets brutally hard, the best way to succeed is to stay focused on your current task as it relates to your mission. Focus on your breathing and take one moment at a time instead of looking at how much more work lies ahead. Let's say your mission is to run three miles and you are halfway there. Your legs are hurting, you are gasping for breath, and every neuron in your brain says you would rather be at home on the couch. If you agonize over the fact that you are only halfway done with the workout, you are in for a long training session.

Fighters often overcome the painful training sessions by staying focused and maintaining a positive mental attitude. Combining overall optimism with gritty determination, MMA warriors dig deep within their reserve of inner strength to achieve their goals in training, in life, and inside the cage. The unwavering commitment to pushing their bodies to the limit is a part of every fighter's mindset.

In the event that you decide to enter an MMA competition, focusing on your pain or fatigue is only going to give your opponent the advantage. The moment you allow yourself to be mentally distracted, your opponent can capitalize on the mistake and put you in a position of disadvantage. To win, you have to be focused on your objective: finishing the fight.

CREATIVITY

Creativity is a natural part of MMA. You've probably already gleaned that MMA fighters use some pretty creative and unorthodox ways to improve their strength and conditioning. This is important because it keeps a fighter on his toes as he prepares for a match.

In fact, some athletes purposely instruct their coaches to mix up their training so that the fighters have no idea what to expect. By doing this, the combat athlete learns to adapt quickly to changes in circumstance. This concept is extremely beneficial inside the cage, where a fight can be incredibly unpredictable.

If a fighter is adaptable, relaxed, and calm during a match, he'll often discover openings and opportunities to exploit his opponent's weaknesses. A fighter can utilize his natural creativity if he has successfully developed the other attributes of his mental game. Drawing on his focus and resolve, a combat athlete can also utilize his creativity to escape from dangerous situations.

WARRIOR MEDITATIONS

The best fighters in the world all have one thing in common: They integrate all of the above mental game components into a singular clear vision of what they want to achieve. The top MMA competitors understand that to be the best, they need to utilize all levels of their training to gain a competitive edge over their opponents. This is where creative visualization comes into play in a warrior's training regiment.

Science has shown that athletes who visualize a successful outcome are significantly more likely to achieve victory. This type of mental practice, called visual motor rehearsal, is an often-underused training technique. In this process, a combat athlete closes his eyes and mentally rehearses the fight. Having developed his ability to focus, the fighter visualizes himself throughout the entire course of events that lead to victory.

Smart athletes who understand how to maximize their training time often incorporate this process as part of their workout. For instance, many of the elite MMA competitors use their resting periods in between training rounds for visualization. This is a great way for fighters to get the most out of their workouts, because they are training their mind and body simultaneously.

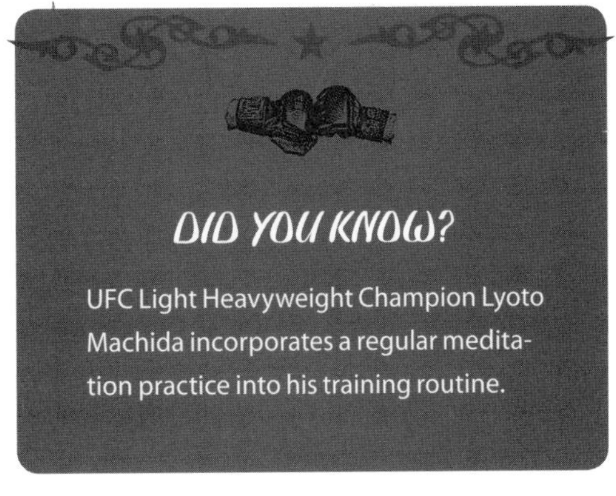

DID YOU KNOW?

UFC Light Heavyweight Champion Lyoto Machida incorporates a regular meditation practice into his training routine.

Another benefit of this process is that it helps to calm the physical body in addition to clearing the mind. By focusing on deep breathing in conjunction with visual motor rehearsal, a warrior can quickly lower his heart rate. This also oxygenates the body and helps to speed his recovery time between rounds. Although it is far from sitting on a rock and contemplating the universe, this technique is a type of meditation for warriors.

Try the following mental exercises as part of your training regimen. Experiment with the particular ways that these meditations work best for you during your workouts. Try a visual motor rehearsal routine for five minutes before you begin your physical training for the day. As mentioned above, you can also use one-minute meditations between your workout rounds. As you end your training for the day, taking another five minutes for visualization is also beneficial. You can use any combination of these methods, or all of them together.

Starting Any Meditation

For each meditation, begin with the following process: Start by becoming aware of your breathing. Spend a few moments feeling the air entering your lungs and try to relax your body as you exhale. Chances are good you'll feel your heart pulsing, so spend another few moments endeavoring to slow your heart rate as you breathe deeply. Repeat in your mind the words *calm* or *center* a few times. Next, count down from five to one as you continue to slow your breathing. Your mind will become clearer, and you can visualize a large, blank, white movie screen.

You can then move into any of the following visual motor rehearsals.

Purpose Meditation

Visualize yourself on the screen, just like you are watching a movie. See yourself fully engaged in the pursuit of your training goals. Feel the sensations of accomplishing those goals and see yourself being congratulated by others. Hear their compliments as they tell you your success was because of staying true to your purpose. Then refocus on the feeling of your purpose—the driving force behind your training. Cement that feeling in the core of your body and visualize it on the screen as the fuel that propels you through your training and helps you achieve your goals.

Focus Meditation

On the screen in your mind, visualize a particular quote or saying that inspires you in your training. It may be something a coach or training partner mentioned or an inspirational anecdote from a fighter you respect. Once you can see it on the screen, hear it being repeated in your mind. Keep your focus on this one saying, seeing and hearing it repeated over and over like a mantra. As you do this, see if you can extend your focus to include your breathing. Focus on nothing else except for your mantra and your breathing until you come out of the meditation.

Confidence Meditation

For this exercise, visualize yourself on the screen at the point in your life where you had the highest level of confidence. It can be anytime when you felt like you could take on the entire world. Visualize and feel yourself completely in that moment in your life. Now visualize yourself taking off a "coat of confidence" from that point in your life and putting it on yourself in this moment. Essentially, you are taking off a jacket from a time when you were supremely confident and wearing it now. By doing this, you are placing yourself in a state of ultimate confidence.

Discipline Meditation

Similar to the confidence meditation, visualize a time in your life when you have been extremely disciplined. A time when you followed a structure that led to your success. Visualize that version of you on the large screen and see the positive outcome of those disciplined actions. Next, visualize stepping into the movie screen and directly into the image of yourself. This process of alignment helps you to reacquire the positive feelings of being disciplined in your life. Lastly, feel yourself inside the movie screen as the scenery changes to your workout area. Sense your new level of discipline that will help you stay on track in your training and lead to triumphing over any obstacle.

Self-Evaluation Meditation

For this exercise, visualize recent training matches or fights on the screen in your mind. Watch the replay like an observer sitting in a movie theater. While other meditations have endeavored to increase your emotional involvement, for the self-evaluation meditation you want to be as detached as possible. Simply notice yourself on the screen and watch the progression of events. Hold your critique until after you've seen the whole event. When finished, reflect on what you witnessed while watching the screen and save your observations in your memory like a computer file. In this way, you learn from your experiences but avoid dwelling on them, which distracts you from the present moment.

Resolve Meditation

In this proactive and visceral mental exercise, put yourself inside the movie screen during one of your toughest training sessions or fights where you came out on top. Feel the deep-seated feeling of resolve as you took whatever punishment was dished out and kept on going. Feel your sense of determination as you gritted your teeth and never lost focus. No matter what happened, you were going to continue pushing through the pain.

Nothing could stop you from succeeding. Hold this sense of unbreakable tenacity until you come out of your meditation.

Creativity Meditation

Start this warrior meditation by visualizing a time during your training where you continually outmaneuvered your sparring partner. No matter what he did, he couldn't submit you or land any effective strikes. You were simply toying with him, causing your partner to get frustrated and lose his focus. Now transfer this feeling as you visualize yourself during an actual match. No matter what techniques your opponent tries, you easily evade him. It's as if you are four or five moves ahead of him, even when he starts to get you in a tight spot. You escape effortlessly and apply your own techniques to quickly secure your victory.

THE PRESENT MOMENT OF FIGHTING

When you calm the body and clear the mind, all of the aspects of a fighter's mental game merge into complete focus on the present moment. When an actual fight is underway, staying fully in the moment is key to success. Get distracted by thinking about the previous round, and your opponent could knock you out while your attention is diverted. Mentally jumping ahead to thoughts of your victory while the match is still happening is equally perilous. The only way to be completely alert and able to capitalize on any situation is to be focused only in the present. This is the mind of the warrior.

Now that you have the necessary understanding of mental game, it is time to move full speed ahead into the incredible cardio training of mixed martial arts.

5 ★★★

A WARRIOR'S HEART: CARDIO TRAINING FOR COMBAT

THE MECHANICS OF CARDIOVASCULAR FITNESS

The importance of cardiovascular fitness in the sport of mixed martial arts cannot be overstated. With MMA becoming more competitive every day, combat athletes must have excellent conditioning in order to succeed. More than that, they need to ensure they have the correct type of conditioning to prevail. Before jumping into that subject, however, let's take a moment to review the inner mechanics of the body that are responsible for these types of exercise.

The circulatory system is made up of the heart, lungs, blood, blood vessels, and arteries. The average adult has about six quarts of blood pumping through the body. The heart pumps oxygen-depleted blood through the lungs and returns oxygenated blood through the process of pulmonary circulation. Systemic circulation then carries the oxygenated blood to the rest of the body, including the muscles. But why is this information important to a combat athlete?

The better the cardiovascular system is at delivering oxygenated blood to the body, the more work the body can perform. This function is critical to the MMA warrior who has to push his body to the limit during a match. As you'll see shortly, fighters train in a specific type of cardiovascular training to increase their bodies' ability to extract oxygen from the air and deliver it via systemic circulation to the muscles.

The average heartbeat in an adult is sixty-five to seventy-five beats per minute. During rigorous cardio training, an athlete's heart rate can get up to two hundred beats per minute. The rate at which a combat athlete's heartbeat returns to his average heartbeat is called the heartbeat recovery rate. This is a critical component of MMA because fighters only get one minute of rest between rounds. The faster a fighter's heartbeat recovers from intense exercise, the better his level of conditioning.

Anaerobic vs. Aerobic Conditioning

As we touched on in chapter three, there are two predominant types of conditioning: aerobic and anaerobic exercise. Aerobic conditioning involves the intake and use of oxygen to perform low to moderate levels of exercise. An example would be distance running because it involves exercising at a continuous pace with an athlete's heart rate staying in a range below his metabolic threshold.

Anaerobic exercise on the other hand is the type of conditioning most used by today's MMA warriors. Anaerobic means "without oxygen" and refers to quick bursts of intense exercise. In this type of conditioning, the body has to perform at high levels without the necessary amount of oxygen to sustain these activities. An example of this would be short-distance sprinting because the body is rapidly deprived of oxygen.

Anaerobic conditioning makes for grueling training but provides excellent results. An important concept to understand here is that anaerobic exercises can also improve a fighter's aerobic fitness. The reverse, however, is not true. Running miles on end won't improve your ability to handle five-minute rounds inside the cage. This is one of the reasons that combat athletes favor sprinting as a part of their cardio programs. Most will limit their running to no more than three miles at a time.

While most exercises are a combination of anaerobic and aerobic, they tend to be one more than the other. Think of it like a sliding scale, where a particular exercise might be 75 percent anaerobic and 25 percent aerobic. Again, the goal is to incorporate as many anaerobic exercises as possible in an effort to imitate the type of conditioning needed for MMA.

In chapter three, we also mentioned that fighters often design their workout routines to mimic the rounds of an actual match. This means that their fitness regimen will typically incorporate hard anaerobic exercises for five to ten minutes without any break. After a short one-minute rest, the combat athlete goes all out again for another five- to ten-minute round. This type of conditioning is the closest thing to athletic self-torture you'll ever come across in physical fitness. Fighters are gluttons for punishment, but it can yield terrific results, and that's one of the reasons they put themselves through this harsh training.

If the combat athlete can cultivate the warrior resolve we talked about in the last chapter, he can push himself past the pain and fatigue that comes with this level of conditioning. Hard-core anaerobic exercise regimens are also very enlightening and help a fighter to come face-to-face with his limits. The reward will be an increased ability to handle the extreme endurance requirements of this sport.

Additional Cardio Considerations

As if this type of training isn't challenging enough, there are a couple of additional elements that fighters can incorporate to increase their conditioning levels. The first is one that is often overlooked by many combat athletes. In an effort to simulate the conditions of an actual match as closely as possible, we highly recommend that MMA warriors wear their mouthpieces during a workout.

Following this simple piece of advice will help reduce the amount of oxygen a fighter can take in while exercising, thereby increasing anaerobic conditioning. It will also help a fighter get used to wearing his mouth guard. Once this becomes comfortable, there is another easy way to make cardio training even more challenging: adhesive tape.

In a sport where getting punched in the face is normal, busted noses are a common occurrence. When this happens in a fight, it generally means that a fighter's only option is to breathe through his mouth. To simulate this during training, use some medical tape to seal the nose and tape it shut. Combine this technique while wearing a mouthpiece and your anaerobic conditioning goes to a whole new level.

Another common practice among professional fighters is what is called high altitude training. Working out at higher altitudes increases the body's ability to extract oxygen from the air and transport it to the muscles. At sea level, normal air has an oxygen content of about 21 percent. Most people know that the higher you go in altitude the "thinner" the air gets. What this means is that the oxygen content of the air is reduced to between 9 percent and 15 percent.

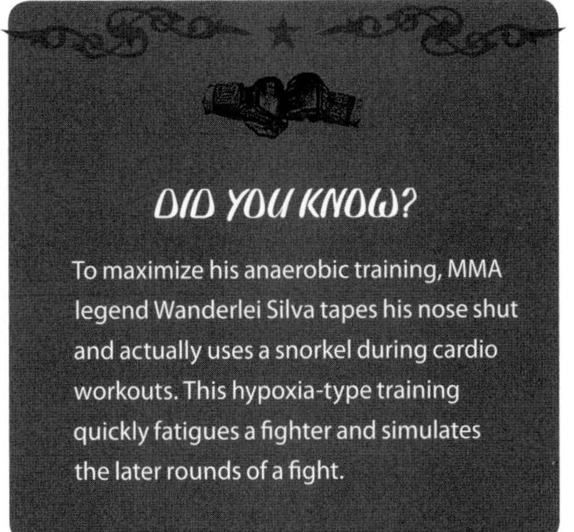

DID YOU KNOW?

To maximize his anaerobic training, MMA legend Wanderlei Silva tapes his nose shut and actually uses a snorkel during cardio workouts. This hypoxia-type training quickly fatigues a fighter and simulates the later rounds of a fight.

Some of the best-known MMA training facilities, including Tito Ortiz's Big Bear camp in California and Greg Jackson's camp in New Mexico, are high-altitude training centers. Another practice that is becoming more common for fighters unable to travel to these high-altitude training camps is the use of personal hypoxicators. These portable devices simulate a high-altitude environment by reducing the amount of oxygen that is consumed.

Although they run several hundred dollars, high-altitude simulators made by AltiPower (www.altipower.com) and AltoLab (www.pharma pacific.com) are gaining in popularity. Some training centers have purchased a hypoxicator to be used by all the fighters on its team. This helps to defray the cost among team members and provides the ability to incorporate regular high-altitude training without having to go to the mountains. Some studies have even shown that a regular hypoxicator training program yields better results than the approximate two-week short-term benefit of training in the mountains.

Measuring Cardiovascular Improvement

While it is easy to measure progress in weight training by tracking how much weight a fighter can lift, measuring cardiovascular fitness can prove difficult. This is where the use of a heartbeat monitor comes into play. These products can now be purchased for around $50 to $150 and provide an excellent resource for the fighter to evaluate his performance.

The best types of heart-rate monitors for combat athletes are ones that have a chest strap and wristwatch combination. The chest strap takes the measurement, and the wristwatch provides the digital readout of the fighter's heartbeat. Although there are many excellent products out there, our top economical recommendation is the Timex Personal Trainer 5G971. There are also higher-end models, like the Polar F11, that have computer software designed to help fighters track all of their workouts.

Heart-rate monitors give MMA warriors the ability to have a biofeedback device that helps them develop sensitivity to their own heartbeats. A fighter begins to understand what it feels like to train at different heart-rate ranges. It also provides the fighter with a way to measure his heartbeat recovery rate.

Seeing a reduction in the athlete's maximum heart rate during the same type of exercise over a period of weeks is an excellent indicator of cardiovascular improvement. Likewise, noticing the trend of a lower heart rate at the end of a one-minute rest period is another positive measurement. Lastly, seeing a decrease in the time it takes to reach a normal resting hear rate also points to enhanced levels of conditioning.

All of the above are ways in which fighters push their bodies to the cardio limit. It is how they measure and build the stamina necessary to endure twenty-five minutes of combat inside a cage. Now that we've covered the basics, let's jump into some of the common exercises that are a part of a MMA warrior's cardio regiment. Are you ready?

CARDIOVASCULAR EXERCISES

In the sport of MMA, athletes and trainers utilize so many different types of exercises as a part of cardiovascular conditioning that it would be impossible to list them all. What is presented here are a number of the more common training elements that comprise a typical cardio regimen. While some of the exercises that follow are a combination of cardio and strength activities, the major difference is in the training format.

As we've already discussed, MMA matches typically have five-minute rounds with one-minute rest periods. In an effort to make their training as sport-specific as possible, fighters use this as a formula for their cardio conditioning. It means that the combat athlete will perform an exercise, or series of exercises, for five minutes and then take a one-minute rest. This constitutes one round; fighters typically complete five rounds during one workout.

Yeah, we know this type of training is a form of self-torture. Our advice? Bring some motivational music or a buddy to help coach and push you through the exercises. This is some of the toughest training in the world, and that's one of the reasons MMA warriors are counted among the best-conditioned athletes on the planet. Oh, and bring a bucket just in case.

Jumping Rope

Jumping rope has been used as a cardio conditioning exercise in boxing for decades. Although it is a simple exercise, it can be a very effective cardio warm-up tool. There are also a number of different techniques and sequences that can be mixed together for an entire cardio session. If you enjoy jumping rope, the best program out there is called Rope Sport. You can find more information at www.ropesport.com.

Mountain Climber Push-Ups

This is a variation of a common exercise called the mountain climber. Start in a push-up position.

Now quickly bring your right knee to your chest while maintaining your balance.

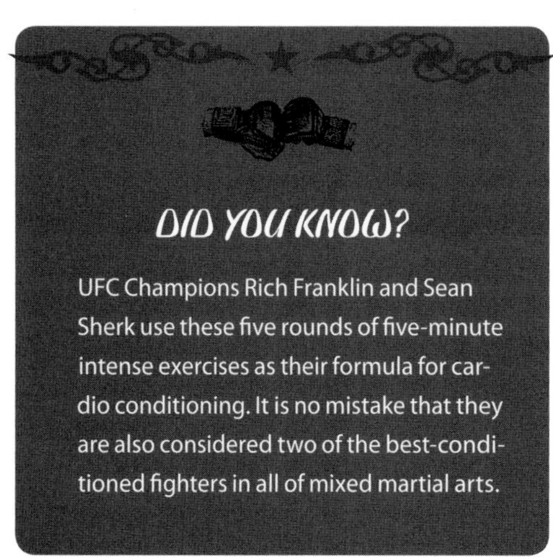

DID YOU KNOW?

UFC Champions Rich Franklin and Sean Sherk use these five rounds of five-minute intense exercises as their formula for cardio conditioning. It is no mistake that they are also considered two of the best-conditioned fighters in all of mixed martial arts.

Next, switch knees by rapidly bringing your right leg back to the starting position and bringing your left knee to your chest. This switch is to be done as fast as possible while still maintaining good form.

Quickly bring your left leg back to the starting position and execute a full push-up.

Upon completing the push-up, you are once again in the starting position and the process repeats. Begin by attempting to do this exercise for thirty seconds and then take a one-minute rest. It is a terrific cardio and upper-body exercise that can be done anywhere. Eventually you can build up your endurance to perform mountain climber push-ups for longer periods.

Partner Closed Guard Sit-Up Reaches

This is a fantastic cardio exercise that also heavily works the core. Start by having your partner get in a low squat position. Then jump to guard by wrapping your legs around his waist and locking your ankles. Lean back until your head touches the mat.

With your feet firmly locked together, start executing a sit-up. Although you can place your hands behind your head, be sure not to pull your head forward, which could cause unnecessary strain on your neck.

Having gone as far as possible with your sit-up, twist your body to your left side and begin to reach over your partner's right arm and shoulder.

Lastly, reach up and over your partner's arm. This portion of the exercise begins to build the muscle memory for the Kimura submission, which will be covered on page 212. To complete the exercise, simply lower your body back down. Then repeat the closed guard sit-up reach, this time twisting your body to the right and reaching over your partner's left arm and shoulder.

Squat Jumps With Medicine Ball

This dynamic plyometric exercise is terrific for developing powerful take-downs, but overdoing the jumping portion can add extra strain on your knees. That is why we recommend only one explosive upward movement for every ten squats. We also advise against doing more than one minute of this exercise per round.

This exercise builds explosive power in the legs while also contributing to cardiovascular fitness. Start by holding a medicine ball above your head.

Next, bring the medicine ball to your chest and then perform a squat. Once you raise back up to your starting position, push the medicine ball back above your head. Repeat steps 1 and 2 for ten repetitions.

On your tenth squat, explode upward and jump with the medicine ball, pushing it as high into the air as you can.

Tire Flip

The tire flip is a phenomenal full-body exercise for the MMA warrior. Involving both the lower and upper body, this explosive cardio activity will take your conditioning to new heights. The only thing you'll need is a giant tractor tire. If you check around with local farmers or at scrap yards, you'll probably be able to locate one for free. Make sure you bring a few buddies to help you transport it because most can weigh between two hundred and four hundred pounds.

With the tire flat on the ground, squat down and get your hands underneath it. Get on the balls of your feet and lean into the tire slightly as you explode upward and slightly forward. Once the tire is elevated above your thighs, switch your grip to push the tire upward and over to complete the flip. Just like the other exercises, do as many tire flips as you can in one minute. You'll definitely be looking forward to your rest period after this awesome exercise.

Heavy Bag Ground 'n' Pound

It's time to practice your beat-down skills! The heavy bag ground 'n' pound exercise is a fantastic way to build your cardio endurance. It also gives you a chance to work on some of your technique while you improve your stamina.

There are a number of ways to format this drill. You can do punches only for one minute and then the same for elbows and knees. Another option is to do punches, elbows, and knees on one side of your body for one minute. The possibilities are numerous, so mix and match them as you like. Just remember to make your strikes as hard and as fast as possible to maximize your cardiovascular workout.

To start, throw your heavy bag on the ground and climb on top in a full mount.

Start off with twenty seconds of punches as fast and as hard as you can deliver them.

Next, it is time to rain down some elbows on the heavy bag. Switch to a knee mount with one knee on the bag and the opposite foot on the floor. Once again, go as hard and fast as you can for twenty seconds.

Now it's your chance to finish the drill with some punishing knees. Slide off from the knee mount and switch into a simulated side mount by putting your chest perpendicular on the bag. Extend and lift your striking leg as high as possible.

Drive your knee forward with as much power and speed as you can muster. Deliver as many knee strikes as you can for the final twenty seconds.

Running

Since we've previously identified why fighters select sprinting over distance running, we can go right into detailing the MMA warrior's running program. Short distance sprinting, whether on a treadmill, at a track, or on an outdoor sports field, is a terrific cardio conditioning exercise. The goal, regardless of the type of sprinting, is to go all out for a short fifteen-second burst followed by a moderate running pace for forty-five seconds. Repeat this process without stopping for five minutes, and you've completed one round and earned yourself a one-minute rest period.

Here are some variations that will mix up your rounds of sprinting:

- **Treadmill:** Complete the above routine, but increase the level of incline by 5 to 7 percent for each round you complete. This would mean that your fifth round is at a 25 to 35 percent incline.
- **Track:** Sprint the straightaway and then lightly jog the curves. Repeat until your five-minute round is up.
- **Outdoors:** If you don't have a buddy for the partner carry 'n' run described on page 72, use a medicine ball or free weights instead. Another option is to purchase a weight vest to add resistance to your running.
- **Stair climb:** Head to a local high school or college stadium and sprint up the stairs. Quickly walk back down and repeat for a full five-minute round.
- **Hill sprints:** There is pretty much the same exercise as above except you're using a hill. For a modification, try "bear crawling" up the hill by putting your hands flat on the ground and using both your arms and legs to make it to the top. Walk back down and repeat for five minutes.

Resistance Run

If you are by yourself, try threading your resistance band through the support straps of your heavy bag and then securing the band around your chest. See if you can run forward, dragging the heavy bag behind you for added resistance. Make sure you have a couple of heavy-duty elastic bands for this exercise.

Another way to achieve the same objective is with a weight-pulling sled. You can purchase a professional one or make one on your own with some plywood and 2 × 4s. Most sleds will have a short one- to two-foot pole on top of the sled on which you can stack plates of free weights. This exercise is great for both the upper and lower body.

Grab your elastic resistance band; it's time for some resistance running. If you have a partner, double up the resistance band around your chest and have your partner lean back as you try to sprint forward.

Partner Carry 'n' Run

This is another terrific running exercise that adds weight resistance. You'll need a partner, preferably someone close to your own body weight.

Start by grabbing your partner's outstretched right wrist with your left hand.

Next, squat down underneath his arm while threading your right arm between his legs. Reach your right hand around your partner's right leg and towards his right wrist.

Grasp your partner's right wrist with your right hand as you move your left hand up to his elbow. Squat down further and make sure your right foot is directly in between your partner's feet.

Lift your partner upwards onto your shoulders as you stand up. Using this position, you'll keep from dropping your partner on his head.

Have your partner lock his ankles together and start your fifteen-second sprint, followed by forty-five seconds of moderate running.

Swimming

Swimming is one of the best all-around exercises on the planet, and it is awesome for MMA competitors. First, it is a rigorous anaerobic workout because you have to hold your breath when your face is in the water. Second, it is a full-body workout, which also gives a fighter complete freedom of movement. Many combat athletes report increased body sensitivity, relaxation, and fluidity of movement in their sparring as a result of a regular swimming practice.

If you are new to swimming, try starting with the basic freestyle stroke. As your skills in the water progress, you can advance to the breast and butterfly strokes. To improve your swimming technique, we suggest checking out the terrific Total Immersion DVD series at www.totalimmersion.net.

While there are a number of excellent swimming strokes to help you get from one end of the pool to the other, there is one rule you absolutely should never break: Always have a swim buddy. Since the type of swimming training a combat athlete undergoes is very intense, the last thing you want to do is take a chance on drowning. So do yourself a favor and make sure there is always a lifeguard or coach to monitor your progress.

Remember, MMA is a sport where you need power, speed, and endurance for up to twenty-five minutes. Thus, any swimming routine you develop should follow the same five-minute round and one-minute rest formula. If you haven't done any swimming in a long time, you can bet on needing to start with one minute of swimming followed by a thirty-second rest. Everyone has to start at his own level, and you'll build up your endurance the more you practice.

Sparring and Grappling

For the aspiring MMA enthusiast, there is absolutely no better way to enhance cardiovascular fitness than through actual sparring. It provides an opportunity to test both your techniques as well as your perseverance.

There are an infinite number of ways to mix and match sparring drills. A great way to start is with light standup sparring. This can be done for one minute or an entire five-minute round.

Next, you can work on closing the distance and attempting takedowns. This really gets your blood pumping and hones your wrestling skills. Once you score a takedown, you can stand back up and go again or keep the fight on the ground.

If you keep things on the ground, work for a dominant position. Groundwork can also be an entire five-minute round of your sparring session.

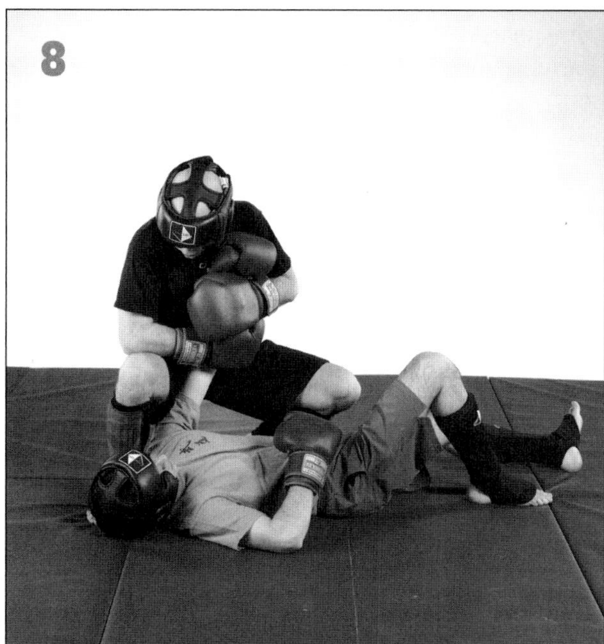

You can also try to make your opponent tap out with a submission. If you submit your partner, just stand back up and start all over again until your five-minute round is up.

If you have multiple training partners, one of the best sparring conditioning exercises is to go with a new partner for each round. This way, each opponent is fresh and ready to give his all for each round. You, on the other hand, have to develop your mental resolve to push through the fatigue. Five rounds of sparring in this format is sometimes called "the shark tank" because you spar against one opponent while the others are circling the mat like sharks waiting to get their turn.

One quick note: Make sure your sparring partners all agree to the level of intensity of the sparring session. The easiest way is to establish a 1 to 10 scale with 1 being shadow boxing and 10 being about 85 percent strength and speed. Of course, this scale should also be evaluated on the amount of sparring gear you are wearing.

Wearing groin protection, a mouthpiece, full shin pads, headgear, and twelve-ounce boxing gloves may mean that you can spar harder without a high risk of injury. Wearing just a cup, mouth guard, and MMA gloves may mean you'll have to tone down the intensity level. The balance between intensity level and threat level provides a multitude of training options during a sparring session.

Having explored the cardio training of combat athletes, we can now examine the other half of an MMA warrior's fitness routine: strength conditioning.

6 ★★★

A WARRIOR'S POWER: STRENGTH TRAINING FOR COMBAT

THE MECHANICS OF STRENGTH CONDITIONING

Now that you've worked up a sweat understanding how fighters improve their cardio conditioning, it's time to learn about the strength training used in MMA. Developing fighting strength, power, and endurance is vital to the well-rounded mixed martial artist. In competition, a fighter uses his entire body in an attempt to best his opponent. As a result, developing full-body muscular strength becomes an important goal of the combat athlete.

There are three types of muscle groups: cardiac, smooth, and skeletal. Both cardiac and smooth muscles are involuntary muscles that are not consciously controlled. Skeletal muscles, on the other hand, are consciously controlled and are used to cause motion and exert force. These muscles are attached to the bone by tendons and are the central focus of a combat athlete's strength conditioning.

Broken down into two major groups, skeletal muscles can be classified as either slow- or fast-twitch fibers. Slow-twitch muscle fibers contract for longer periods of time, but with far less force that fast-twitch muscles. If you've ever seen a picture of the muscular tissues of the body, the slow-twitch fibers are bright red. This is because they are dense with capillaries and carry more oxygen. As a result, slow-twitch fibers are the muscles used to support aerobic activity.

Fast-twitch muscles contract rapidly, exerting a large amount of force, but they also fatigue quickly. These muscles are generally lighter in color and are responsible for anaerobic activity. When used, fast-twitch fibers produce more lactic acid buildup than slow-twitch fibers. This type of skeletal muscle also plays an important part in developing a fighter's speed and agility, which we will cover in more detail in chapter eleven.

BASIC STRENGTH-TRAINING CONCEPTS

While many fighters develop a muscularly toned athletic physique, the full-body strength of fighters is different than that of bodybuilders. Using resistance training as well as basic weightlifting exercises, competitors can build muscle strength and bone mass without accumulating overly large muscle groups. This helps fighters to maximize functional strength while maintaining the speed necessary for the sport. Utilizing whole-body exercise also burns significantly more calories and speeds up a fighter's metabolism.

In addition to achieving a high level of strength output, the MMA warrior also has to keep that output going for up to five rounds. This type of strength endurance is usually referred to as strongman training. If you've seen the World's Strongest Man competition on TV, you know that many of the contests revolve around this strength endurance concept. And while combat athletes may not need to lift cars or pull airplanes, having a high degree of strength in the later rounds of a fight could be the difference between winning a championship and losing one.

MMA warriors typically use a combination of weight and resistance training to build their overall strength. Weight training utilizes free weights to oppose muscle contraction, forcing the muscle to overcome the inertia of the mass in order to move the weight. This means that the majority of the strength development occurs at the beginning movement of the exercise. Examples of basic weight training exercises are the bench press, clean and jerk, and barbell squats.

Resistance training involves the use of elastic or hydraulic tension to provide resistance to muscle contraction. In contrast to free weights, elastic resistance training provides the greatest opposition at the end of an exercise movement. Most gyms have resistance machines, and if you've ever seen an infomercial for the Bowflex you know that these types of equipment utilize elastic resistance to develop strength.

Exercises that move a body part against a force are called *isotonic*. Most people are more familiar with exercises that hold a body part in place against a force which are called *isometric* exercises. Isometric exercises are actually quite important for a combat athlete because there are numerous times in a match where one fighter may have to hold a certain position for an extended period of time. A good way to train isometric strength is to simply pause for five seconds during parts of a weight- or resistance-training exercise.

THE FOUR PILLARS OF MMA STRENGTH

In MMA, a fighter needs to develop four main types of strength: explosive, pulling, pushing, and lifting. Each of these categories is an important part of a combat athlete's overall strength-training program. Typically, fighters will use both free-weight and resistance-training exercises to develop their power in each of these areas.

1. **Explosive strength.** The ability to explode into action is a crucial part of securing an advantage in this sport and is what an MMA warrior seeks to develop through anaerobic conditioning. Fighters want to develop their explosive strength to be able to rapidly take an opponent to the ground. They also want to be able to land a series of rapid strikes that may lead to a knockout victory.

2. **Pulling strength.** This type of power is needed in all three levels of the match. While standing up, pulling an opponent into a Muay Thai clinch could gain a fighter an upper hand in the striking game. Similarly, wrestling for position and pulling his opponent off balance can lead to a successful takedown. And when the bout goes to the ground, pulling his opponent into the guard can be an important defensive maneuver.

3. **Pushing strength.** This form of strength is responsible for the power in a fighter's strikes. It is also key in pushing away from an adversary's clinch, as well as pinning an opponent up against the cage. Pushing strength is also used to keep a foe on the ground and unable to stand up when the fight goes to the mat. If an MMA warrior ends up on the bottom, pushing strength may help him sweep his opponent and reverse the position.

4. **Lifting strength.** Being able to lift an opponent for a throw or sweep can earn a fighter valuable points should the match go to a judges' decision. Lifting power is also required for takedowns as well as scrambling against an adversary in an attempt to stand back up if a match went to the ground.

STRENGTH-TRAINING EXERCISES

There are numerous ways to structure a strength-training regiment. Some fighters break their workout down by body part, dedicating an entire session to a handful of muscle groups. In this approach, a combat athlete likely uses a combination of free-weight and resistance-training exercises to develop strength over a weekly routine. For example, the fighter may choose to work the neck, arms, chest, and shoulders on day one. Day two could be back, core, and hip exercises. And day three could focus on lower body strengthening.

Other MMA warriors work on one type of strength conditioning per session. Using this formula, a fighter may work on strictly explosive exercises on one day followed by only pulling exercises on the next day. The succeeding third and fourth sessions could consist of pushing and lifting conditioning. By using this routine, a combat athlete can work the entire body in one session with a specific focus on one application of strength training.

A third method involves integrating the four pillars of strength into one workout. A typical workout in this format could utilize the five-minute round formula described in the last chapter. For example, a fighter could start off with a non-stop five-minute cardio round followed by a one-minute rest. The second round could be dedicated solely to five minutes of explosive strength exercises. Round three could consist of pulling exercises, followed by pushing drills for round four. Lastly, the final five-minute round would be lifting exercises. This routine, lasting only thirty minutes, would provide the fighter with a full-body workout using the most important types of strength conditioning for MMA.

You may also choose to mix and match all of the above strategies in order to form your workout routine. Whatever method you decide is best for your body and schedule, it is best to avoid going longer than a week without training a muscle group. This is because the muscles need to be regularly worked in order to progressively accumulate strength. In the next portion of this chapter, we've outlined some of the best strength-conditioning exercises for MMA athletes.

NECK EXERCISES

Developing multi-dimensional strength in the neck is an often-overlooked portion of training. MMA warriors need to have strong neck muscles in order to maintain posture against a Muay Thai clinch (see page 147) and defend against common submissions like the guillotine choke (see page 217). Fighters should take a gradual, long-term approach to developing the neck and avoid using sharp movements during any exercise. Instead, slow movements performed against light resistance are the preferred method of developing this part of the body.

Isometric Exercise

For this neck exercise, start by simply placing both of your palms on your forehead. Now try to push your head forward as you resist with your hands for fifteen seconds. Then place both hands behind your head and push your head backward while resisting with your hands for another fifteen seconds. Next, place your left hand on the left side of your head and try to push your head to the left for fifteen seconds. Then switch and do the same on the right side of your head.

For the second rotation of this exercise, repeat the same process as above, but instead try to move your head by pushing with your hands. For example, when your palms are on your forehead, try to push your head backwards while you resist this pressure with your neck. This works a different set of neck muscles and helps to develop both pushing and resisting fibers in the neck.

Free-Weight Neck Exercise

This exercise will require a free-weight plate and a harness. Begin with a minimal amount of weight, perhaps only a five- or ten-pound plate. It is also highly recommended that you have a friend or partner spot you for this exercise. Thread the harness through the center hole of the plate and then sit down on a chair or the workout bench. Put the harness around the back of your head and begin to slowly move your head up and down, lifting and lowering the plate.

Muay Thai Scarecrow

This is a fantastic neck-strengthening exercise that also incorporates the Muay Thai clinch that will be covered in chapter eight. It is best to do this drill with someone who is of equal or greater body weight and size. The object is to keep your neck straight with good posture as your partner climbs all the way around your body without touching the floor. Once in a stable position, the partner doing the climbing clinches his hands around the head of the person doing the scarecrow. He then begins to slowly pull towards himself as the standing partner resists.

This drill, while it may seem simple, is anything but easy. The scarecrow exercise builds functional strength in both partners. Even though he is just standing there, the first athlete has to support the full body weight of his training partner. It also develops multi-dimensional neck strength, teaching a fighter how to maintain his neck posture when an opponent is trying to get an advantage.

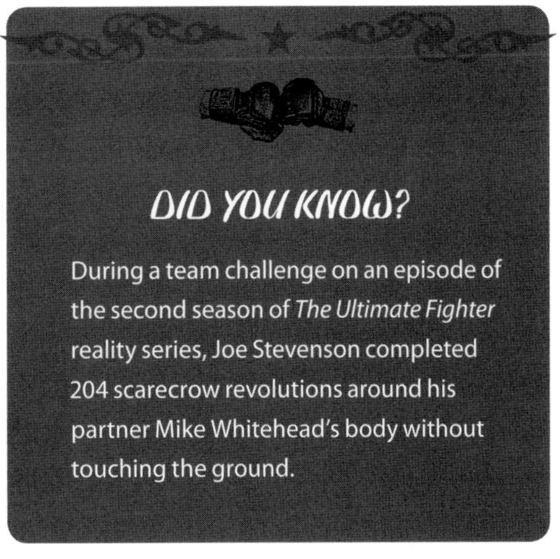

DID YOU KNOW?

During a team challenge on an episode of the second season of *The Ultimate Fighter* reality series, Joe Stevenson completed 204 scarecrow revolutions around his partner Mike Whitehead's body without touching the ground.

This drill begins with one partner standing in one place with his arms outstretched, just like a scarecrow.

The second partner hooks his left arm underneath the right shoulder of the scarecrow. Next, he wraps his right arm around the scarecrow's neck. Then, he hooks his left leg around the scarecrow's waist.

The second partner then climbs onto the first and clinches his hands around the scarecrow's neck. He then slowly applies resistance, trying to pull the scarecrow's head forward. This is typically done for about ten seconds at a time.

Without touching the floor, the second partner starts to spin counterclockwise around the scarecrow's body. He adjusts his grip and then slowly begins pulling in a new direction for another ten seconds.

Continuing to spin around the body, the second partner slides his head underneath the outstretched left arm of the scarecrow. He then locks his hands around the right side of the scarecrow's head and pulls it toward himself for another ten seconds.

Lastly, the moving partner completes his rotation around to the right side of the scarecrow's body. At this point, note that the second partner can also go over the top of the scarecrow's outstretched arm. After pulling toward the scarecrow's body for ten seconds, the moving partner can get down or keep going for another full rotation.

The moving partner now climbs behind the scarecrow and latches his hands around the scarecrow's forehead. Once again, he slowly pulls for approximately ten seconds.

SHOULDER EXERCISES

Having strong shoulder muscles adds power to punches and helps a fighter to maneuver his opponent when in a clinch. Developing these muscles also helps to prevent shoulder related injuries, which can sideline a combat athlete and keep him from competing.

Handstand Push-Ups

This exercise requires little explanation. Simply find yourself a wall and move into a handstand position where your back is facing the wall. Have your heels gently touching the wall as you lower your body downward and then press yourself back up to the original starting position. This is a great exercise, but don't overdo it because you don't want too much blood rushing to your head.

Military Press

The military or shoulder press is an excellent weight-training exercise for the MMA warrior. It helps to build strength in the deltoid and trapezius muscles and can be performed with a pair of dumbbells or a barbell. If you don't have a pair of dumbbells or barbell, use your medicine ball instead. This overhead press starts by bringing the dumbbells or barbell to your chest with your elbows pointed towards the floor. Then press the weights directly upward over your head. This exercise is most effective from the seated position where it isolates the shoulder muscles more effectively.

Shoulder Shrug

For this weight-training exercise, hold a pair of dumbbells down by the sides of your legs. If you are using a barbell, hold the weight in front of your quadriceps. Keeping your arms in the downward position, simply shrug your shoulders. Although it may seem easy, a few repetitions of this exercise will get your shoulders burning.

Dumbbell Shoulder Fly

Start out with your pair of dumbbells at the sides of your legs. Then raise one arm directly out to the side and lower it slowly. Repeat with the opposite arm and then try to raise both dumbbells simultaneously. This is a great shoulder workout.

ARM EXERCISES

Arm strength is obviously an integral part of building explosive, pushing, pulling, and lifting strength. The following exercises will help you develop significant strength in your arms and add tremendous power to your punches.

Weight Sled Pull

This exercise requires a weight sled and a rope. Add a few plates to the weight sled and then attach the rope. Start at the opposite end of the rope and begin using your arms to pull the sled towards you as quickly as possible. This is a phenomenal arm workout because it requires continuous movement.

Medicine Ball Push-Ups

Set your medicine ball on the ground and then place your right hand on the ball and your left hand on the ground. Make sure your feet are shoulder-width apart, and execute a push-up. Then switch by placing your left hand on the ball and your right hand on the ground. Do another push-up and then switch back and forth for a full minute.

The Bus Driver

This exercise is great for building arm strength. Also known as an "around the head plate drill," all this activity requires is a barbell plate. If you are just beginning, start with a twenty-five-pound plate and increase the weight as necessary. As an added challenge, you may want to perform this exercise holding two or three smaller plates, which increases your grip strength.

Just like the exercises mentioned in the last chapter, a great way to train this drill is to do it without stopping for a full minute.

Start by bringing the plate to the center of your chest.

Next, extend the plate straight out in front of your chest.

Rotate the plate counterclockwise and begin to bring it toward your left shoulder. Bend your left elbow down and in towards your side as you raise your right arm.

Continue moving the plate around your left shoulder as you pass your right arm above your head.

Bring your left elbow upward as you simultaneously bring your right elbow down and move the plate directly behind your head.

Now move the plate around to your right shoulder, as you lower your right elbow and raise your left arm to complete the revolution.

WRIST EXERCISES

Since boxing techniques are a significant part of standup striking in MMA, it is vital to develop your wrist strength. Unfortunately, the wrists are definitely one of the most overlooked parts of a combat athlete's strength training regiment. Make sure you integrate some wrist exercises in your program to avoid some of the common injuries received from punching.

Knuckle Push-Ups

While this may seem like an old-school karate movie exercise, doing push-ups on the knuckles actually strengthens the smaller tendons in the wrists. For added difficulty, place the back of one fist on the ground. As you complete the push-up, switch and place the back of your other fist on the ground. Be sure to go slowly, but these unconventional push-ups can dramatically improve your wrist strength.

Dumbbell Rotations

Start this exercise by holding a pair of dumbbells vertically in front of your core.

Rotate your wrists outward so the dumbbells are parallel with the ground.

Continue rotating your wrists outward until the dumbbells are directly in front of your body.

Next, flex your wrists upward as you return the dumbbells to their original starting position. Then repeat the exercise, this time rotating your wrists inward.

CHEST EXERCISES

Having powerful chest muscles are a key to developing your pushing strength. Remember that you'll need this kind of strength for both defense and offense. The extra time you spend building strength in your chest could be the factor that allows you to break away from a competitor's clinch and win the fight.

Fitness Ball Pike Press

This exercise works your chest and shoulders while also forcing you to maintain your balance. Start by placing your hands on the floor and your toes just behind the center of the fitness ball. You'll want your body to be at a right angle to begin this exercise.

Lower yourself toward the ground, bending your head backward as you attempt to bring your chest to the floor. Then press yourself back up to the original starting position. For added difficulty, try to balance on one foot instead of two.

Dumbbell Chest Fly

This weight-training exercise can be performed inclined, flat, or declined depending on your preference. Bring the pair of dumbbells together directly over the center of your chest. Keep your arms relatively straight, with just a slight bend to avoid locking out the elbows. Then move the dumbbells away from each other and out toward your sides. Bring the dumbbells downward until your arms are parallel with your chest. To finish the exercise, bring your arms back to the starting position.

Bench Press

This classic weight-training exercise is a terrific way for MMA warriors to develop their chest strength. As with the dumbbell fly, the bench press can be done inclined, flat, or declined. Make sure that you have a partner to spot you during this exercise. Grab the barbell with a closed grip and lower the weight to your chest while bending your elbows to a 90-degree angle.

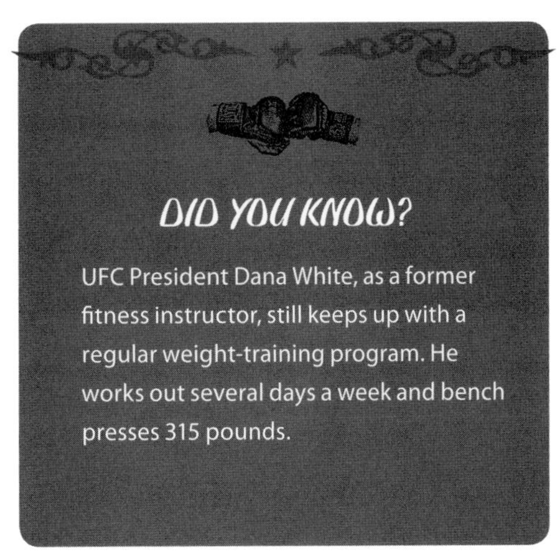

DID YOU KNOW?

UFC President Dana White, as a former fitness instructor, still keeps up with a regular weight-training program. He works out several days a week and bench presses 315 pounds.

BACK EXERCISES

Developing the back muscles greatly enhances a fighter's pulling strength. Keeping an opponent pulled in tight while looking for takedown opportunities or openings for strikes can put you in the dominant position to win the match.

Pull-Ups

Developing the back muscles greatly enhances a fighter's pulling strength. There are numerous variations of pull-ups. Do a few repetitions with a wide grip and then switch to a narrow grip. Another option is to do behind-the-neck pull-ups instead of the traditional chin-ups. For more resistance, add a weight vest or belt. Any way you do them, this exercise is a terrific way to build strong back muscles.

Back Extensions

This weight-training exercise requires a gluteal-hamstring (or "glute-ham") machine that allows you to secure your feet so that your body is parallel to the ground. Lower yourself to a 45-degree angle and then raise your torso back to the original starting position. Your hands are crossed in front of your chest and can be holding a weight plate for added resistance if necessary. This is a great exercise to build the muscles in the lower back.

Romanian Dead-Lift Barbell Row

Another valuable weight-training activity for the back is this exercise, which combines a Romanian dead lift with a barbell row. Start by setting the barbell on the floor and squatting down with your legs shoulder-width apart until you can grip the barbell.

Lift the barbell with your arms extended as you begin to stand up. Keep your hips, back, and chest forward. Your upper body should be at a 45-degree angle from the standing position.

Now row the barbell to your chest while you contract your shoulder blades. This portion of the exercise works directly on the upper back.

Next, extend your back as you come to a full standing position. Try to keep the barbell in the center of your torso as you rise up. This helps to strengthen the lower back.

From the standing position, begin the decline portion of the exercise. Lower yourself down into the previous 45-degree position, with the bar still held against your mid-section.

To finish the exercise, slowly allow the barbell to descend in a reverse row so that the arms are fully extended. Then return the barbell to the ground and repeat. Do this exercise slowly to prevent injury.

ABDOMINAL EXERCISES

Building a strong core is one of the most important parts of a fighter's strength-training regiment. The abdominal muscles aid in positioning the upper body to avoid or deliver strikes. The core is also vital to a combat athlete's movement while on the ground.

Sit-Ups

Sit-ups and crunches are some of the most rudimentary abdominal exercises around, but they are also very effective. There are countless variations to these simple exercises. If you want some creative conditioning activities for your abdominal muscles, check out a local Pilates class. You might even see an MMA athlete there because, believe it or not, fighters take their core training seriously.

Leg Lifts

Leg lifts can easily be done with or without a partner. Simply lie flat on the floor with your legs together. Keeping them straight, slowly lift them upward until your feet are directly above your core at a 90-degree angle. As you lower them back down to a 45-degree angle, you may choose to hold them here for an isometric exercise. Flutter kicks in this position are also fantastic for building the abdominal muscles.

Ab Roller

Nothing quite works the core like an ab roller. This inexpensive piece of equipment can be found at your local sporting goods store for less than $25. You don't need to splurge for the fancy models, because a basic ab wheel will work perfectly.

For beginners, this exercise can be done on the knees. If you've been doing regular sets of sit-ups and leg lifts, however, you may want to give it a try from the standing position.

With the wheel on the floor, place your hands firmly on the wheel grips. Start to push the ab roller forward as you keep your feet in the same place.

Extend as far forward as you can while maintaining your form.

Then begin to retract as you pull the wheel and yourself all the way back towards your feet. Repeat this exercise as many times as possible, but don't overdo it because this exercise will definitely make you sore the next morning.

HIP EXERCISE

Some combat athletes completely forget to develop their hip strength. Strong hips allow a fighter to quickly reposition himself to capitalize on an opponent's movement. Flexible hips are also a key element in executing several ground submission techniques.

Resistance Band Guard Pull

This exercise is one of the best ways to increase your strength in this part of your body.

Start by lying on the ground with your feet up and having your partner hook a resistance band in the crook of your ankle. Be sure to keep your feet flexed to keep the band in place. When you are ready, have your partner pull backward as you try to keep your legs as close to your body as possible. Start with twenty seconds of resistance.

Then rotate onto your left side as you continue pulling with your hips for twenty seconds.

Lastly, you can switch to your right side and finish out with another twenty seconds.

LEG EXERCISES

The leg muscles are vital to developing explosive strength. A necessary part of executing rapid takedowns, leg strength is very important to MMA fighters. Naturally, strong legs are also better able to deliver powerful kicks.

Squats

The squat is a commonly used exercise that is awesome for building leg strength. Mainly focused on building the quadriceps muscle, squats can be done a plethora of ways. They can be done by bending the back or keeping the back straight. Squats can also be performed with or without weights. Be as creative as you want with this exercise, but definitely make it a part of your strength-training routine.

Partner Shoot 'n' Carry

This leg-building exercise has similarities to the partner carry 'n' run from the last chapter. In this exercise, however, we'll specifically focus on building the leg muscles.

Start by standing across from your partner and beginning to shoot in toward his body.

Lower one knee to the ground and then wrap both of your arms around the back of your training partner's legs.

Next, come up to both feet as you press your left shoulder against his torso.

Explode upward as you lift your partner into the air and then begin to walk around as you carry your partner in this position for fifteen seconds. Then put your partner down and repeat the exercise.

Leg Curl

This particular weight-training exercise focuses on strengthening the hamstring muscles. The hamstrings play a crucial role in MMA, helping a fighter to have the necessary strength to take down an opponent. Performed on a leg curl machine, this activity can be performed one leg at a time or both legs simultaneously. Hamstring injuries are common in most athletic sports, and MMA is no exception. Make sure you take the time to work these very important leg muscles.

ANKLE EXERCISE

Having strong ankles is another portion of strength training that is perpetually neglected. The ankles help to balance the body, coordinate mobility, and proving the explosive spring for takedowns. Inside the cage, the mat can be slippery and taking the time to develop ankle strength can help prevent an ankle related injury.

Resistance-Strap Ankle Flex

This exercise helps to develop multi-directional strength in the ankles, which is key for defending against a potential submission by ankle lock. You can use a towel for this exercise, although a yoga strap tends to work better.

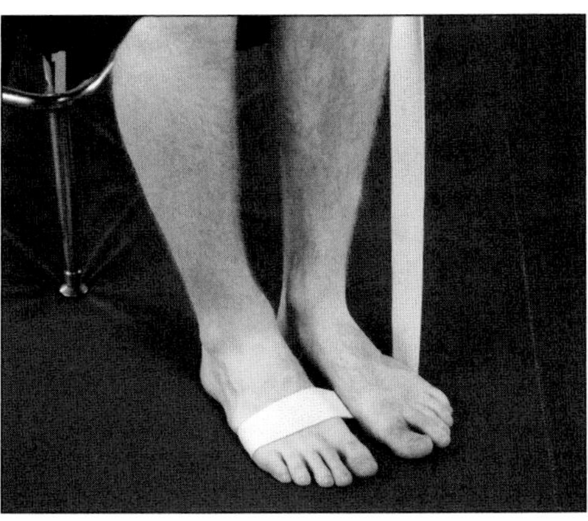

Start by sitting on a chair and wrapping a loop around the instep of your right foot. Then put the sole of your left foot on top of the band to keep it in place.

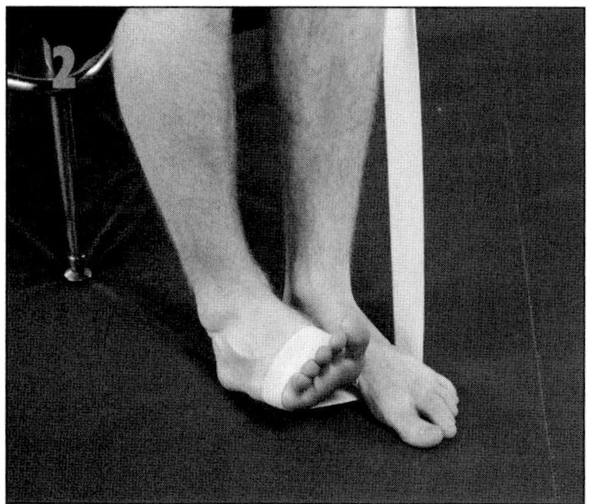

While pressing down with your left foot, try to flex your right foot upward. Make sure your feet are close together to provide the necessary resistance. Try this isometric resistance exercise for approximately thirty seconds.

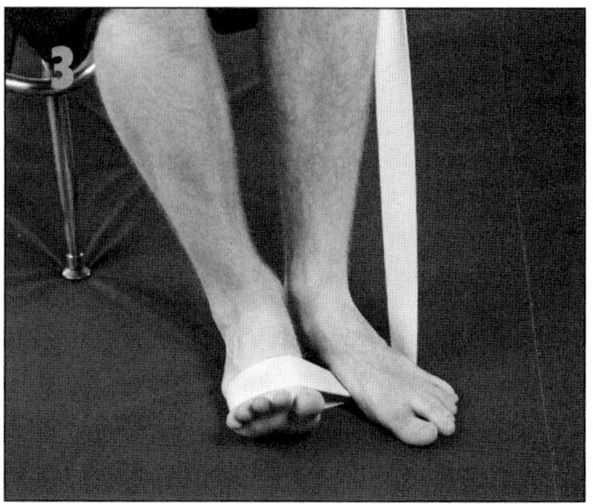

Now try to flex your right foot outward toward your right side. See if you can continuously keep flexing your foot to the right for thirty seconds. Then repeat the entire exercise on the other foot.

7 ★★★

THE STANDUP GAME: BOXING AND MUAY THAI TECHNIQUES

As MMA continues to evolve, the standup striking game is quickly becoming a favorite topic of study among fighters. Everybody can throw basic kicks and punches, but combat athletes have to learn the intricacies of accurate striking techniques in order to win inside the cage. Although it may seem simple, the standup striking portion of MMA is one of the most technical aspects of the sport.

When two competitors are standing and slugging it out, there are a few different ways to achieve a victory. Although it doesn't happen often, a powerful strike could open a deep facial cut that causes significant bleeding. After examination, this could prompt the ringside physician to indicate to the referee that a fighter is unable to continue due to injury.

A fighter may also incapacitate his opponent through a series of punches, kicks, knees, or elbows. This could result in a total knockout, which means that a fighter is knocked unconscious. It could also result in a technical knockout, in which a fighter is mostly conscious, but unable to intelligently defend himself.

THE EVOLUTION OF STRIKING IN MIXED MARTIAL ARTS

In the early days of MMA, striking may have lacked the technical finesse fighters possess today, but it didn't stop warriors from slugging it out. One of the first strikers to rise to prominence was UFC bad boy Tank Abbott. Known for his incredibly heavy hands, Abbott established his presence in his debut in UFC VI by knocking out John Matua cold in only eighteen seconds. Although he had incredible striking power, Abbott lacked good physical conditioning and often suffered losses when fights lasted longer than a few minutes. Competitors quickly realized that even great striking ability was useless without the cardio necessary to endure a tough match.

Another noted striker during the infancy of the UFC was Marco Ruas, winner of UFC VII. Ruas combined his grappling skills with kickboxing and became a well-known fighter. He was also one of the first MMA competitors to effectively employ the Muay Thai leg kick as part of an overall striking strategy. Ruas successfully used this thigh kick to wear down and defeat Paul Varelans and capture the tournament.

Don Frye, a wrestler and professional boxer, showed the effectiveness of good boxing technique just one event later in UFC VIII. Frye won the event after knocking out his first opponent in only ten seconds. This KO still stands as one of the fastest knockouts in MMA history.

The perfect combination of punching technique, accuracy, and lightning-fast speed was demonstrated a year later in the boxing skills of nineteen-year-old Vitor Belfort. Nicknamed "The Phenom," he blasted through his competition in UFC XII and also defeated Tank Abbott in UFC XIII. Belfort showed fight fans just how valuable a fine-tuned boxing skill set could be for an MMA warrior.

Meanwhile, kickboxer Maurice Smith had been racking up wins in Battlecade Extreme Fighting, proving his kicking skills by defeating Marcus Silveira with a head kick. Smith was soon earning a name for himself as an excellent striker and proving that well-placed kicks were an important part of a fighter's striking arsenal.

As UFC ownership changed hands, Chuck Liddell emerged as one of the preeminent strikers in the world. With over a dozen career knockouts, Liddell's powerful right hand is typically set up by his great footwork. While it may seem trivial, footwork is an often-overlooked component of the MMA standup game. Having excellent footwork is an important element of striking and separates the champions from everyone else.

While Liddell was demolishing everyone in his path in the UFC, Wanderlei Silva was doing the same in Japan's PRIDE Fighting events. Known for his vicious Muay Thai knees, Wanderlei has won over twenty fights by knockout. Although not a relation, another Muay Thai fighter named Anderson Silva was also making a name for himself in PRIDE. Anderson signed with the UFC in the spring of 2006 and burst onto the scene with a string of victories. Displaying a complete range of powerful punches, elbows, knees, and kicks, Anderson Silva is considered one of the most accurate and talented strikers in all of MMA.

The current standup striking techniques of MMA are a fusion of traditional boxing and Muay Thai kickboxing. Effectively integrating the accuracy of boxing punches with powerful kicks from kickboxing and devastating Muay Thai knees and elbows, today's fighter has an abundance of strikes to choose from during a match. But knowing how to land great strikes is only half the equation. A combat athlete must also know how to defend against all of these potentially dangerous threats to be a complete fighter.

Jab

The jab is one of the most basic and effective punching techniques for a combat athlete. Although it may not have knockout power, a good jab can make for a powerful strike because MMA gloves are smaller than those used in boxing. This straight punch can also help a fighter to gauge his distance from his opponent. Lastly, the jab is a good boxing technique to help you close the gap between you and your opponent in preparation for a takedown.

Using the same side hand as your lead leg, the jab should be thrown level. Turn your hip towards your target, which also brings the shoulder forward to generate the power for the strike. At the same time your hip and shoulder move toward your opponent, extend your fist forward to execute the punch. Tighten your fist prior to impact and make contact with the middle and index knuckles. Remember to keep your chin tucked and your non-punching hand high to protect your face.

Cross

The cross is another great punching technique, often used in combination with a jab. More powerful than the jab, the cross derives its strength from the longer rotation of the hip and shoulder. This punch is executed with your rear hand and thrown with the force of your body weight behind it. If it lands on your opponent's chin and you see his eyes start to go cross-eyed, you did it right. A key point is not to telegraph this punch too much because it is slightly slower than a jab, and your adversary may have a chance to evade or counter.

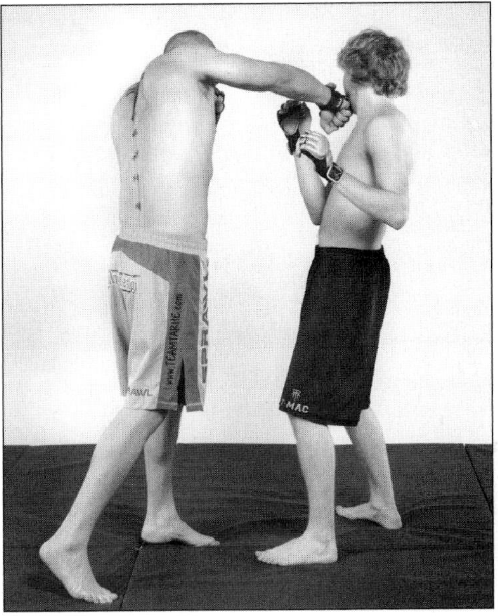

Hook

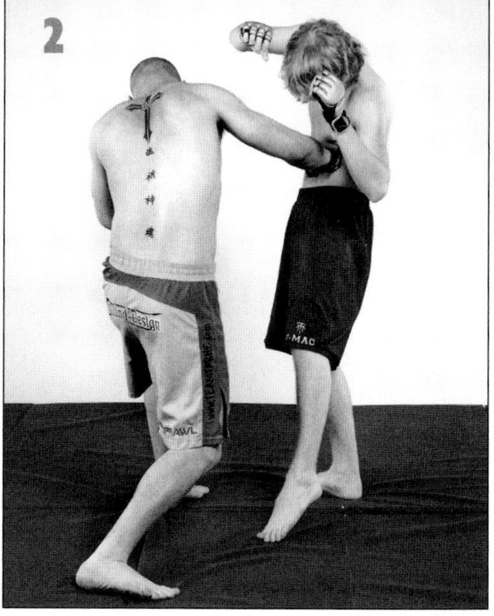

The hook, delivered either to the body or the head, can be a devastating strike. This awesome punch generates power from the full rotation of the hip, torso, and shoulder in one fluid movement. Keep your elbow relatively in line with your fist as you turn your shoulder into the strike. This punch also travels a circular path vs. the linear path of the jab and cross. It makes the hook more elusive as well as being a more difficult punch to block.

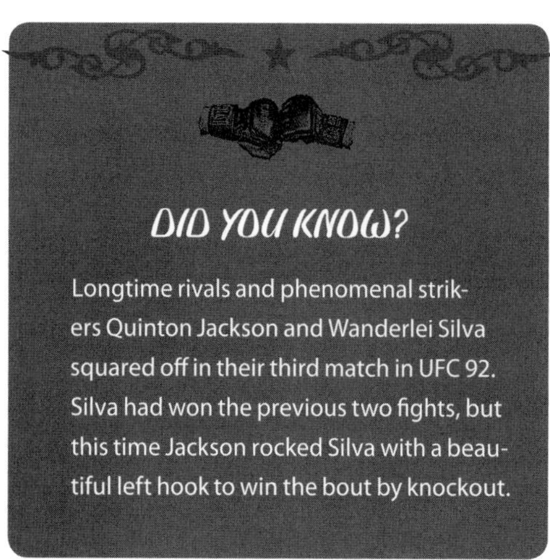

DID YOU KNOW?

Longtime rivals and phenomenal strikers Quinton Jackson and Wanderlei Silva squared off in their third match in UFC 92. Silva had won the previous two fights, but this time Jackson rocked Silva with a beautiful left hook to win the bout by knockout.

Overhand

When it comes to knockouts, the overhand punch takes the cake. Delivered from the rear fist, this strike is often a great way to come over the top of your opponent's hands if his defense gets sloppy. It is also a terrific counterpunch to a jab. As you extend your fist forward, raise the shoulder of the striking hand and rotate your hips into the target. Exhale as you land the punch, and again, remember to keep your non-punching hand high to guard your head.

Uppercut

If you land it on your opponent, this punch is beauty in motion. This terrific strike can be thrown effectively to your adversary's body or head. When you see an opening, drop down slightly in your stance and use your hips to explode your rear hand forward. This punch will have your weight behind it and should be thrown upward at an angle to cause the maximum damage. The uppercut is often used to sneak in underneath an opponent's arms if they are too far apart. It makes for a great strike from the dirty boxing clinch (described on page 146), as well as from the defense against the hook and overhand.

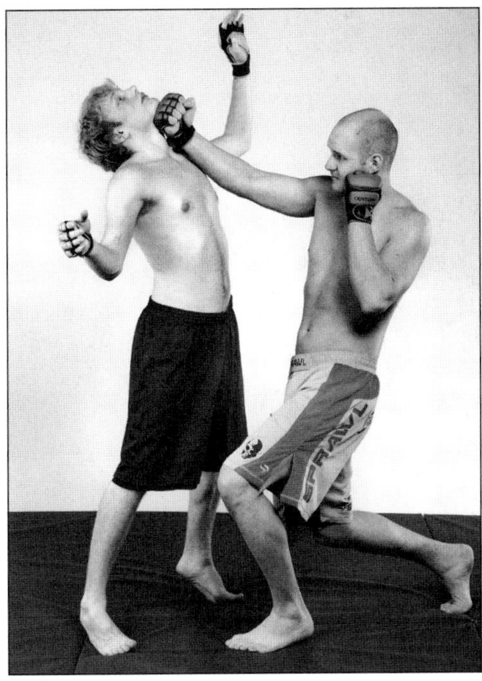

Backfist

Although it isn't employed often, the backfist can be used as a setup technique similar to the jab. It is also thrown from the lead hand like the jab. The movement is circular like the hook, except that it originates close to the body and moves outward and away from the body. It is a quick strike with limited power, but it is useful for creating an opening for a hook or uppercut. The best target is your opponent's jaw line or temple.

DID YOU KNOW?

In May 2001, Shonie Carter knocked out Matt Serra with a spinning backfist at UFC 31.

Rear Spinning Backfist

A flashy variation is the rear spinning backfist. It is seldom used but has significant power because of the momentum generated from the hips. Place your rear leg toward the outside of the lead leg and spin backward as you snap your hand around into a backfist. If you attempt this move in competition, remember to keep your shoulder high to prevent getting tagged with an overhand punch.

Elbows

Elbows are some of the most dangerous strikes a fighter can throw. They can cause significant damage to an opponent, often opening up deep cuts. Elbows are extremely powerful and most often used when fighters are in a clinch, either standing up or on the ground. Some fight leagues have specific rules about striking downward with the point of the elbow, so if you are going to compete, make sure you get the details before stepping into the cage.

In the following scene, Kevin, in the dark shorts, is controlling his opponent's head with a Muay Thai clinch. His opponent has his left hand on Kevin's right leg to defend against a possible right knee.

Feeling his opponent trying to straighten his neck to break the clinch, Kevin senses an opportunity to deliver an elbow strike. Because his opponent's left hand is low guarding against a knee, Kevin releases the Muay Thai clinch and lets his opponent bring his head upward. In perfect position for the strike, Kevin pulls his right elbow back and turns his palm slightly outward.

Kevin, still grasping his opponent's head with his left hand, turns his hips and delivers a powerful elbow strike. This is an excellent position, allowing Kevin to return to controlling his opponent's movement.

Muay Thai Knee

Another famous strike used in MMA is the Muay Thai knee. When it lands, the knee is a powerful strike that can end a fight very quickly. Knees can be delivered to the body or face, although the Unified Rules of Mixed Martial Arts do not allow knees to the head of a grounded opponent.

Just like elbows, knee strikes are often thrown from the Muay Thai clinch.

In preparation for the strike, Chris drops back in stance, pulling his opponent off balance and rapidly forcing his head downward.

Chris can then explode his right knee forward, delivering a powerful knee right to the face of his opponent.

If Chris doesn't knock his opponent out with this strike, he knows that his foe won't want to take much more of this punishment. His adversary will likely try to pull himself back up to a standing position. Knowing this, Chris can regain head control and keep his opponent from standing up.

Feeling his opponent resisting hard and trying to break free, Chris can suddenly release his downward pressure and drill his opponent with a knee to the midsection as his foe tries to escape.

Flying Knee

A variation of the previous strike is called the flying knee. The move is pretty much exactly what it says, a knee strike while flying through the air. This unconventional move has caught more than a few MMA competitors off guard. If timed well, this strike can be a very unique and effective way to close distance. The flying knee is usually targeted to the head of an opponent and can definitely cause its fair share of damage.

Front Kick

The front kick executed with the front leg is often used in the same manner as a jab. Done with the back leg, the front kick can generate greater power, similar to a cross. It can help a fighter gauge distance, inflict some pain, and potentially get an opponent to lower his hands. It is also a great setup for additional striking combinations. The main target for a front kick is the solar plexus. Done with speed and sharpness, it can knock the wind out of an opponent, creating other striking opportunities.

Round Kick

The round kick is as powerful as it is versatile. A fighter can target the inside or outside of his opponent's lead leg, as well as the body and head. It can also be thrown either by the front or the back leg. The more flexible a combat athlete's hips, the stronger and faster this kick can be executed. Here's the basic starting position for most kicks.

Inner Thigh Kick Using the Front Leg

Targeting his opponent's inner thigh, Kevin shifts his weight to his back leg as he brings his front foot upwards.

As Kevin twists his hips to the right for increased speed, he strikes his opponent's inner thigh with the lower part of his shin. While this front leg round kick doesn't have a tremendous amount of power, it can be a terrific setup for an overhand right punch.

Outer Thigh Kick Using the Back Leg

To execute a back leg round kick, Kevin will target his opponent's outer thigh.

Kevin twists his hips to the left, bringing the back leg forward as he raises his knee. He keeps his hands high to protect his head.

Now Kevin drops his hips downward, changing the direction of his knee so that it is pointed at his opponent's outer thigh. This alters the trajectory of the kick to a downward angle, which has a more punishing effect.

Completing the turn of his hips, Kevin drills the middle of his opponent's outer thigh with his shin. Getting hit with this kick feels like it does when you have a charley horse in your leg. A fighter often changes his lead leg after being hit repeatedly with this kick.

Head Kick Using the Back Leg

Often, as a result of several outer thigh kicks, a fighter will instinctively lower his hands. This mistake sets him up for a round kick to the head. To begin this move, Eric starts by pivoting his lead foot towards the outside, which will help him turn his hips easier. He then brings his knee up to start the kick.

As he brings his leg high, Eric points his knee toward his opponent's head while keeping his hands up for protection.

Fully extending his leg, he lands the kick with the lower portion of his shin across his opponent's head. The force of this round kick will inevitably knock his opponent in the direction of the kick, setting him up well for a left hook.

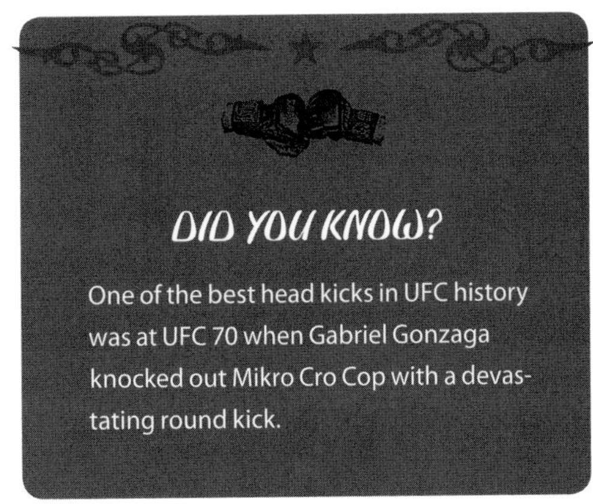

DID YOU KNOW?

One of the best head kicks in UFC history was at UFC 70 when Gabriel Gonzaga knocked out Mikro Cro Cop with a devastating round kick.

DEFENSE TECHNIQUES

Defense Against the Jab and Cross

The best defense against a jab or cross is to simply raise your elbow upward on the same side as the strike. This covers your head as you move it away from the strike.

If you look at this angle, you can see that Eric has successfully deflected his opponent's jab. He is also in a great position to throw an uppercut with his left hand.

Defense Against the Overhand

Similar to the defense against the jab and cross, Eric raises his elbow to the outside while ducking down and away from the strike. Just like the previous defense, this movement also sets him up well to execute an uppercut.

Defense Against the Muay Thai Knee

We've already established that the Muay Thai knee is a powerful strike. Since more fighters are implementing this technique in their standup games, it is also important to know how to defend against it.

In this photo, his opponent has Kevin (in the dark shorts) in a Muay Thai clinch. To defend against possible knees, Kevin presses his hands into his opponent's thighs. Kevin also straightens out his back leg, which helps him to align his hips, shoulders, and head in a straight line. This is an important key because even though he is slightly bent over, keeping strong posture will help Kevin protect himself.

Because of the dynamic movement of a fight, a fighter's grip may slip off his opponent's leg and make him vulnerable to a knee. In this scenario, Kevin crosses both of his forearms in front of his body to jam the knee and prevent it from landing. It is much better to take the brunt of the force with your forearms instead of blocking the knee with your face. Notice that Kevin is still maintaining great posture with his back and neck.

If a fighter throws one knee, chances are high that he'll throw a second. As he readied himself for the second knee, Kevin prepared to shift his body to the outside of the strike. Instead of fully absorbing the blow with his forearms, he deflects it to his right, much like a fighter might parry a non-committed jab. As he does this, Kevin drops his hips and moves to the outside of his opponent in perfect position to execute a takedown.

Defense Against the Round Kick

The best defense against a round kick to the thigh is to raise the leg and point the knee. This relaxes the leg muscles and absorbs the kick across the whole outside of the leg rather than just thigh. As his opponent tries to execute a round kick, Chris raises his knee to deflect the strike.

As his opponent's leg fully extends, Chris brings his knee to his elbow and keeps his hands high. This protects the whole outside of his body, no matter where his opponent is trying to kick. Often, the fighter who is kicking will slightly drop one of his arms, making him vulnerable to a hook punch.

WINNING COMBINATIONS

The key to success in the standup game is to deliver a combination of strikes in rapid succession. The fighters who implement this strategy will have an enormous advantage over the strikers who only throw one technique at a time. Executing a series of strikes in combination helps a fighter to dominate the match. The following combinations are some of the most commonly used in MMA.

Combination One: Jab + Cross + Round Kick

Kevin starts off by throwing a punch between the hands of his opponent, landing a straight left jab.

As his opponent is reacting to the jab, Kevin follows up with a powerful right cross.

With his opponent rocked, the timing is perfect for a powerful outer thigh round kick executed with the back leg.

Combination Two: Lead Front Kick + Jab + Overhand

This combination is great for closing the distance. Chris starts out by landing a front kick to the solar plexus, forcing his opponent to temporarily drop his hands.

Capitalizing on the mistake, Chris lands a straight left jab to his opponent's chin.

This sets him up perfectly to finish closing the distance and land a knock-out overhand right.

Combination Three: Jab + Overhand + Muay Thai Knee

Chris starts off this combination by landing a quick left jab.

He then quickly follows up with a right overhand punch.

His opponent dazed from the strikes, Chris capitalizes on the opportunity and grabs his opponent in a Muay Thai clinch.

Launching forward with a powerful right knee, Chris blasts into the body of his opponent.

As you can see, a lot goes into the standup striking game. Fighters have to continually perfect their boxing and Muay Thai skills in order to be successful. Now that you understand more about the art of striking in MMA, it is time to move on to another important component of the sport. In the next chapter, you'll learn about how wrestling skills play a pivotal role in MMA.

8 ★★★

WRESTLING AND TAKEDOWN TECHNIQUES

Although they may not be as aesthetically beautiful as a knockout strike or a great submission, wrestling techniques are an integral part of MMA. When fighters successfully close the striking distance, they often end up in a clinch vying for position. Once competitors clinch, the fight often ends up going to the ground as a result of a takedown. Excellent wrestling skills help a combat athlete execute and defend against takedowns. They also help a fighter end up in a dominant position once the action goes to the mat.

THE EVOLUTION OF WRESTLING IN COMBAT SPORTS

As you learned back in chapter one, Dan Severn was the beginning of the wrestling movement in MMA. Holding more than seventy amateur records, Severn displayed his impressive Greco-Roman wrestling skills against Royce Gracie in the finals of UFC IV and went on to sweep the tournament in UFC V. Severn proved the importance of wrestling fundamentals in combat and became a legend in the sport. He was even inducted into the UFC's Hall of Fame.

Only ten months after UFC V, Severn's protégé, Don Frye, entered the Octagon. Severn had coached him at the collegiate wrestling level, and after Frye saw his former mentor in the UFC, the two reunited and became training partners. Although Frye didn't have the vast wrestling experience of his coach, he nonetheless did extremely well in competition, demonstrating effective clinching technique and defending against his opponent's takedown attempts.

On the heels of Frye winning UFC X, Mark Coleman came to prominence. A former freestyle Olympic wrestler, Coleman had explosive takedowns and always dominated the wrestling portion of a fight. Coleman went on to win the UFC heavyweight title and was later inducted into the UFC Hall of Fame. Soon other Olympic-level wrestlers like Kevin Randleman, Mark Kerr, Matt Lindland, and Kevin Jackson joined the ranks of MMA competitors.

The next wrestler to take the MMA world by storm was four-time national Greco-Roman wrestling champion Randy Couture. Couture won the heavyweight tournament in UFC XIII and went on to become a legend in the sport. His biggest strength was the ability to end up in a dominant position every time the fight went to the ground. A three-time UFC heavyweight champion, two-time UFC light-heavyweight champion, and UFC Hall of Fame inductee, Randy Couture is arguably the most decorated veteran in the history of MMA.

Matt Hughes, a two-time All-American wrestler, also dominated opponents with his powerful slams in the 170-pound division and became the UFC welterweight champion. Some of the top contenders in MMA with wrestling backgrounds are nationals contender Sean Sherk, Olympic wrestler Dan Henderson, and NCAA wrestling champions Matt Hamill, Josh Koscheck, and Brock Lesnar.

WRESTLING BASICS

There are two major components of wrestling that are essential for a fighter to master: the clinch and the takedown. A clinch occurs when two fighters grapple for position and lock hold of one another. The clinching techniques found in MMA are often derived from Greco-Roman wrestling and Muay Thai kickboxing. In Greco-Roman wrestling, attacks below the waist are not allowed. As a result, more throws and sweeps are utilized in this Olympic style of the sport.

The second component of wrestling in MMA is the takedown. Many fighters have adapted the takedown techniques of freestyle wrestling, which is the second version of Olympic wrestling. This style incorporates the use of the legs for both offense and defense and has its origins in catch wrestling. To take the match to the ground, a fighter often shoots in against his opponent and tries to secure a takedown. The most widely practiced techniques are the single- and double-leg takedowns.

THE CLINCH

When two fighters close the distance and begin to grapple, they usually end up in some kind of clinch. There are a few main types used in MMA including the wrestling, dirty boxing, and Muay Thai clinch.

Wresting Clinch

In wrestling, there are a handful of different types of clinches. The most common is the *over-under clinch*.

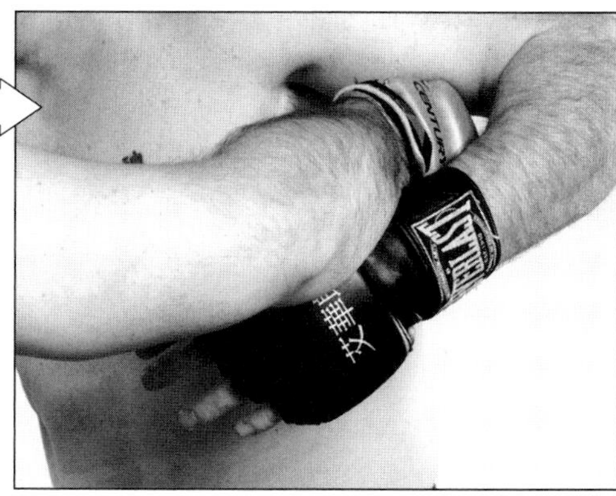

After closing the striking distance, Ryan (in the white shorts) controls his opponent's right hand while continuing to press forward into a clinch. As Ryan is moving forward, he will try to slip his right arm to the inside of his opponent's left arm. This gives him the best opportunity to gain an underhook by sliding his right hand underneath his adversary's arm.

Ryan is able to secure an underhook and wraps his right arm around his opponent's body. His opponent, however, is able to do the same, so Ryan wraps his left arm over the top of his adversary's right arm to secure an overhook. Ryan then positions his head on the same side as his overhook, pressing forward in order to put more weight on his opponent's right arm. This reduces his foe's ability to effectively use his underhook.

Since both fighters are mirror images of one another, the over-under clinch is a neutral position where neither athlete has an advantage. To gain the upper hand, Ryan leans into his opponent and lowers his weight. This defensive move prevents the forward progress of his opponent and gives Ryan the leverage to push his adversary backward into the cage. It also disrupts the balance of his opponent, which could set Ryan up for a successful takedown.

From the over-under clinch, many fighters progress to a bodylock sometimes called a *pinch grip tie*. To secure the bodylock from the above position, Ryan would try to bring his underhooked right hand high on his opponent's back, reaching upward toward the back of his adversary's head. Next, he'd switch his head position to the right side where the underhook is secured. Lastly, he'd bring his overhooked left hand over the shoulder of his opponent and latch onto his own right hand.

If an opponent successfully counters and mirrors a fighter's movement, the pinch grip tie would also end up being a neutral position. From this position, however, fighters often try to throw one another to the ground. If unsuccessful, a combat athlete may try to switch to another clinching position called the *collar tie*.

In this clinch, a fighter releases his hands from a pinch grip tie and pulls back slightly, securing his overhooked hand around the back of his opponent's neck. If his foe counters with the same motion, the competitors end up in a *collar-elbow tie*. This is where each fighter has collar tie with one hand and is grasping his opponent's elbow with his opposite hand.

The collar-elbow tie is another neutral position, and now both fighters will be wrestling for the advantage. A fighter may try to explode forward and secure double underhooks, where both of his arms are underneath his opponent's armpits. From here, a combat athlete usually looks to secure a bear hug bodylock by latching his hands together around the body of his adversary. This type of bodylock is one of the most dominant wrestling positions because it allows an MMA warrior to take down or throw the other fighter with greater ease.

Dirty Boxing Clinch

Since MMA also involves striking, a fighter may also transition from the collar-elbow tie into what is known as the *dirty boxing clinch*. Advancing into this dominant position gives an MMA warrior the chance to land some close-range strikes. Overhand punches, crosses, hooks, uppercuts, and elbows are all great striking opportunities from the dirty boxing clinch.

In the following scene, Chris has a collar tie with his right hand around the back of his opponent's head. He has just released his left hand from the elbow of his adversary.

Pulling back and away from his opponent, Chris adjusts his stance and has the proper range to begin landing strikes. He still controls his opponent's head as he begins to deliver punches and elbows. Chris also keeps his footwork light in case his opponent tries to attempt a single leg takedown on his lead leg. This gives him the ability to defend the takedown as we'll see later on page 167.

Muay Thai Clinch

From the pinch grip or the collar-elbow tie, the fighters may also try to advance to another dominant position known as the *inside double collar tie*. This is also affectionately known in MMA as the *Muay Thai clinch*. The Muay Thai clinch is one of a striker's favorite clinching techniques.

By clutching the head of his opponent, a fighter can move his opponent around the cage at will. This dominant position allows a combat athlete to control his foe while setting up some of the fantastic strikes we covered in the last chapter. Knees, elbows, punches—it's all there. It also gives a fighter the best opportunity to completely disengage from the clinch and resume his striking game.

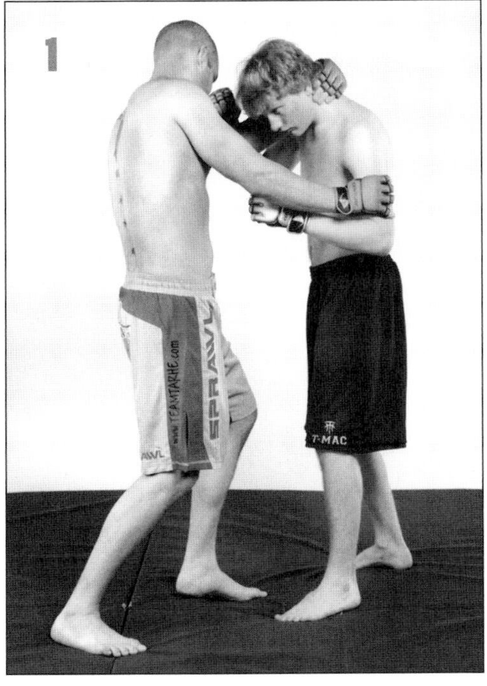

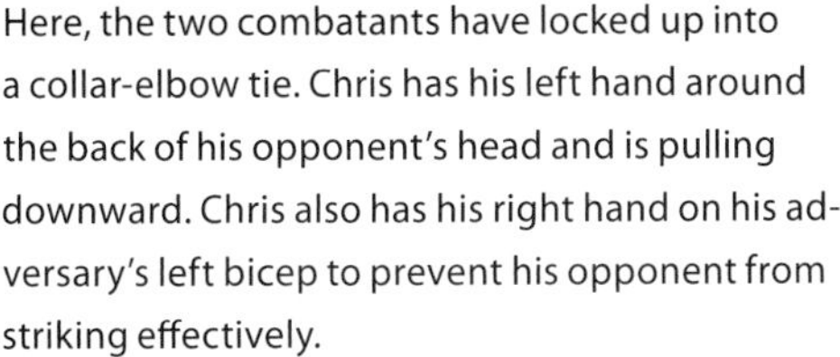
Here, the two combatants have locked up into a collar-elbow tie. Chris has his left hand around the back of his opponent's head and is pulling downward. Chris also has his right hand on his adversary's left bicep to prevent his opponent from striking effectively.

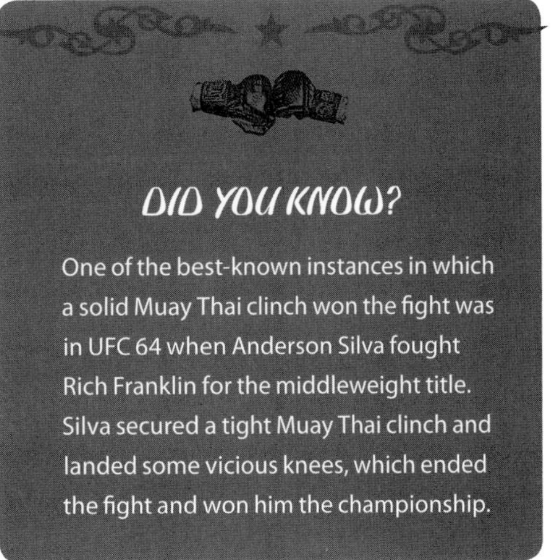

DID YOU KNOW?

One of the best-known instances in which a solid Muay Thai clinch won the fight was in UFC 64 when Anderson Silva fought Rich Franklin for the middleweight title. Silva secured a tight Muay Thai clinch and landed some vicious knees, which ended the fight and won him the championship.

Chris releases his right hand and slides it upward to also lock around the back of his opponent's neck, securing the double collar tie. His opponent resists as Chris begins to pull forward with both hands.

To secure the Muay Thai clinch, Chris drives his elbows into his opponent's chest and pulls downward with his grip. This forces his opponent's head down and takes him off balance, setting Chris up perfectly for the Muay Thai knee covered on page 120.

COUNTERING THE CLINCH

Just as it is important to understand how to execute and capitalize on a clinch, it is also valuable to know how to defend against one. Learning how to escape a clinch is a vital defensive wrestling skill and could mean the difference between winning and losing a match.

Countering the Wrestling Clinch

As we discussed earlier, most MMA competitors will end up in the over-under position when they first clinch. Oftentimes, as fighters vie for advantage, they'll transition into a collar-elbow tie. Here, both fighters are in a modified version of this position.

To counter this clinch, combat athletes try to get double underhooks and secure a bear hug. Ryan (in the white shorts) has an underhook with his left arm and releases his right hand from behind his opponent's neck. He then slips his right hand to the inside of his adversary's left arm and drives his arm forward.

After successfully sliding his right arm underneath the armpit of his opponent, Ryan wraps his arm around the back.

He then pushes forward, driving his left underhook around the back of his competitor and latching both hands together in a bear hug. In preparation for a takedown, Ryan locks his arms around the lower back of his opponent and starts to stand up.

As he rises, Ryan pulls toward his own body with his arms and pushes his shoulders forward. This two-way action compromises his opponent's posture, and Ryan can spring forward to take his adversary to the ground.

Countering the Dirty Boxing Clinch

If you're the one who gets caught in it, the dirty boxing clinch can be a dangerous place. With the opportunity for a lot of strikes to come your way, it is best to counter this move to avoid getting hit repeatedly.

Here, Chris finds himself on the losing end of a dirty boxing clinch and starts to counter right away to avoid any damage. He tries to lean his head forward into his opponent's left shoulder and places his right palm underneath his opponent's left elbow. Simultaneously, Chris grabs his competitor's bicep with his left hand. This temporarily prevents his opponent from landing any effective strikes with his right arm.

Next, Chris drives his opponent's right elbow into his body, which makes his foe tense his right arm as he tries to resist. This distraction allows Chris to rapidly raise his right palm upward, which lifts his adversary's left arm. By driving forward with his legs, Chris now has the opportunity to duck underneath Eric's left arm.

Having successfully cleared the dirty boxing clinch, Chris slides his left arm around his opponent's waist and grabs his right hand. He also drops his knee to lower his body weight, pressing his head against the midsection of his competitor's body. This position minimizes the chance of being caught in a guillotine choke and gives Chris the leverage he'll need to execute the takedown.

Chris then lifts up and drives his weight forward while pulling in with his arms to secure the takedown.

Countering the Muay Thai Clinch

The Muay Thai clinch is something you want to defend against quickly before you end up on the receiving end of your opponent's strikes. A modified version of the counter to a dirty boxing clinch works well to defend against this position. Once again, Chris is on the losing side of the clinch. He takes quick action by placing his right palm underneath his opponent's left elbow, while putting his left hand on the opponent's right thigh. This prevents any knee strikes from his competitor's lead leg and sometimes baits his foe into preparing to knee with his rear leg.

This misdirection is intentional because as soon as his opponent prepares to knee with his rear leg, Chris launches into his counter move. He pushes up rapidly with his right palm, elevating his competitor's arm and creating an opening. As he begins to duck under his opponent's arm, Chris checks his opponent's rear knee with his forearm to prevent getting a knee to the face as he continues this maneuver.

With his head successfully clear, Chris bridges his neck backward, pressing into the back of his opponent's shoulder. This movement, combined with throwing his opponent's left elbow behind him, gets Chris through the opening. It also spins his opponent to the right, which sets up the next part of the counter.

Chris continues pressing his head into his opponent's shoulder as he rolls and turns towards his left. He lets his left arm slide off his opponent's thigh and wrap around his midsection. Chris then reaches around his competitor's back with his right arm and grabs his left hand.

Continuing his movement around the back of his foe, Chris secures a rear bear hug. This puts him in perfect position to execute a throw or even a suplex.

TAKEDOWNS

The takedown techniques used in MMA are often from freestyle wrestling and judo. The main focus of a takedown is to bring the fight to the ground while landing in a superior position. Most of the time, fighters set up their takedowns from a series of strikes. This helps to misdirect their opponents into focusing on the standup game while also helping a fighter to determine the proper distance.

Single Leg Takedown

After throwing some punches, Ryan changes his level by dropping close to the ground. He springs forward, beginning to thrust his right arm between the legs of his opponent while protecting his face with his left hand.

Ryan closes the distance, putting his chest against the thigh of his competitor's lead leg. He also puts the side of his head against his adversary's midsection, which minimizes the chance of a guillotine choke. Simultaneously, he wraps his left arm around the back of his opponent's lead knee while shooting his right arm upwards. This is known as the *high crotch position* and gives Ryan the leverage necessary for the takedown.

Ryan then drives his weight forward, pulling his opponent's leg out from underneath with his left arm. At the same moment, he also pushes forward with his right shoulder to take his foe to the ground.

Double Leg Takedown

Ryan also sets this takedown up with a series of strikes and once again drops his level as he prepares to close the distance.

He then wraps both of his arms around the outside of his opponent's legs as he presses his right shoulder into his competitor's midsection.

After he successfully locks his grip around the back of the opponent's legs, Ryan comes into a low squat. This will give him lots of leverage to execute the takedown.

Ryan now explodes upward into the standing position as he lifts his foe into the air.

To finish the takedown and slam his opponent to the mat, Ryan turns to the right and drops his body weight to the ground. Done in this manner, Ryan will end up in dominant side mount position after completing this move.

Shoot Takedown

A variation of the double leg takedown is what MMA athletes often refer to as a *shoot takedown*. Although shooting often just refers to the movement of attempting a takedown, this particular maneuver is a modification that is sometimes identified as a separate technique.

The beginning of the move starts in the same way, with Ryan executing some strikes and then dropping his body and changing his level.

After closing the distance, Ryan wraps his right arm around the upper thigh of his opponent's lead leg. His left arm goes around the hip of his competitor.

Ryan then begins to push off his left leg and starts to drive his weight toward his right side. This movement begins to break the balance of his opponent.

To secure the takedown, Ryan drives his momentum forward and to the right while keeping his right arm locked around the opponent's lead leg. Since his chest is pressed into his adversary's rear leg, Ryan's body weight and forward movement keep his foe from stepping backward to prevent the takedown.

Hip Throw

The *hip throw* is often found in judo and is a great technique to execute from a clinch. This particular movement involves using the hip as a pivot point by placing your hip in a lower position than your competitor's center of gravity. The hip throw is often executed from the over-under clinch we illustrated earlier on page 144. Ryan has an underhook with his right arm and has his left arm wrapped in an overhook.

Ryan steps forward and through with his right leg, getting his hip underneath the opponent's midsection. He then leans toward the ground to lift his foe onto his hip.

Pulling his arms to his left, Ryan executes the throw by tossing his opponent over his hip and toward the ground.

Having slammed his adversary into the mat, the move puts Ryan in a knee mount and at a perfect angle to throw some punches.

DEFENDING TAKEDOWNS

If an opponent is quick and powerful, stopping a takedown can be challenging to say the least. However, if a combat athlete practices these defenses repeatedly, the move may become second nature. Staying alert and being familiar with counters is the best way to prevent getting taken down during a match.

Defense Against the Single Leg Takedown

Ryan's opponent has shot in against him, grabbing his lead leg and trying to score a single leg takedown.

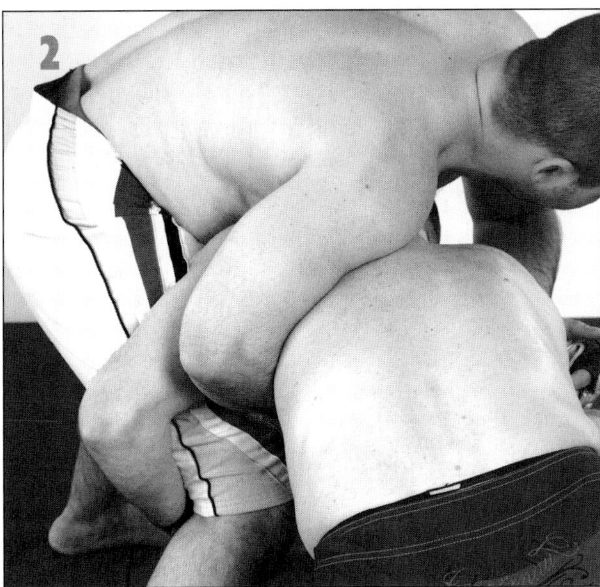

To begin to counter the takedown attempt, Ryan hooks his right arm behind and underneath his opponent's left arm. This move is often called a *whizzer* in freestyle wrestling.

Ryan then turns his hips counterclockwise, deflecting the forward movement of his adversary. He simultaneously begins to sprawl both of his legs to the right while driving his right shoulder and arm into the mat. This movement shoves his opponent's head toward the ground.

Having successfully driven his foe to the ground, Ryan continues to move his legs around toward his right while pressing his body weight on top of his opponent's left shoulder.

Ryan now swings his right leg over his opponent's hip and traps his arm to complete the technique and put himself in a dominant position.

Defense Against the Double Leg Takedown

Ryan's opponent has started to move in for a double leg takedown. To defend against the takedown, Ryan moves his hips back and checks his opponent's shoulders by pushing forward with his palms. This momentarily stops his adversary's movement, giving him chance to sprawl.

With his opponent still moving forward, Ryan sprawls his legs backward as he leans his chest forward on top of his opponent's shoulders.

Ryan then secures double overhooks and straightens out his legs as he drops his hip to the ground. This puts all his weight on the back and neck of his foe, driving him face first to the mat.

Defense Against the Shoot Takedown

Although you can also use a sprawl to defend against this type of takedown, there is another alternative if you are quick on your feet. Here, Joel sees the takedown coming and starts to move to his left as he grabs his opponent behind the neck with his left hand. An important key element of this defense is at this crucial moment. Joel presses his left forearm into his opponent's right shoulder while he moves his hips back, making it more difficult for his adversary to secure the takedown.

As his foe tries to capture his legs, Joel swiftly moves to his left and out of range for the takedown. His takedown attempt thwarted, the opponent turns towards Joel in an effort to keep pressing forward.

Joel anticipates this movement and counters by latching onto his competitor's head with both hands and delivering a devastating knee strike to his face.

Defense Against the Hip Throw

The counter to this throw starts in the wrestling clinch. Both competitors are locked in an over-under clinch, and Joel's opponent begins to step forward to start the throw. Joel has an underhook with his right arm and an overhook with his left arm. Instead of having his left overhook high on his opponent's shoulder, however, Joel has the overhook on his opponent's right elbow.

As his opponent steps through to execute the throw, Joel straightens his spine and squats down to get his center of gravity lower than his competitor's. Joel lets his opponent's movement help him to wrap his right arm around his adversary's waist. As he does this, Joel slides his left hand behind his opponent's elbow and around his back, securing a bear hug. This effectively traps his opponent's right arm against his own body.

Exploding straight upward, Joel comes to a standing position and lifts his opponent into the air while maintaining a tight grip.

He then throws his body weight to the left and slams his opponent to the mat. Notice that his competitor's right arm is still trapped as he lands.

Joel lands in side mount and protects his face by keeping his head down and checking his opponent's left hand.

He can then rise up into a knee mount and prepare to rain down some strikes on his opponent.

9

★★★

GROUND WORK: JIU-JITSU TECHNIQUES

The ground game in MMA is one of the most fascinating and intricate portions of this sport. Among other things, the ground provides the most opportunities to successfully win a match. First, a fighter can use striking on the ground to win the same way he can by standing up. A flurry of accurate punches can cause a technical knockout, prompting the referee to stop the contest. A series of strikes could also open a large cut, and the match can be called due to doctor stoppage.

Secondly, a fighter can also secure a victory with a wide variety of different submission techniques. The large number of joint locks and chokes make ground fighting a very strategic aspect of competition. A fighter has to learn to look for finishing techniques while at the same time defending against the submission attempts of his opponent. This is one of the reasons why MMA is often referred to as "human chess." The winning fighter is often trying to improve position by thinking four and five moves ahead of his opponent.

There are numerous ways a fighter can end up on the mat during a match. From takedowns, throws, and slams to just plain slipping or getting knocked on your butt from a hard strike, a fight can be on the ground in a matter of seconds. As a result, a vast majority of fights end up on the mat at some point during the match. To become a successful MMA competitor, it is absolutely essential to study the elements of fighting on the ground.

THE EVOLUTION OF JIU-JITSU FOR MMA

The importance and value of ground work was proven at the very beginning of the UFC with Royce Gracie. As Gracie submitted opponent after opponent, it became clear that learning how to fight on the ground was a necessity. The introduction of Brazilian Jiu-jitsu paved the way for this aspect of the sport and has forever changed how fighters prepare for MMA competitions.

In the earlier days of the UFC, competitors were allowed to wear traditional martial art uniforms, often called a *gi*. Brazilian Jiu-jitsu was one of the styles that utilized the

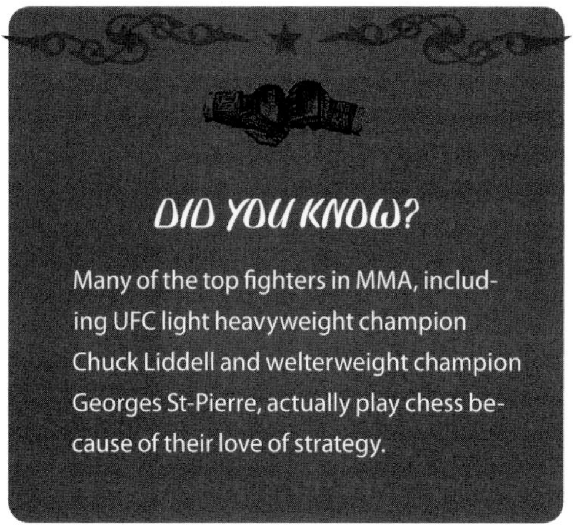

DID YOU KNOW?

Many of the top fighters in MMA, including UFC light heavyweight champion Chuck Liddell and welterweight champion Georges St-Pierre, actually play chess because of their love of strategy.

gi to its advantage. A gi allowed a jiu-jitsu practitioner to hold his opponent better and keep him from slipping away during competition. A uniform also provided extra ways to grip and could be utilized for different submissions, such as a gi choke.

When Gracie was competing in the UFC, very few fighters knew what to do when they ended up on the ground. Even fewer knew how to actually defend against arm bars and chokes, and, as a result, Gracie cleaned up the tournaments. It wasn't long before fighters started learning Brazilian Jiu-jitsu and understanding how to escape from certain positions. As a result, the skill level of the competitors increased dramatically.

As the sport continued to evolve, a UFC rule change was implemented that prevented a gi from being worn in competition. Fighters could now only wear MMA shorts or kickboxing trunks. This eliminated numerous setups, sweeps, passes, and submissions from the classical jiu-jitsu playbook. To adapt to the new rules, many competitors began to study no-gi jiu-jitsu and submission grappling. These newer versions of old techniques did not involve the use of the gi. Moves in no-gi jiu-jitsu also took into account that an opponent would be able to strike while on the ground.

Those jiu-jitsu fighters who failed to make changes in their ground game soon found themselves in precarious positions, often losing matches as the skill sets of the MMA practitioners became more advanced. Up until this point, jiu-jitsu practitioners had been very successful at fighting effectively from their back using the guard position. Due to an opponent's lack of jiu-jitsu knowledge, they could avoid strikes and also set up numerous submissions. Ground fighting was essentially being used in a very aggressive and offensive way.

Eventually, fighters with kickboxing and wrestling backgrounds learned enough jiu-jitsu to defend against submissions while simultaneously being able to land effective strikes. This allowed a fighter to be in the guard but still punch his opponent and win matches by the "ground and pound" method. The MMA world witnessed a shift in training focus. Competitors acquired the defensive jiu-jitsu skills necessary to avoid getting tapped out, but were also able to maximize their own striking capabilities while on the ground.

Today, the ascent of no-gi jiu-jitsu training in MMA is once again turning the tables, as new variations of submissions are added to the fighter's arsenal of techniques. These intricate and unique new moves are once again elevating the skill level of the sport. Fighters are now consistently executing submissions amid their opponent's strikes. For MMA fans, submission artists have become the underdogs, and the crowd loves to see a fighter pull off a lock or choke just as much as they love to see a knockout.

GROUND BASICS

Although there are a multitude of positions on the ground, a good fighter should know all the basic ones, including the top mount, side mount, rear mount, full guard, and half-guard. There are also numerous submissions that MMA competitors have to learn, including arm bars, shoulder locks, leg locks, and chokes. In addition to understanding how to apply these submissions, fighters must learn how to defend against them as well.

Just as with standup fighting, there are offensive and defensive components of ground fighting. Knowing how to escape from positions of disadvantage and submission attempts is crucial to a fighter's defense. Generally speaking, a fighter does not want to be on the bottom when the match goes to the ground. A fighter on the bottom has fewer options and is more vulnerable to strikes. Most of the time, the fighter on the bottom attempts to create space between himself and his opponent. This gives the fighter on the bottom the opportunity to escape this vulnerable position and get to his feet so the match can return to standing.

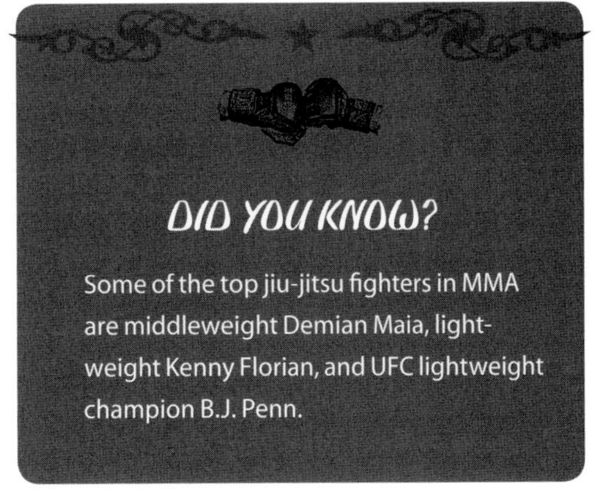

Learning how to advance to the more dominant positions and secure submission techniques is the offensive portion of ground work. When a fight goes to the mat, both competitors try to come out on top and vie for top control. The most dominant position is the *top mount* in which the fighter on top is sitting on his opponent's abdomen. From this position, he can strike with both hands and has several submissions at his disposal. During the ground game, the fighter in top control tries to advance his positioning and secure the top mount.

Knowing how to escape from non-dominant positions and advance towards top control while avoiding and applying submissions takes a lot of hard work and practice. That effort usually pays off big because understanding both the offensive and defensive portions of the ground game gives a fighter a significant chance to achieve victory. Both elements are also critical to analyzing an opponent's strengths and weaknesses and creating a winning fighting strategy.

POSITIONS

To start learning about the aspects of jiu-jitsu in MMA, you first need to know the positions that fighters end up in when the bout goes to the mat. Although a fight on the ground is always in motion, these are the common positions that you will see during a match.

Full Mount

The *full mount* occurs when one fighter is on top of another with his hips on an opponent's midsection. This is the most dominant position on the ground in MMA. In this first photo, Joel is chest to chest in the low full mount with his knees on either side of his competitor's body. He also has his foe secured with double underhooks to limit the opponent's striking ability.

Posturing up to the high full mount, Joel can now effectively rain down punches on his adversary. Because Joel is sitting in the mount position, he has the reach advantage and can punch his opponent in the face without getting hit there himself.

Knee Mount

In this modification of the full mount, Joel has his left knee on the abdomen of his opponent. His right leg is sprawled out straight, creating a solid base from which he can maintain his balance while throwing strikes. Fighters will often end up in the *knee mount* when attempting to pass from the side mount position.

Side Mount

The *side mount* is another dominant position in which the combat athlete on top is perpendicular to the fighter on the bottom. Joel sinks his upper body weight directly into his opponent's chest and sprawls his knees outward so that his hips are close to the ground. One knee is typically by the opponent's hip while the other is by his head. Joel also has his head down and his arms clinched around his competitor's left arm to protect against any strikes.

Closed Guard

The *guard* is the jiu-jitsu position made famous by the Gracie family. In a strictly sport jiu-jitsu match, the guard can be a neutral or even dominant position. In MMA, however, it can be a position of disadvantage due to the ability to throw strikes. In this photo, Joel has his legs wrapped around his opponent's midsection with his ankles locked in the full guard. To secure this defensive position he controls his adversary's head, locking his arms around and pulling him in close.

Open Guard

In this guard modification, Joel's legs are not wrapped around his opponent. Most fighters in this position will try to control their competitors' arms in an effort to attempt a submission or transition to a better position.

Butterfly Guard

Another variation of the open guard is called the *butterfly*. In this position, a fighter can have one or both of his feet inside his opponent's upper legs. This allows a technically proficient ground practitioner to control the hips of his foe and set up a sweep or reversal. In this photo, Joel has both of his feet high inside his competitor's legs.

Half Guard

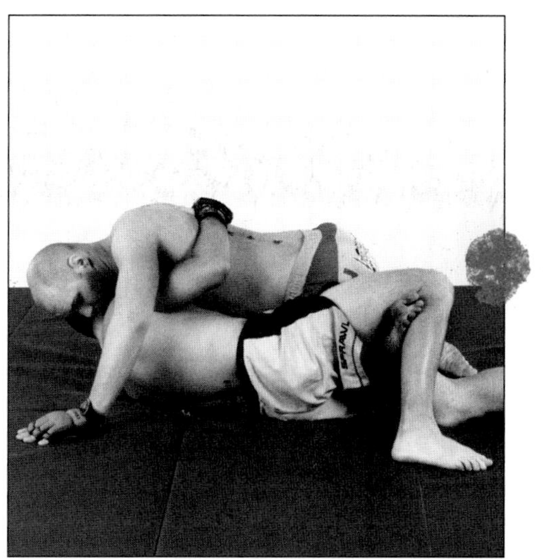

In this position, the fighter on the bottom has both of his legs wrapped around one of his opponent's legs. The MMA athlete on top is halfway between a mount and the guard, so the position is known as the *half guard*. The higher your leg can be wrapped around your competitor's leg, the better your defensive position because it makes it harder for him to pass.

ESCAPES

As we mentioned earlier in the chapter, knowing how to escape from bad positions is critical to a fighter's ground defense. Although the world of jiu-jitsu escapes is vast, we've featured some of the more common escapes used in MMA.

Escaping the Full Mount

Here Joel is on bottom and his opponent is on top in the full mount position. To start the escape, Joel puts his right hand on his opponent's hip because he will be escaping to that side first. Joel also straightens out his legs to begin the move.

Next, he pushes his opponent's right leg downward while sliding his right leg out from underneath.

In this critical part of the move, Joel turns onto his left side and slides his hip out from underneath his opponent. Joel's left leg is still straight, while his right leg bases to the outside.

Simultaneously, Joel pushes downward on his competitor's right leg with his left hand as he bends his knee towards his chest and out from underneath his opponent. This part of the technique is often referred to as "shrimping."

Once his leg is clear, Joel immediately shifts onto his back and brings his left leg over his opponent's hip. He also tries to reacquire his opponent's right hand to prevent getting hit with punches.

Joel then brings his right leg around the midsection of his opponent, locking his ankles and wrapping his arms around his opponent's upper body to secure a full closed guard.

Escaping the Knee Mount

With his opponent on top in the knee mount position, Joel attempts to deflect any strikes while quickly reaching across his body with his left hand, placing his left palm on the side of his opponent's left knee. Notice that Joel also bends his right knee and bases his right foot on the ground. This is an important key in this move and will give Joel the leverage to escape.

Joel then pulls his adversary's knee to his left while pushing off of his right foot. He slides his hips out from underneath and shifts onto his left side.

Next, he continues his movement, twisting his hips further to the left. This helps Joel to clear his left leg while pressing his right knee into the midsection of his opponent. The placement of the right knee is vital because it prevents his opponent from coming over the top and forces him to move around to the right.

As his opponent tries to move around to the right, Joel pushes backward and switches his hips to the right. This moves Joel onto his back and gives him the opportunity to bring his left leg through to block the sideways movement of his competitor. From this position, Joel can bring his foe into a closed guard or attempt a submission.

Escaping the Side Mount to the Guard

Most of the time, fighters who end up on the bottom with their opponent on top in a side mount try to maneuver themselves into the guard position. In this photo, Joel is on the bottom and immediately turns onto his right side as he brings his left elbow into his opponent's chest and his right arm into the hip.

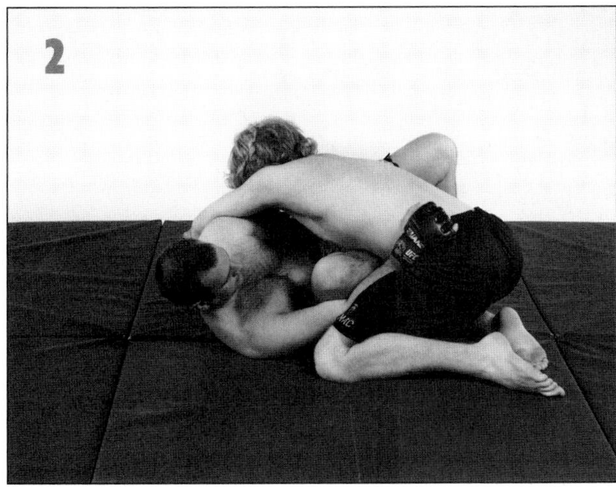

Joel then pushes his opponent off with his left arm and pushes away from his opponent's hips with his right arm. This turns Joel's hips to the right and allows him to bring his right knee underneath his competitor's midsection.

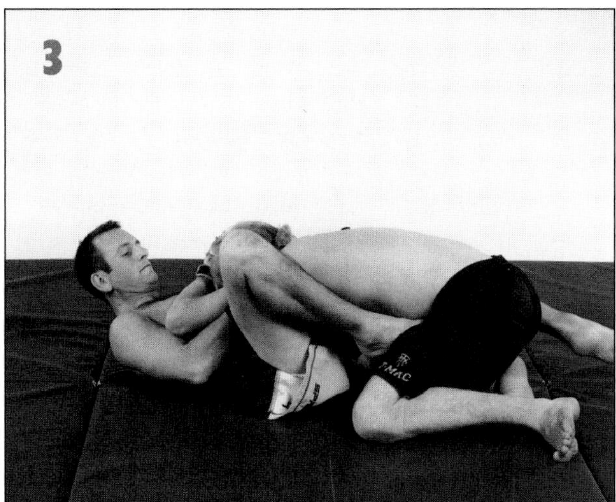

Continuing to slide his right leg through, Joel pushes away from his foe as he moves toward his left. This spins him around to the left and gives Joel the option to secure a butterfly, open, or closed guard.

Guard to Standing

So far, we've shown you how to escape from the full, knee, and side mount by transitioning into the guard position. Now we'll explain how to get from the guard back to your feet so you can resume a standup striking game. Joel is on the bottom and begins by opening his guard and starting to turn towards his left side. He creates a base with his left forearm on the ground while maintaining control of his opponent's head with his right hand. As Joel starts to sit up, he straightens his left leg, which will help him clear his competitor's right arm.

Joel bends his right knee and bases his right foot on the floor. He then sits up, basing all his weight on his left arm and right foot. At the same time, Joel retracts his left leg underneath his own body while still pushing down on his opponent's head with his right hand.

After planting his left foot on the ground, Joel rises to a low crouch and then comes to the full standing position. Note that he controlled his competitor's head the entire move, pushing downward and making it difficult to stop Joel's escape.

Sweeping From the Butterfly Guard

This is a great reversal technique using the full butterfly guard. Joel is on the bottom and has both his feet inside his opponent's hips. He also has double underhooks and keeps his right arm tucked in around his adversary's body while raising his left arm upward. This stretches out the right arm of the opponent, which keeps him from stopping the sweep. At the same time, Joel hooks the inside of his competitor's right thigh with his left foot and pushes upward. This elevates his opponent's hips and momentarily suspends him in the air.

With his right foot hooked inside his opponent's left thigh, Joel explodes his right leg upward and thrusts his body to his left side. His right underhook helps to provide additional leverage, and Joel continues to raise his left arm as he rolls, keeping his opponent's right arm trapped.

Rolling all the way to his left and on top of his opponent, Joel successfully reverses the position and ends up in a full mount. Notice that Joel's right hand is still underhooked underneath his opponent's left arm, which leaves him in a good position to attempt a head and arm triangle choke.

Sweeping From the Half Guard

There are a number of intricate no-gi jiu-jitsu counters from the half guard. This is just one of many possible escape maneuvers, but it is a very effective technique often used in MMA matches. In the first photo, Joel is on the bottom and has his opponent's left leg trapped with both of his legs wrapped around it. Trying to push forward and squeeze through Joel's half guard, his opponent bases his right foot on the ground. Capitalizing on this common mistake, Joel slides his left arm underneath the back of his opponent's leg.

Having fully wrapped his left arm around his opponent's right leg, Joel uncrosses his legs and opens his half guard. He immediately brings the inside of his right leg to the outside of his adversary's left knee. This sets him up to take his opponent's balance by providing a lever to create two-way action. As he does this, Joel also bases out by putting his left foot on the mat, which will help him generate the power to execute the sweep.

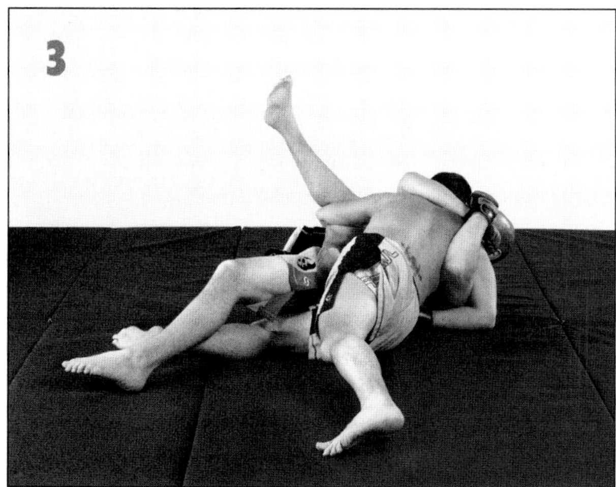

In one explosive movement, Joel pushes to the right off of his left foot as he brings his opponent's right knee upward. At the same crucial moment, Joel scissors his right leg inward causing his opponent's left knee to be swept out from underneath. Joel continues to roll to the right, putting his opponent on his back.

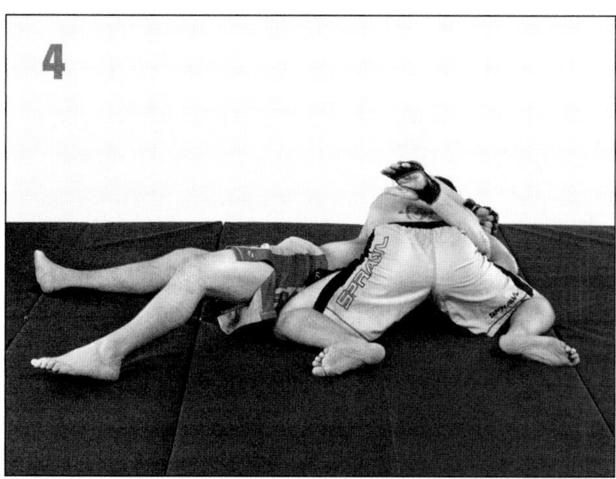

To finish the move, Joel slightly lifts up his left leg and slides his right leg underneath his body and out to the side mount position. With practice, this move can get you out of a precarious spot and into a much better position with more options. From here, Joel can disengage and return the fight to standing, look for a submission, or pass into the full mount and advance his position.

PASSING

In jiu-jitsu and MMA, passing refers to advancing from one position to another, more dominant one. In MMA especially, fighters try to advance their movements and end up in the mount. Passing is a proactive process and part of the offensive strategy of the ground game.

Passing the Closed Guard

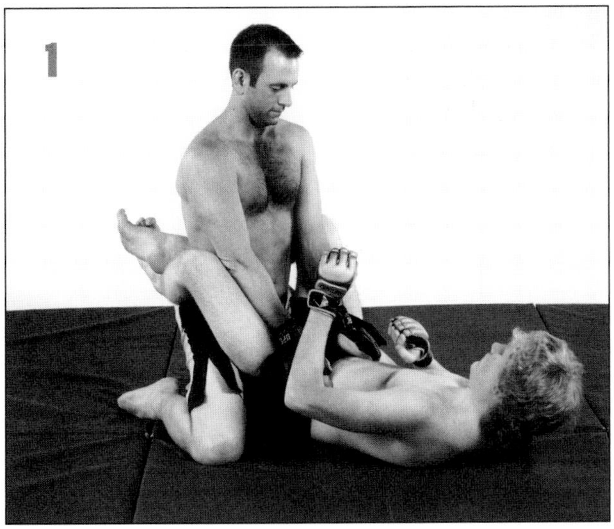

To pass the closed guard, the first thing Joel does is called *posturing up*. As he sits back and brings his hips forward, Joel's shoulders are squarely over his hips with a straight spine. This prevents his opponent from grabbing and locking him up.

Next, Joel pushes down with his right hand, pinning his opponent's left knee to the mat. Then Joel brings his right knee forward, riding his shin over the inside of his competitor's left thigh.

197 ➡

Having opened his opponent's guard, Joel switches knees, bringing his left knee forward, and places his left shin on the inside of his opponent's left thigh. As he does this, Joel turns his hips to the right and prepares for the next part of the move.

Joel controls his adversary's hip with his left hand to prevent him from rolling upwards and then swings his right leg over his opponent's left leg. Notice that Joel is still pinning that leg with his left shin, which averts his opponent from blocking the pass.

Continuing his movement to the right, Joel turns onto his right side and scissors his hips so that his right leg is alongside his opponent. Joel also presses his weight down into his competitor's chest, keeping his foe pinned to the ground. From this position, Joel can quickly retract his right leg and swing his left knee towards his opponent's hip, ending up in a side or even a full mount.

Passing the Open Guard

To pass this position, Joel gets low in his opponent's half guard and secures an underhook by slipping his right arm underneath his opponent's left leg. Joel brings his right arm close into his chest to defend against being put in an arm bar or triangle choke. He then begins to push his weight forward onto his competitor.

Next, Joel drives his opponent's knee upward into the opponent's chest and begins to sprawl and move around to his right side. He continues to put all of his weight on his adversary's leg as he spins to the right.

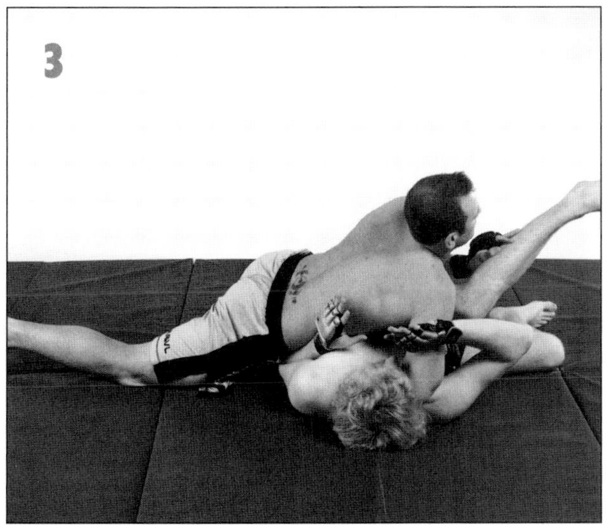

Joel then arches his back, clearing his head from underneath his opponent's left leg. He brings his left hand up and pushes his opponent's leg to the ground. Note that Joel is looking away from his opponent to avoid being hit in the face by any punches. Once his competitor's leg is pinned to the ground, Joel will be in a side mount and in a much more advantageous position.

Passing the Half Guard

Stuck in his opponent's half guard position, Joel maintains good posture and shifts his hips towards the right. He also keeps his foe stationary by pinning the opponent's face to the ground.

In an explosive move, Joel jerks his hips to the left and brings his right knee upward. This breaks the grip of his opponent's legs and gives Joel the opening he needs to pass.

Joel immediately switches the position of his knees, planting his left foot and driving his right knee downward. This pins his competitor's right leg to the mat and makes the pass possible.

Turning onto his right side and putting his body weight on his opponent, Joel slides his right leg over the top of the opponent's right leg. As he brings his left leg back, Joel drops his right hip to the ground and completes the pass.

Side Mount Passing to Mount

Joel is in the top position and wants to pass to the full mount so he can finish the fight by ground-and-pound striking. His opponent, however, has wisely brought his right knee up to prevent Joel from simply stepping over him. To execute the pass, Joel puts his left hand on the back of the opponent's left tricep and puts his right hand on the outside of his opponent's right knee.

Joel then pushes his competitor's right leg all the way to the left and pins it against the ground. This essentially twists his opponent's lower body and sets up the next part of the move.

Swinging his right knee over his adversary's hip, Joel slips his right knee underneath his right arm. Note that he is still pinning his opponent's right knee to the ground as he executes the maneuver.

Having completed the pass, Joel is now in the full mount and able to land a flurry of strikes in hopes of finishing his opponent.

Winning Submissions

Just like every other part of the ground game, submissions are an art form all their own. There are a multitude of techniques that can be used to force your opponent to tap out, but the ones included here are some of the more common used in MMA competition.

Arm Bar From the Mount

The *arm bar* is a crowd favorite among MMA fans. Surprisingly, this technique is fairly simple to execute. Along with chokes, the arm bar is responsible for a majority of submission victories in MMA. In the first photo, Joel is in full mount and landing a solid right punch to his opponent's face. In a vain attempt to defend against further strikes, Eric extends his right arm straight upward. Joel recognizes the mistake and quickly traps his adversary's wrist with his left hand.

Joel then springs forward on his left leg and moves his opponent's arm to his right, where he reinforces his grip by grabbing the arm with his right hand.

To sink the arm bar, Joel swivels his hips and swings his left leg over Eric's head. He keeps his knees pressed tightly together to prevent his opponent from sitting up between his legs. Holding Eric's arm tight against his chest, Joel drops his hips to the ground and sits back. This locks his opponent's arm out straight; now Joel can thrust his hips upward to put the elbow in danger of being hyperextended. His foe knows the arm bar is secure and taps out, giving Joel the win.

Key Lock From the Side Mount

This winning submission is often referred to as the *key lock*. It can be applied from the mount or side mount positions and also has a number of different variations. Joel has landed on top in the side mount position and has his opponent's left arm pinned to the ground. He traps his adversary's wrist with his left hand, which will set him up for the next stage of the move.

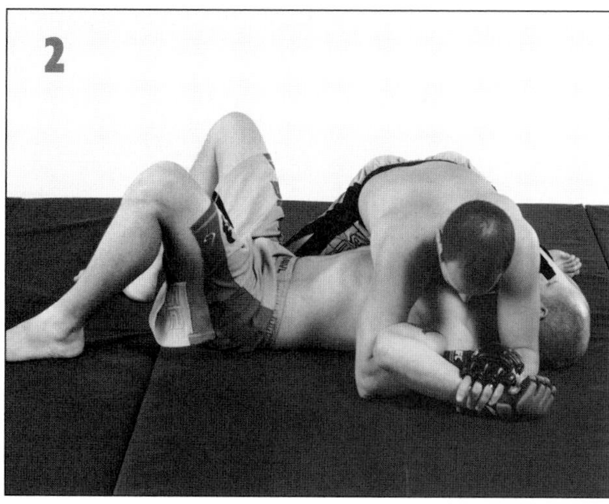

Joel now slides his right arm underneath his opponent's left elbow and then grabs his own left wrist with his right hand.

To execute the lock and put his foe in excruciating pain, Joel lifts his right elbow upward while dragging his opponent's hand toward his own hip. By keeping his adversary's hand on the ground, this movement raises his elbow and puts tremendous torque on the shoulder. Even though his arm is partially pinned, his opponent taps out with his right hand to prevent a dislocated shoulder.

Arm Bar From the Guard

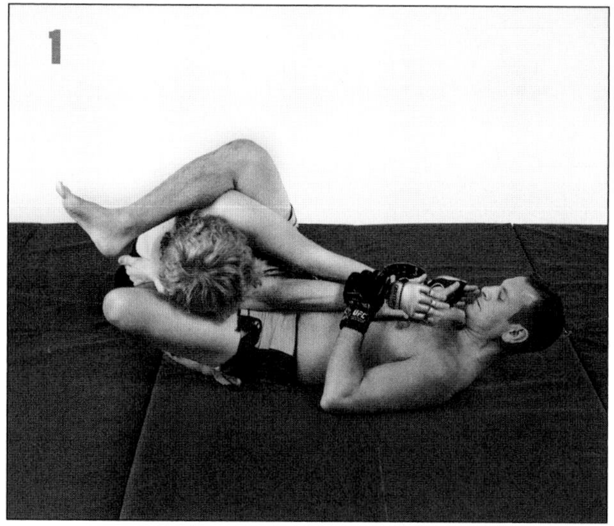

The arm bar submission can also be achieved from the open guard position. Here, Joel has his opponent in his open guard. To start the technique, Joel traps his competitor's right arm to his chest and places his left foot on his opponent's right hip. This creates a leverage point that enables Joel to shift his hips as he brings his right leg upward. He catches underneath his opponent's left shoulder with the inside of his leg, forcing his opponent to move to Joel's left side. Joel performs the motion as if he is trying to plant his right foot on the ground, which turns his opponent onto his right side.

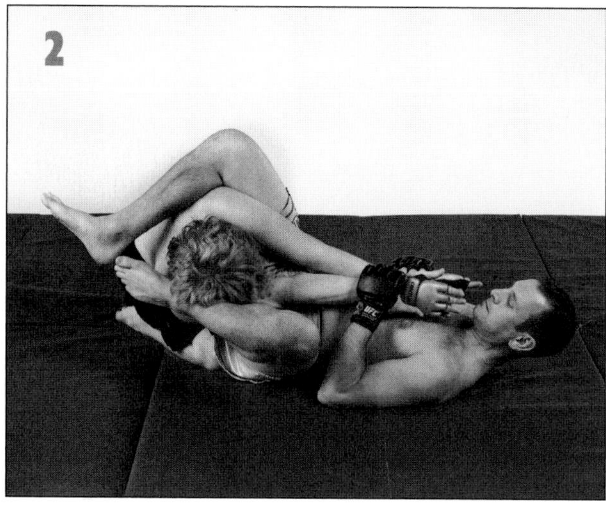

In the next step of the move, Joel retracts his left knee in order to get it out from underneath his foe while still pressing towards the ground with his right leg.

Joel completes the submission by swinging his left leg over his opponent's head and pressing down with both legs while raising his hips upward. With practice, this entire move can be done very rapidly, resulting in a quick tap out.

Kimura From the Guard

In the MMA ground game, this popular winning submission is called the *Kimura*. It is sometimes also referred to as a *reverse key lock*, *hammer-lock*, or *ude-garami*. This painful shoulder lock can be applied from many different positions, making it a key part of a fighter's submission arsenal.

Joel is on the bottom and has his opponent in a closed guard. Joel's left hand is grabbing his opponent's right wrist. He is also controlling his opponent's head with his right hand, which limits the foe's ability to throw effective punches.

Next, Joel opens his guard while still controlling his opponent's right wrist. He then sits up and twists his upper body toward the trapped arm. Simultaneously, Joel extends his right arm and reaches over his opponent's right shoulder.

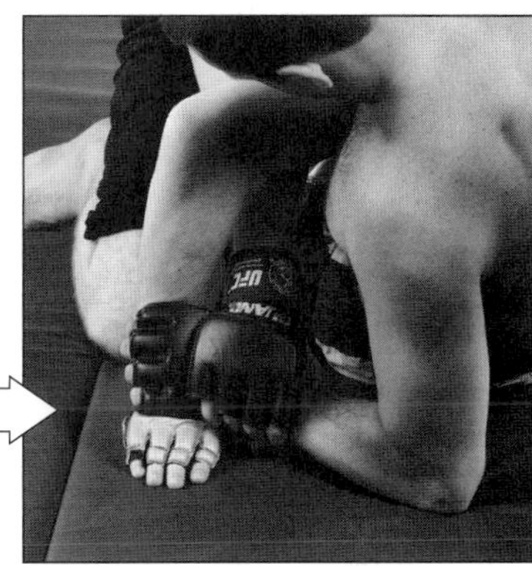

Joel takes his right arm over his opponent's right tricep and then snakes his right hand underneath his opponent's arm. Joel's right hand then grabs his own left wrist. He also turns his upper body further left to secure the lock tight against his chest. This prevents his opponent from defending the technique by straightening his arm.

To secure the Kimura lock, Joel pivots his hips and upper body toward his opponent's trapped arm while dropping his back towards the mat. Joel uses his downward momentum to drive his opponent's face into the ground while elevating his opponent's arm at the same time. Joel also keeps his opponent's arm tight into his chest and presses his left leg into the opponent's lower back to prevent him from rolling away. To inflict pain and force the tap out, Joel presses his opponent's hand upward toward the head.

Omoplata From the Guard

Another painful shoulder lock submission is called the *omoplata*. This move is similar to the Kimura, but it can be tricky to execute and requires a lot of practice to pull it off during an actual match. Joel is on the bottom and has his opponent in his open guard. He grabs his opponent's right wrist with his left hand while cross-facing him with his right hand. This temporarily makes it more difficult for his foe to land effective punches and gives Joel the opening to start the technique.

Next, Joel sharply pivots his entire body to his left and pushes his opponent's head toward the mat. At the same instant, he raises his left arm and swings his left leg upward, forcing his opponent's right shoulder toward the ground.

Continuing to spin to the left, Joel clears his right leg out from underneath his opponent. He also traps his adversary's right arm with both hands, plants his left foot on the mat above his opponent's right shoulder, and drives his opponent's upper body into the floor.

Forcing his opponent's right arm up toward his own head, Joel sits upward, leaning onto his left hip and swinging his legs around to the right. The opponent's arm is trapped over Joel's left thigh and ultimately caught between Joel's legs as Joel sits up.

Joel then leans his chest forward all the way to his opponent's back and cross-faces his opponent while locking his hands together. The two-way action to force the tap out occurs as Joel pulls his left leg backward while forcing his hips forward. The omoplata is an extremely painful technique, so be sure to practice it carefully when working with a training partner.

Guillotine From the Guard

Now that we've covered some arm bars and shoulder locks, it is time to explore the world of submission chokes. This is a common choke found in MMA, which can be performed standing up or on the ground. The *guillotine choke* often occurs when one fighter attempts a takedown but leaves his neck exposed. In this photo, Joel's opponent just performed a takedown and tried to put Joel on his back. To put himself in position for the submission, Joel grabs his opponent's right wrist with his left hand and sits up towards his opponent's right shoulder.

Turning slightly onto his left hip, Joel wraps his right arm around the neck of his opponent.

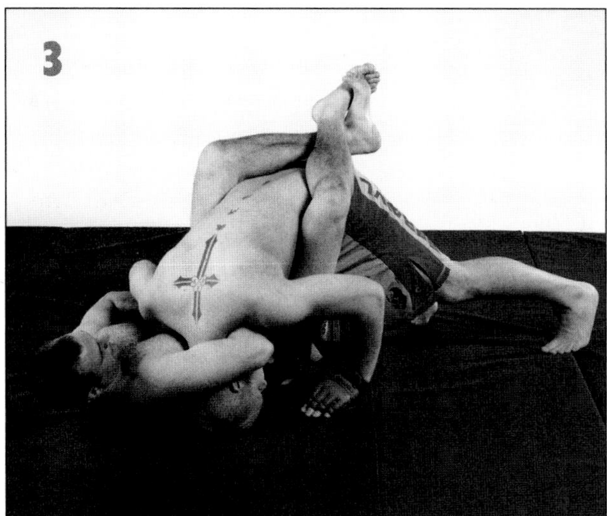

He then leans back and locks his hands together to generate more leverage. As Joel pulls his foe into his closed guard, he arches his hips upward while forcing his opponent's head downward. This two-way action across the opponent's neck causes him to tap out or risk losing consciousness.

Triangle Choke From the Guard

This particular choke is a favorite among MMA practitioners and is called the *triangle*. Joel is on the bottom and has his opponent in his open guard. To control the right side of his adversary's body, Joel has his left foot on his opponent's right hip and is pinning his right wrist. Note that the opponent's right arm is trapped diagonally across Joel's chest so that his right hand is near Joel's right shoulder. To begin the technique, Joel slightly lowers his right leg toward the ground as he pushes his opponent's left hand downward.

Having passed his competitor's arm inside his leg, Joel brings his right leg straight upward alongside his opponent's neck. Joel also shifts his hips slightly to the right, which will help him set up the choke.

He then bends his right knee, taking his right foot across the back of his opponent's neck. Next, Joel swings his left leg around his opponent's right shoulder and clamps it down over his right foot to secure the choke. As you can see, Joel's opponent is already getting ready to tap out due to the pressure around his neck.

To lock the choke in deeper, Joel grabs his opponent's head with both hands and pulls downward. His foe is forced to tap out fast or get put to sleep.

Arm Triangle From the Half Guard

The *arm triangle*, sometimes also called the *head and arm choke*, uses a similar principle as the last technique. This time, the move is applied with the arms instead of the legs. It is important to note that the arm triangle can be done from both the top and bottom half-guard position.

Here, Joel is on the bottom and has his opponent in his half-guard. To begin the technique, Joel pushes the right arm of his adversary toward his right side with his left hand. Joel also reaches up with his right arm and puts it alongside his opponent's neck.

Next, Joel wraps his right arm around the back of his opponent's neck and brings his left arm up in preparation for the choke.

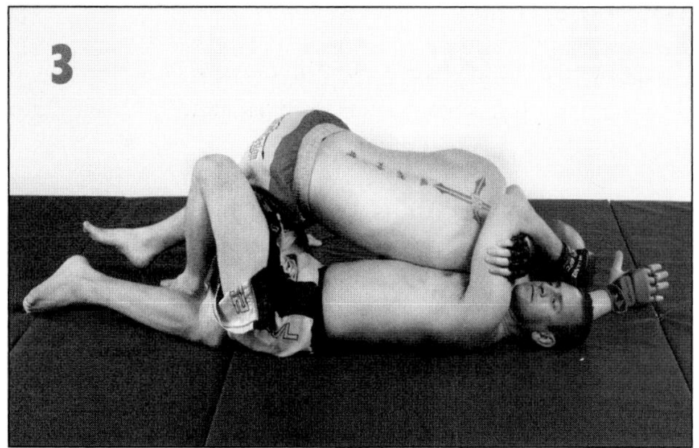

Joel grabs his left bicep with his right hand and bends his left elbow to cinch the technique. He then applies pressure by squeezing his arms together.

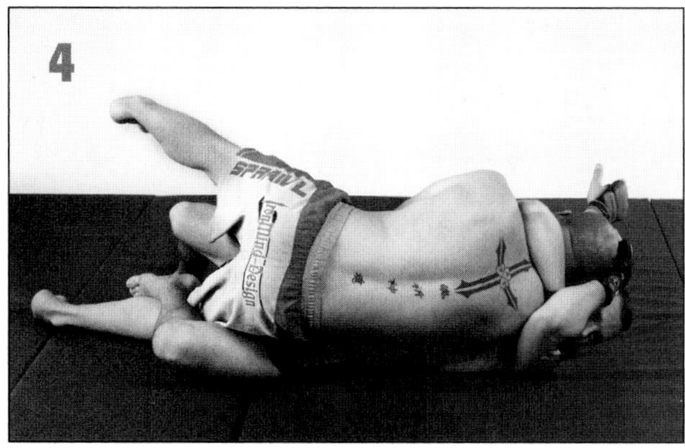

Next, Joel unlocks his feet and places his right foot on the mat while still pinning his opponent's right leg to the ground by bending his left leg. Joel then pushes upward and to the left off of his right foot, which starts to roll his adversary. He maintains the choke during the entire roll, continuing to increase the pressure around his competitor's neck.

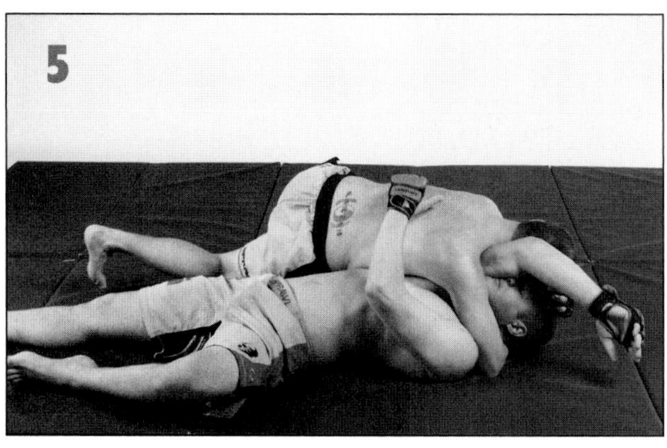

Completing the reversal and putting his opponent on his back, Joel ends up in the side mount and presses his head into the back of his opponent's tricep. This further increases the intensity of the choke and causes his opponent to tap out.

Rear Naked Choke From the Back

Getting to the back of your opponent is one of the most dominant positions on the ground and sets you up for this classic technique. Although it is a simple submission, the *rear naked choke* is a crowd favorite.

Here, Joel has already gotten on his opponent's back and has locked his feet inside of his opponent's hips. This is known as "getting your hooks in" and allows Joel to stretch his legs backward and flatten out his opponent on the mat. To start the choke, Joel locks his left forearm across his adversary's face and pulls his head backwards. This exposes his competitor's neck and sets him up for the choke.

Next, Joel slides his right arm all the way underneath his opponent's exposed neck.

To lock in the choke, Joel bends his right elbow and squeezes his competitor's neck between his right bicep and forearm. He then grabs his left bicep with his right hand, bends his left elbow, and puts his left hand on the back of his opponent's head. Joel squeezes his arms together and drives his opponent's head forward, forcing a quick tap out.

Leg Lock

During the ground game, the legs are also susceptible to attack and vulnerable to submissions. In this photo, Joel is standing and his opponent is on the ground. To set up the lock, Joel pushes his opponent's left leg to the side while moving the right leg upward.

Joel then steps his right leg through, placing his foot to the outside of his adversary's right hip. He then begins to squat down as he traps Chris's outstretched leg between his inner thighs. Joel also maintains pressure behind his competitor's right ankle to prevent his opponent from bending his leg and making sure it stays straight.

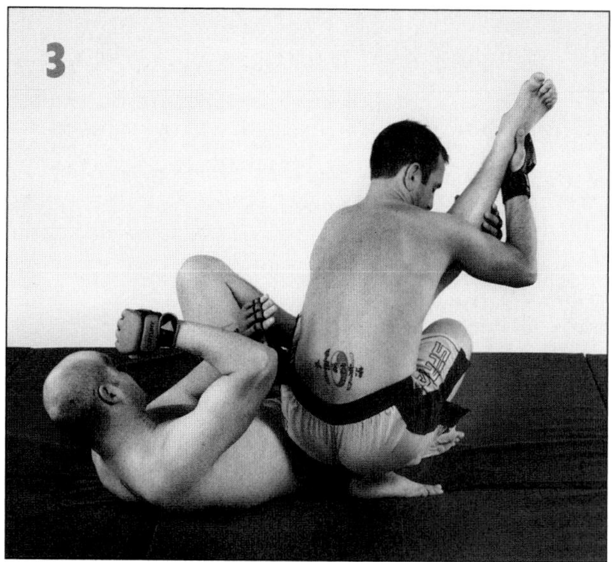

In the next part of the move, Joel continues to spin to his right as he slides down his opponent's leg and lowers his hips to the mat. While doing this, Joel now has both hands behind his opponent's leg as he pulls the leg toward his chest.

Dropping all the way to the ground, Joel pulls his opponent's leg downward while driving his hips upward. This two-way action is similar to the arm bar and puts enormous pressure on the knee joint, prompting his opponent to tap quickly before his leg is injured.

Ankle Lock

Joel is sitting back in his opponent's open guard and sees an opportunity for an ankle lock. He postures up to stay out of striking range and squats up on his right knee, which pins his adversary's left leg between his quadriceps and ribs.

Next, Joel hooks his right arm around and underneath his opponent's left ankle and starts to sit back.

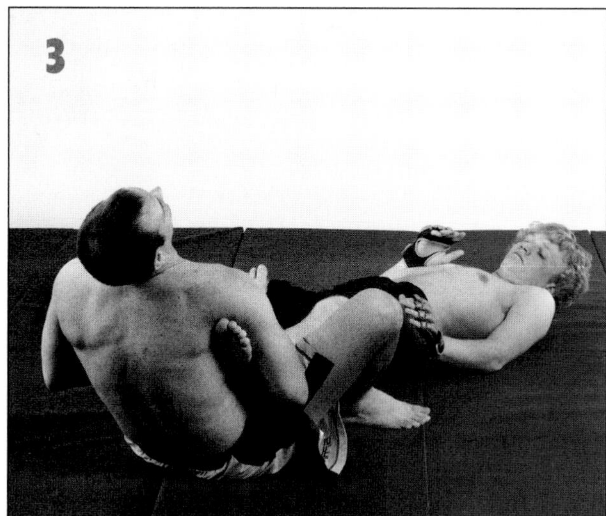

With his arm behind his adversary's Achilles tendon, Joel grabs his right hand with his left and drops his back to the floor. This two-way action extends his opponent's ankle beyond its normal range of motion and forces a quick tap out to avoid permanent damage.

The ground game in MMA is incredibly technical and even a small mistake can lead to defeat. This is one of the reasons that so many fighters train diligently in jiu-jitsu in order to maximize their success when the fight goes to the ground.

10 ★★★

THE MMA TRIATHLON: ULTIMATE TRAINING WORKOUTS

If you've read this far, you have a good understanding of the cardio and strength training regimens that MMA athletes use to get their bodies prepared for battle. You've also learned about the fundamental striking, wrestling, and jiu-jitsu techniques used in mixed martial arts. Now it's time to put all that knowledge into practice with some explosive workout routines that will put your mind, body, and spirit to the test.

Welcome to what we call the MMA Triathlon. Nope, this isn't your typical biking, swimming, and running triathlon. Instead, it refers to the three fighting ranges of MMA: standup striking, wrestling, and ground fighting. By integrating training drills focused on these three ranges with the cardio and strength exercises you've already learned, we've created a series of workouts like no other.

CIRCUIT TRAINING

The beautiful thing about all of these exercises is that they can be combined into what are called circuits. Circuit training involves doing a number of exercises at different stations to compose a full workout. The benefits for combat athletes are numerous. First, this format of training promotes cardiovascular fitness as well as muscle endurance. It can also provide a full-body workout using numerous muscle groups.

As we've described in earlier chapters, MMA warriors endeavor to simulate the conditions of a real match as closely as possible. For a hard-core anaerobic workout routine, this means adopting the nonstop, five-minute-round formula. To maximize our circuit training, we've combined a series of exercises and drills into rounds. This greatly improves a fighter's ability to adapt quickly and develop the all-around stamina needed for a real match.

ULTIMATE WORKOUTS

The ultimate training workouts described below are designed to use specific drills to sharpen your abilities. They also represent a series of skill-building activities to develop and improve an athlete's knowledge of the fight game. Not to mention the fact that they will make even the most well-conditioned athlete think about quitting. But remember, fighters aren't your average athletes, and "quitting" isn't in the warrior vocabulary.

At first glance, they may seem simple and that is the point. Sometimes, a person new to the sport will try to overcomplicate his training regimens, which only leads to poor results. These workouts are simple, yes, but far from easy. Just like you should never underestimate an opponent, you shouldn't underestimate how tough these routines will actually be when you are going through them.

We recommend a twelve-week training program using the ultimate workouts. These are broken down into three different cycles: beginner, intermediate, and advanced. You can follow the samples in this chapter or mix and match various rounds to create your own program. Just remember, the goal is to work the entire body by using cardiovascular exercises, combined with the four types of strength training (see chapter six) and skill-specific drills. Here is the progressive format that we suggest:

BASIC LEVEL: FOUR WEEKS

- Week One: Two days of three-round workouts
- Week Two: Three days of three-round workouts
- Week Three: Four days of three-round workouts
- Week Four: Five days of three-round workouts

INTERMEDIATE LEVEL: FOUR WEEKS, FIVE DAYS EACH WEEK

- Week One: Four three-round workouts and one five-round workout
- Week Two: Three three-round workouts and two five-round workouts
- Week Three: Two three-round workouts and three five-round workouts
- Week Four: One three-round workout and four five-round workouts

ADVANCED LEVEL: FOUR WEEKS, FIVE DAYS EACH WEEK

- Week One: Four five-round workouts and one ten-round workout
- Week Two: Three five-round workouts and two ten-round workouts

- Week Three: Two five-round workouts and three ten-round workouts
- Week Four: One five-round workout and four ten-round workouts

Even if you are already in great shape, starting with the basic level is the best way to begin training in MMA. The basic workouts are three five-minute rounds with one-minute rest periods in between rounds. These routines only last seventeen minutes and can be ideal if you only have a limited amount time to exercise. The intermediate workouts gradually phase in five rounds and work all the way up to a total of ten rounds for the advanced level.

If you follow this progression, not only can you expect to be in phenomenal shape at the end of twelve weeks, but you will also have a great base of MMA techniques in your repertoire. Put simply, this program works. We call it Battle Ready Fitness.

BASIC LEVEL: WEEK FOUR SAMPLE

Day 1: Seventeen-Minute Workout

Three rounds of five minutes each with one-minute rest between rounds.

ROUND ONE: CARDIO

- One minute of jumping jacks
- One minute of jump rope
- One minute of regular push-ups
- One minute of jump rope
- One minute of mountain climber push-ups
- Rest period of one minute

ROUND TWO: STRENGTH—PULLING

- One minute of Muay Thai scarecrow
- Thirty seconds of shoulder shrugs
- Thirty seconds of bicep curls
- One minute of weight sled pull
- Thirty seconds of pull-ups
- Thirty seconds of resistance band guard pull
- One minute of leg curls
- Rest period of one minute

ROUND THREE: STANDUP STRIKING AND CARDIO

- One minute of boxing combinations
- One minute of kicking and knee combinations

- Three minutes of running on treadmill (flat grade)
- End of workout: rest, recover, and stretch

Day 2: Seventeen-Minute Workout

Three rounds of five minutes each, with one-minute rest between rounds.

ROUND ONE: CARDIO

- Three minutes of running on a treadmill (flat grade)
- One minute of mountain climber push-ups
- One minute of jump rope
- Rest period of one minute

ROUND TWO: STRENGTH—PUSHING

- Thirty seconds of handstand push-ups
- One minute of fitness ball pike press
- Thirty seconds of bench press
- One minute of ab roller
- One minute of squats
- One minute of tire flip
- Rest period of one minute

ROUND THREE: STRIKING

- One minute of boxing punches
- One minute of Muay Thai knees
- One minute of kicks
- One minute of heavy bag ground 'n' pound
- One minute of hill sprints or treadmill at 30 percent incline
- End of workout: rest, recover, and stretch

Day 3: Seventeen-Minute Workout

Three rounds of five minutes each, with one-minute rest between rounds.

ROUND ONE: STRENGTH—FULL BODY

- Thirty seconds of free weight neck exercise
- Thirty seconds of dumbbell wrist rotations
- Forty-five seconds of military press
- Forty-five seconds of dumbbell shoulder fly
- Forty-five seconds of medicine ball push-ups

- Forty-five seconds of bus driver plate drill
- Thirty seconds of leg lifts
- Thirty seconds of squats
- Rest period of one minute

ROUND TWO: STRIKING

- Thirty seconds of boxing punches
- Thirty seconds of elbows
- Thirty seconds of Muay Thai knees
- Thirty seconds of kicks
- Thirty seconds of ground 'n' pound
- Two and a half minutes—*repeat sequence*
- Rest period of one minute

ROUND THREE: STRENGTH—EXPLOSIVE

- One minute of tire flip
- One minute of mountain climber push-ups
- One minute of partner closed guard sit-up reaches
- One minute of squat jumps with medicine ball
- One minute of partner shoot 'n' carry
- End of workout: rest, recover, and stretch

Day 4: Seventeen-Minute Workout

Three rounds of five minutes each, with one-minute rest between rounds.

ROUND ONE: CARDIO

- Thirty seconds of resistance run
- Thirty seconds of sprinting
- One minute of stair climb
- One minute of partner carry 'n' run
- Two minutes of focus pad striking
- Rest period of one minute

ROUND TWO: COMBINATION

- One minute of practicing shoot takedowns
- Thirty seconds of neck isometrics
- One minute of defending shoot takedowns
- Thirty seconds of resistance strap ankle flex
- One minute of heavy bag ground 'n' pound

- One minute of running on the treadmill (10 percent grade)
- Rest period of one minute

ROUND THREE: WRESTLING AND STRIKING

- One minute of practicing single leg takedowns
- One minute of boxing combinations
- One minute of defending single leg takedowns
- One minute of Muay Thai knees
- Thirty seconds of practicing single leg takedowns
- Thirty seconds of defending single leg takedowns
- End of workout: rest, recover, and stretch

Day 5: Seventeen-Minute Workout

Three rounds of five minutes each, with one-minute rest between rounds.

ROUND ONE: CARDIO AND WRESTLING

- One minute of jumping rope
- One minute of practicing double leg takedowns
- One minute of squat jumps with medicine ball
- One minute of defending double leg takedowns
- One minute of partner closed guard sit-up reaches
- Rest period of one minute

ROUND TWO: CARDIO AND JIU-JITSU

- One minute of hill sprints
- One minute of practicing escaping mount
- One minute of stair climb
- One minute of practicing escaping knee mount
- One minute of mountain climber push-ups
- Rest period of one minute

ROUND THREE: CARDIO AND SPARRING

- Thirty seconds of sprinting on the treadmill
- Two minutes of standup sparring
- Thirty seconds of sprinting on the treadmill
- Two minutes of ground sparring
- End of workout: rest, recover, and stretch

INTERMEDIATE LEVEL: WEEK FOUR SAMPLE

Day 1: Twenty-Nine-Minute Workout

Five rounds of five minutes each, with one-minute rest between rounds.

ROUND ONE: CARDIO

- Two minutes of jump rope
- Three minutes of running on treadmill (15 percent grade)
- Rest period of one minute

ROUND TWO: STRENGTH—LIFTING

- Forty-five seconds of military press
- Forty-five seconds of bus driver plate drill
- Forty-five seconds of bench press
- Forty-five seconds of Romanian dead lift barbell row
- One minute of leg lifts
- One minute of partner shoot 'n' carry
- Rest period of one minute

ROUND THREE: STRIKING

- One minute of focus pad elbows
- One minute of focus pad kicks
- One minute of heavy bag ground 'n' pound
- One minute of focus pad Muay Thai knees
- One minute of focus pad boxing combinations
- Rest period of one minute

ROUND FOUR: WRESTLING

- One minute of practicing countering wrestling clinch
- One minute of practicing shoot takedowns
- One minute of defending shoot takedowns
- One minute of practicing single leg takedowns
- One minute of defending single leg takedowns
- Rest period of one minute

ROUND FIVE: JIU-JITSU

- One minute of escaping mount
- One minute of passing closed guard

- One minute of escaping knee mount
- One minute of passing half guard
- One minute of practicing arm bar from mount
- End of workout: rest, recover, and stretch

Day 2: Twenty-Nine-Minute Workout

Five rounds of five minutes each, with one-minute rest between rounds.

ROUND ONE: STANDUP STRIKING AND CARDIO

- One minute of boxing combinations
- One minute of kicking and knee combinations
- Three minutes of running on treadmill (15 percent grade)
- Rest period of one minute

ROUND TWO: CARDIO

- Two minutes of jumping rope
- One minute of mountain climber push-ups
- One minute of partner closed guard sit-ups reaches
- One minute of fitness ball pike presses
- Rest period of one minute

ROUND THREE: ESCAPING DRILLS

- One minute of practicing escaping side mount
- One minute of practicing escaping dirty boxing clinch
- One minute of practicing escaping knee mount
- One minute of practicing escaping wrestling clinch
- One minute of practicing escaping guard (to standing)
- Rest period of one minute

ROUND FOUR: CARDIO

- Five minutes of running on treadmill
- Rest period of one minute

ROUND FIVE: STANDUP STRIKING AND JIU-JITSU

- One minute of focus pad boxing combinations
- One minute of practicing arm bar from mount
- One minute of focus pad Muay Thai knees
- One minute of practicing arm bar from guard
- One minute of heavy bag ground 'n' pound
- End of workout: rest, recover, and stretch

Day 3: Seventeen-Minute Workout

Three rounds of five minutes each, with one-minute rest between rounds.

ROUND ONE: STRENGTH AND CARDIO

- One and a half minutes of regular squats
- Thirty seconds of fitness ball pike presses
- Thirty seconds of regular sit-ups
- Two and a half minutes of running on treadmill (10 percent grade elevation)
- Rest period of one minute

ROUND TWO: JIU-JITSU

- One minute of passing closed guard
- One minute of passing open guard
- One minute of practicing arm bar from guard
- Two minutes of jiu-jitsu sparring
- Rest period of one minute.

ROUND THREE: SPARRING

- Two minutes of standup sparring
- One minute of wrestling
- Two minutes of ground fighting
- End of workout. Rest, recover, and stretch

Day 4: Twenty-Nine Minute Workout

Five rounds of five minutes each, with one-minute rest between rounds.

ROUND ONE: STRENGTH—PUSHING

- One minute of squats
- One minute of tire flips
- Thirty seconds of handstand push-ups
- One minute of fitness ball pike press
- Thirty seconds of bench press
- One minute of ab roller
- Rest period of one minute

ROUND TWO: STRIKING

- One minute of heavy bag ground 'n' pound
- One minute of focus pad elbows
- One minute of focus pad kicks

- One minute of focus pad boxing combinations
- One minute of focus pad Muay Thai knees
- Rest period of one minute

ROUND THREE: WRESTLING AND JIU-JITSU

- One minute of practicing double leg takedowns
- One minute of passing closed guard
- One minute of practicing single leg takedowns
- One minute of passing open guard
- One minute of practicing hip throws
- Rest period of one minute

ROUND FOUR: DEFENDING

- One minute of defending against jab and cross
- One minute of defending against Muay Thai knee
- One minute of defending against round thigh kick
- Two minutes of defending against random strikes
- Rest period of one minute

ROUND FIVE: CARDIO AND SPARRING

- Thirty seconds of running on treadmill (20 percent grade)
- One minute of ground fighting
- Thirty seconds of running on treadmill (15 percent grade)
- One minute of standup sparring
- Thirty seconds of running on treadmill (10 percent grade)
- One and a half minutes wrestling
- End of workout: rest, recover, and stretch

Day 5: Twenty-Nine-Minute Workout

Five rounds of five minutes each, with one-minute rest between rounds.

ROUND ONE: STRENGTH AND CARDIO

- One minute of medicine ball push-ups
- One minute of dumbbell chest fly
- One minute of sit-ups
- One minute of back extension
- One minute of stair climb
- Rest period of one minute

ROUND TWO: STRIKING AND WRESTLING

- One minute of countering wrestling clinch
- One minute of focus pad boxing combinations
- One minute of defending hip throw
- One minute of focus pad elbows
- One minute of your favorite striking combinations
- Rest period of one minute.

ROUND THREE: STRENGTH AND CARDIO

- One minute of hill sprints
- Two minutes of jumping rope
- One minute of Muay Thai scarecrow
- One minute of weight sled pull
- Rest period of one minute

ROUND FOUR: NEEDS IMPROVEMENT

- Thirty seconds of practicing your worst strike
- One minute of practicing your worst takedown
- One minute of practicing your worst takedown defense
- One minute of practicing your worst jiu-jitsu escape
- One minute of practicing your worst jiu-jitsu submission
- Rest period of one minute

ROUND FIVE: CARDIO AND YOUR BEST

- Thirty seconds of practicing your best striking combinations
- Thirty seconds of practicing your best takedown
- Thirty seconds of practicing your best takedown defense
- Thirty seconds of hill sprints
- Thirty seconds of practicing your best jiu-jitsu escape
- Thirty seconds of practicing your best jiu-jitsu pass
- Thirty seconds of practicing your best jiu-jitsu submission
- Thirty seconds of stair climb
- One minute of practicing your best striking combinations
- End of workout: rest, recover, and stretch

ADVANCED LEVEL: SAMPLE TEN-ROUND DAY

ROUND ONE: STRENGTH AND CARDIO

- One minute of jumping rope
- Thirty seconds of neck isometrics

- Thirty seconds of dumbbell wrist rotations
- One minute of dumbbell chest fly
- One minute of running on treadmill (flat grade)
- One minute of dumbbell shoulder fly
- Rest period of one minute

ROUND TWO: VARIOUS DRILLS

- One minute of boxing combinations
- One and a half minutes of defending against strikes
- Thirty seconds of resistance band guard pull
- One minute of leg curls
- One minute of resistance strap ankle flex
- Rest period of one minute

ROUND THREE: WRESTLING AND GROUND WORK

- One minute of countering dirty boxing clinch
- One minute of defending double leg takedown
- One minute of sweeping from butterfly guard
- One minute of passing from side mount to mount
- One minute of heavy bag ground 'n' pound
- Rest period of one minute

ROUND FOUR: DEFENDING AND STRIKING

- One minute of partner shoot 'n' carry
- Thirty seconds of defending against strikes
- One minute of defending against random takedowns
- Thirty seconds of Muay Thai knees
- Two minutes of standup sparring
- Rest period of one minute

ROUND FIVE: SUBMISSIONS

- One minute of Kimura from guard
- One minute of heavy bag ground 'n' pound
- One minute of omoplata from guard
- One minute of triangle from guard
- One minute of heavy bag ground 'n' pound
- Rest period of one minute

ROUND SIX: STRENGTH AND JIU-JITSU

- One minute of partner closed guard sit-up reaches
- Two minutes of passing closed and open guard

- One minute of Muay Thai scarecrow drill
- One minute of practicing escape from guard (to standing)
- Rest period of one minute

ROUND SEVEN: JIU-JITSU

- One minute of striking combinations
- One minute of continuous takedowns
- Thirty seconds of arm triangle from half guard
- One minute of passing half guard
- Thirty seconds of practicing key lock from side mount
- One minute of sweeping from half guard
- Rest period of one minute

ROUND EIGHT: VARIOUS DRILLS

- One minute of tire flips
- One minute of defending against Muay Thai knee
- One minute of countering random clinches
- One minute of practicing flying knee
- One minute of practicing triangle from guard
- Rest period of one minute

ROUND NINE: VARIOUS DRILLS

- One minute of sparring (all levels)
- One minute of practicing omoplata from guard
- Thirty seconds of defending against random takedowns
- Thirty seconds of practicing guillotine from guard
- Thirty seconds of practicing rear naked choke from back
- Forty-five seconds of practicing leg lock
- Forty-five seconds of practicing ankle lock
- Rest period of one minute

ROUND TEN: THE END

- Five minutes of sparring (all levels)
- End of workout: rest, recover, and stretch

11 ★★★

SPEED TRAINING: FASTER, FASTER, FASTER!

Having learned many of the techniques used in MMA, it is now time for you to understand another crucial component of this sport. In a word: speed. An athlete's ability to be faster than an opponent is found in almost every competitive sport. MMA is no different, and given the circumstance of two fighters with equal technical ability, speed can be a determining factor for victory.

Training for speed focuses on the refinement of technique and efficiency of movement. Fighters are continually looking for ways to improve their techniques. They know that the more they hone their skills, the faster they will be inside the cage. For combat athletes, developing speed is not about being in a hurry. They don't confuse rushed and sloppy movements with quick and precise strikes.

Building lightning-fast speed, reflexes, and timing will almost always give a fighter an edge over his competitor. Speed can save you from being hit while allowing you to out-strike your opponent. In this chapter, we'll show you some training exercises to increase your speed output while maintaining the high degree of accuracy necessary for combat. Before we delve into that topic, however, let's take a look at the anatomy and mechanics of speed to better understand how to become as fast as possible.

ANATOMY AND MECHANICS OF SPEED

Speed is basically defined as the distance covered divided by the time taken to cover the specified distance. This measurement isn't really important to combat athletes. What is important is being able to move and strike faster than your opponent. A fighter's speed is essentially determined by the ability of his nervous system to signal muscles to contract.

Since combative sports are anaerobic events, they require a predominance of fast-twitch muscle fibers. These fibers contract quickly during brief, high-intensity exercises that require an above-average amount of strength output. So if you thought all of those anaerobic exercises from earlier chapters were just to torture you, you were mistaken. They also help a fighter to increase his speed by developing fast-twitch muscles through exercises like sprinting and weightlifting.

Building fast-twitch muscle fibers through anaerobic exercise is also a precursor to speed-specific training drills. The reason is that weak muscles are more susceptible to injury as a result of speed training. And if there is anything a fighter wants to avoid, it is unnecessary injury.

Another important component to consider is the adverse affect of tense muscle groups. Tense muscles take longer to respond to nerve impulses than relaxed muscles. Essentially, the excess tension slows down the message from the brain as it travels along the nerve en route to a specific muscle fiber.

If you've ever read or seen interviews with Bruce Lee, he often promoted the concept of muscle relaxation until the moment of the strike. The more relaxed a fighter is physically, the faster his movements will be against his opponent. To keep their muscles loose and relaxed and promote good nerve conductivity, many fighters get regular sports massages.

The mechanics of speed involve two elements: perception speed and reaction speed. Both are a function of the communication between the visual and nervous systems of the body. Perception speed involves the amount of time it takes to recognize a potential threat. In the case of a fighter, it refers to how rapidly they become aware of an impending strike. Seeing that your opponent is throwing a kick or punch, however, is only half of the equation.

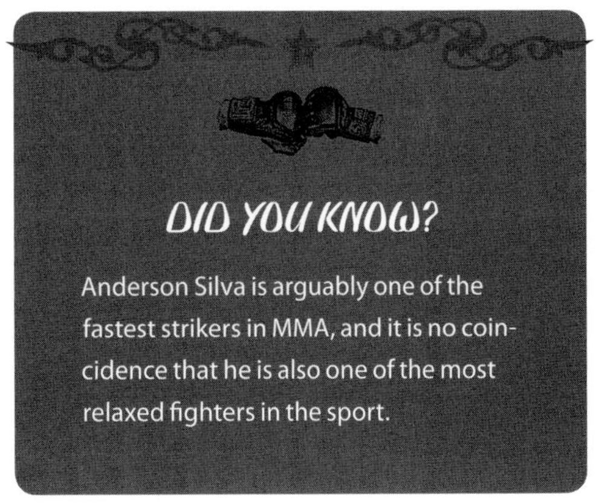

DID YOU KNOW?

Anderson Silva is arguably one of the fastest strikers in MMA, and it is no coincidence that he is also one of the most relaxed fighters in the sport.

Reaction speed is your ability to initiate a response to a particular threat. In MMA, this can mean blocking, evading, or countering an incoming strike. Alertness is a key to reaction speed because knowing a threat is imminent puts the body into a high-functioning state. A fighter knows his opponent isn't there to sing songs or write poetry. MMA warriors are already in a naturally alert state of mind because they know they are stepping into a cage to face an opponent who will be trying to beat them.

SPEED DEVELOPMENT DRILLS

When training to develop faster reflexes, fighters incorporate specific drills to increase their overall perception and reaction speed. They then focus their efforts on sport-specific moves to refine their techniques and reduce excess movement. The cleaner that a combat athlete's execution of a technique is, the less time his opponent has to perceive the attack.

Perception-Speed Drills

In order to build perception speed, a fighter has to expose himself to situations that require instant analysis. A great way to do this is to have a training partner put on some sparring gear and start throwing strikes. Instead of countering, limit yourself to blocking and evading only. Not only does this get you comfortable with being hit, it also improves your ability to see the small initial movements that precede a strike.

Start out with your training partner slowly throwing only one specific strike at a time. As you build your confidence and ability to evade and block a particular strike, ask your partner to start increasing his speed. When you become comfortable dealing with one particular strike, switch to another. You can also limit yourself to only evading or only blocking for any given round. After you are at ease with handling pretty much any singular strike, have your partner begin to throw combinations.

This uncertainty of where the next strike will be coming from will help you read the entire body as a whole. You'll then begin to detect those minor precursor movements, which will help take your perception speed through the roof. Remember, it's not about being so slick that you avoid every strike. That's just pure arrogance. In a match, both fighters are going to get hit. But if you can avoid a majority of the strikes then you'll be in a far better position to capitalize on an opponent's mistakes. This leads us to the next part of speed training.

Reaction-Speed Drills

It may seem strange but to begin to develop reaction speed, we'll build on the perception drills by slowing things down. Have a training partner put on his actual fight gloves and then begin throwing slow singular strikes. Think Tai Chi speed. Although this may feel silly, slow sparring is one of the best ways to begin to improve your reaction speed. By training slowly with a partner who is using real fight gloves, you also reduce your fear of being hit.

Fear is one of the biggest inhibitors of reaction time because it causes your muscles to tense. As we've already discussed, this slows your ability to respond and decreases your chances of countering effectively. As you evade or block a strike, stop and look to see where your opponent is open. Then execute a strike of your own and start the process all over again. This type of red light, green light exercise will improve your ability to sense an opening and deliver a great counterstrike.

Water Training

While other people in the pool may give you weird looks, practicing your striking skills in the water can really help you to improve your speed. Water training provides constant resistance throughout the entire range of motion of a strike. It also allows a fighter to uncover flaws in his striking techniques.

Almost every fitness center with a pool has some sort of water aerobics class. If you've never tried one, give it a shot, and you'll see the benefits that training in water offers. Additionally, if you've suffered a joint injury, water training is also great for joint rehabilitation. So stop worrying about what other people think and just jump in and start practicing.

PUNCHING-SPEED DRILLS

These punching drills, albeit extremely simple, will help you build and develop your hand speed. By singling out the retraction of your strikes, you will improve how fast your body prepares to deliver another punch. This is one of the most commonly overlooked training elements, which is why taking the time to work on these drills will give you an advantage over your opponent. Most fighters think that punching speed is about how fast you can throw the jab or cross, but in reality it's how fast you are ready to throw a second one that really counts.

Jab Retraction

Stand in a fighting stance with your lead hand extended in a full jab. This is the starting position for this particular drill. Remember to keep your opposite hand up to properly defend your face.

Next, retract your fist as quickly as possible back towards your head to a normal fighting position. Think of this as the reverse of actually throwing the punch.

Once your arm has returned to a normal fighting position, slowly extend your punch back out to the starting position and repeat for a series of ten repetitions. Remember, it is the retraction of your jab that helps improve your punching speed.

Cross Retraction

This is the same drill as the last one, only we are working on the cross instead of the jab. Get in your fighting again and extend your rear fist for a full cross.

Now retract your fist as rapidly as possible, allowing your hips to return as well, leaving you in a fighting position with both of your hands up to protect your head.

Slowly return to the starting position and then repeat this drill for ten reps. The more you practice this exercise, the faster your punches will get and the quicker you will be when you get into the cage.

KICKING-SPEED DRILLS

To develop kicking speed, we use the same retraction method as we do for punching. This may seem awkward at first, but implementing these drills in your training regimen will give you a leg up on your competition. The more you practice, the faster your kicks will get. When you combine these exercises with the punching drills, you'll be able to deliver much faster striking combinations. As we discussed in chapter seven, using combinations is the way to dominate your opponent and drive the pace of the match.

Front Kick Retraction

Start by extending a front kick at hip level. Make sure both hands are up protecting your face.

Next, retract the kick as fast as possible into the chambered or ready position.

To complete additional repetitions, simply extend your leg back out to the original starting position and repeat for a set of ten retractions.

Round Kick Retraction

To begin, extend your rear leg forward into a round thigh kick. As always, practice keeping those hands up to protect your face.

Next, keep your upper thigh at the same angle but bend your knee and retract the lower part of your leg as fast as possible.

For the last portion of this speed exercise, retract your upper leg as you turn your hip away from your target as rapidly as you can. This portion of the drill specifically works on developing speed in the hips.

RESISTANCE TRAINING

Remember that elastic resistance band you've been using for some of the cardio and strength training exercises? Well, guess what, it's a great tool to use in the development of your speed training as well!

Resistance Drill #1

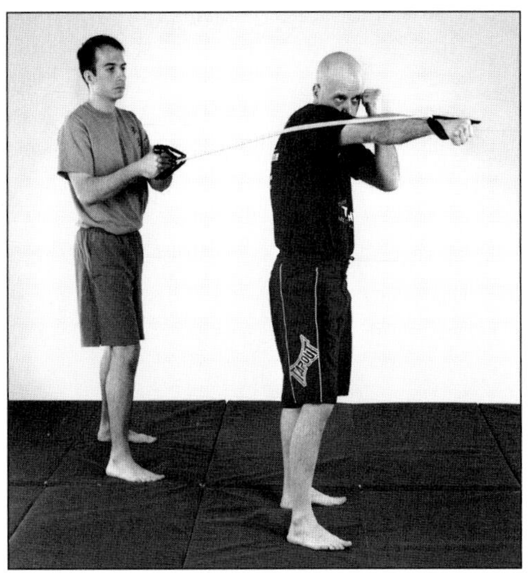

Attach one end of the band to a non-movable object or have one of your training partners help you out. Strap the other end around your wrist or hold it in your fist to work on your punches. Start in your normal fighting stance and then push your fist forward through the resistance as you extend into a full jab or cross. As you pull your fist back, retract it slowly as you resist the pull of the elastic band. Make sure to do repetitions on both arms to build your punching speed on both sides of your body. If you have a third training partner, you can also have him hold a focus pad, giving you an opportunity to actually strike with the resistance band on as you build your speed.

Resistance Drill #2

You can also use the elastic band to improve your kicking speed. With a training partner holding one end, wrap the other end around your foot and start executing some kicks. Remember that the band will be adding resistance, so make sure you are prepared for the faster retraction.

Resistance Drill #3

Another variation using the resistance band is to allow it to snap your leg or arm back using the retraction drills illustrated earlier. The elastic band helps you retract your kick or punch faster than you can on your own. This creates a muscle memory of how quickly your body should retract a strike, helping you improve your overall speed.

FOCUS PAD TRAINING

There are a number of excellent focus pad drills to help you improve your speed. A favorite among fighters is a moving and countering exercise that helps MMA warriors improve both their perception and reaction speed. In this drill, the coach moves around the mat or practice area at regular speed, simulating the movements of an opposing fighter.

Focus Pad Drill

As the coach moves around, he quickly and randomly presents a striking target for the combat athlete. From a fighting position, perhaps the coach quickly extends his left arm, presenting an opportunity for a jab. The fighter must perceive the opening and strike as quickly as possible. This develops speed by increasing a fighter's ability to perceive an opening and then react accordingly to capitalize on an opponent's mistake.

Even though the coach is holding the focus pads, he should also initiate offensive movements of his own to simulate counters by an opponent. This can be everything from strikes to clinching to attempting a takedown. In this way, a coach keeps his fighter alert to all possibilities. An example would be having the coach throwing a hook just a moment after the fighter executed a jab. The fighter has to react by blocking or evading the incoming strike, enhancing his reaction time.

Having evaded, the fighter is now encouraged to rapidly deliver a counterstrike of his own. Not only does this help a combat athlete to develop speed, it helps him to see openings even as he is on the defensive. This shortens the time span between defensive and offensive movements and instills in a fighter the ability to continue to press the action.

Building striking speed can be a valuable asset to any MMA fighter. Sometimes competitors are so evenly matched that speed becomes the deciding factor of fight. When combined with accuracy, speed can give a combat athlete a tremendous advantage over an opponent.

12 ★★★

NUTRITION AND SUPPLEMENTS

For the combat athlete, proper nutrition is an absolute essential part of training. Food is the fuel of the MMA warrior. How and what a fighter eats is an important element of success. Proper nutrition helps to keep the body performing at peak levels. Think of it this way: There is a difference in the type of high-test fuel that goes into a Ferrari and your everyday sedan. High-performance vehicles require high-performance fuel. The same is true for any athlete.

We've already established that mixed martial artists aren't just your typical athletes. They require an even higher level of performance than someone who is working out just to stay in shape. A fighter's diet and nutrition intake is often very specific to ensure he is operating at his peak. Keep in mind, of course, that you should always consult with your physician before starting a new fitness plan or taking supplements.

Here are a some quick nutritional basics utilized by combat athletes:

- **Hydration:** Staying hydrated is critical. When an athlete first becomes thirsty, he may already be dehydrated by as much as 2 percent. This can result in a 5 to 10 percent reduction in performance output. Drinking lots of water, even when not thirsty, is vital during training.

- **Meal frequency:** While most people eat three large meals per day, fighters typically increase the number of meals to five or more. This helps them keep up with their body's demand for energy during intensive training by delivering a steady supply of nutrients. This process also elevates the metabolism, helping fighters burn more fat throughout their workouts.

- **Extra calories:** Due to the rigorous workouts used in MMA, a combat athlete needs to consume significantly more calories than the average person. Many fighters double their daily calorie intake during preparation for a match.

- **High-performance diet:** To make sure that they are giving their bodies what is required, many pro fighters consult a professional nutritionist to assist in monitoring their diet. Most also avoid highly processed foods in favor of more natural and organic foods.

Quality meals are an important part of training for a couple of very good reasons. First, having a high-performance body with minimized fat levels allows for increased speed and endurance. Fat is nonfunctional, and carrying around extra amounts of it will make a fighter's reaction time slower.

Think of it in this way: A combat athlete who weighs in at 185 pounds with 14 percent body fat has a lean body mass of 159 pounds. A fighter who also weighs in at 185 pounds, but has only 7 percent body fat will have a lean body mass of 172 pounds. The second fighter, in addition to probably having quicker reaction time, is also 13 pounds more muscular than the first athlete. In a highly competitive sport like MMA, this kind of advantage can make a huge difference in a fight.

The second reason eating healthy is important to the MMA warrior is because it assists in the prevention of injury. A body that is receiving ample amounts of proper nutrients is less susceptible to damage. Additionally, performance nutrition can aid considerably in decreasing the body's recovery time from extreme training. The faster the recovery time, the stronger the athlete will be for competition.

FUNDAMENTALS OF A FIGHTER'S DIET

During active training, meals are typically consumed a certain amount of time before or after a workout. This process helps a fighter have sufficient energy for intense exercises, while avoiding the lethargic feelings that come with overeating. Likewise, it also helps a fighter to replenish his energy following a tough workout. We'll discuss this in detail toward the end of the chapter.

All athletes need a good balance of protein, carbohydrates, and even fat to function properly. But how much should a mixed martial artist eat? In other words, how many calories are in the daily diet of a fighter? That is a great question, and it depends upon a number of variables, including how much a fighter weighs, the intensity level of his workouts, and whether he is trying to cut or gain weight.

The normal male needs approximately 2,100 to 2,500 calories per day. For a female, the approximate range is 1,800 to 2,000 calories per day.

To get an estimate using an online calorie intake calculator, go to www.mayoclinic.com/health/calorie-calculator/NU00598.

You can also calculate your approximate calorie intake using the following formula. A normal person with an average exercise level can simply multiply his body weight by 12. For example: 200 pounds times 12 = 2,400 calories per day. If you are just beginning your training in MMA, add 25 percent as you start your workout regimen and adjust from there.

If a fighter is trying to cut weight, he will reduce his calorie intake as the fight approaches. We'll address this in more detail in chapter thirteen. To gain weight, an MMA warrior needs to increase his caloric intake by an estimated 500 calories per day to gain one pound of muscle per week. Keep in mind that the combat athlete will have already increased his caloric intake to compensate for the strenuous workouts. This 500-calorie increase is in addition to the extra calories added for training.

Using the above example, a 200-pound MMA athlete would be consuming an average of 3,000 calories per day. To gain one pound of muscle per week, the fighter would have to ramp up to 3,500 calories per day while training. These extra calories should come primarily from carbohydrates with small increases in protein and fat. To facilitate muscle gain, most combat athletes increase their weightlifting routine and use heavier weights with fewer repetitions. This is because the caloric burn is relatively small compared to more active aerobic exercise, resulting in increased muscle mass.

NUTRITION FOR WARRIORS

Now that we've laid out the preliminary components of a how a fighter eats, it's time to understand *what* a fighter eats. While combat athletes have their own individual diet plan, the following information will provide you with an excellent overview of what makes up that plan.

Protein

Amino acids are the building blocks of protein within the body. Proteins help to build muscle tissue and increase muscle mass. There are two major types of protein: animal protein and vegetable protein. Animal protein is found in eggs, milk, cheese, and lean meats, such as chicken, turkey, and beef. Vegetable proteins are found in wheat, rye, and green vegetables.

During rigorous training, physical exertion begins to affect the muscle tissue. To keep the muscle tissue healthy and build strength, the body needs a steady supply of protein. If protein levels are inadequate, the body will begin to pull the amino acids from the muscles during strenuous workouts, resulting in muscle breakdown. Obviously, fighters want to increase their power as much as possible.

To keep their bodies supplied with proper levels of amino acids, fighters typically allocate 10–15 percent of their daily calories from protein. This means that a 200-pound fighter will consume an average of 300 to 450 calories from protein per day. Why not more you ask? The body can only process a certain amount of protein at any given time. If an excess is taken, it will not be absorbed into the body and will be released as waste.

Carbohydrates

Carbohydrates are the energy source that helps to run the human body. They are the first and most continuous source of power and provide the primary fuel for muscles to function. Generally speaking, carbs should make up 55–65 percent of a fighter's daily caloric intake. There are two types of carbohydrates: simple carbs and complex carbs.

Simple carbs are broken down and processed immediately in the body. They can be found in fresh fruit, soda, candy, and cookies. Because they are absorbed quickly, these simple carbohydrates give the body a quick rise in energy. This means that simple carbs are best used when the body needs a boost of nutrients, such as for breakfast and after a challenging workout.

The second kind of carbs are called complex carbohydrates. These are processed over time in the body and provide a prolonged source of energy. Complex carbs are found in vegetables, brown rice, whole grain breads, cereals, and nuts. These starches and fibers give the body longer lasting fuel so that an athlete can train for longer periods. Good choices include oatmeal and potatoes. These carbs are better for snacks, lunch, and dinner because the body stores them as muscle glycogen to be used when energy is needed during training.

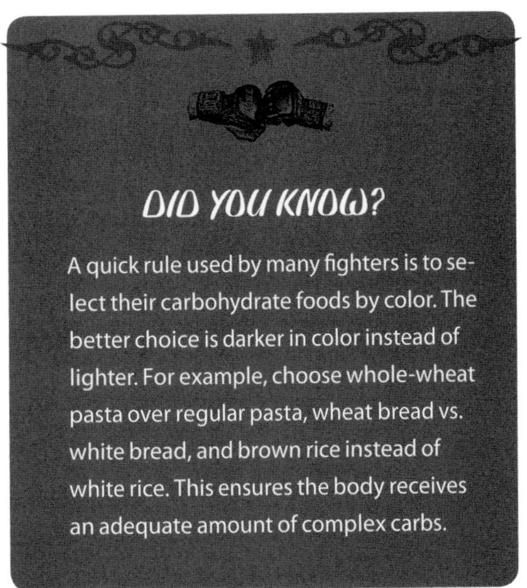

DID YOU KNOW?

A quick rule used by many fighters is to select their carbohydrate foods by color. The better choice is darker in color instead of lighter. For example, choose whole-wheat pasta over regular pasta, wheat bread vs. white bread, and brown rice instead of white rice. This ensures the body receives an adequate amount of complex carbs.

Fats

Although fats usually get a bad rap, the truth is that some fats are an important part of our overall health. Fats play a critical role in the body's metabolism and supply energy to muscles during extended periods of exercise. Generally speaking, the body begins to burn fat as energy about forty-five minutes to an hour into a workout. There are different types of fats; some of them are good and some of them are absolutely terrible for your body.

Saturated fats, like the fats in steak and butter, are solid at room temperature. This is the type of fat most used by manufacturers of processed foods to increase a product's shelf life. Saturated fats are something you want to avoid because they increase your cholesterol and your risk of heart disease.

Trans fats are another type of fat you want to stay away from if you are trying to eat like a combat athlete. Hydrogenation takes a fat and converts it into a trans-fatty acid. This is the stuff found in fast food. Eating a bunch of this junk is another way to increase your health risk.

Unsaturated fats, on the other hand, can be beneficial for your body. Good examples of foods with unsaturated fats are avocados, almonds, walnuts, and olive oil. Another example of a healthy fat is Omega-3 fatty acids. Omega-3s are excellent for improving insulin activity and providing anti-inflammatory benefits. As you can imagine, the latter is particularly valuable for MMA warriors. Good food choices for Omega-3s are fish oil and flaxseed oil.

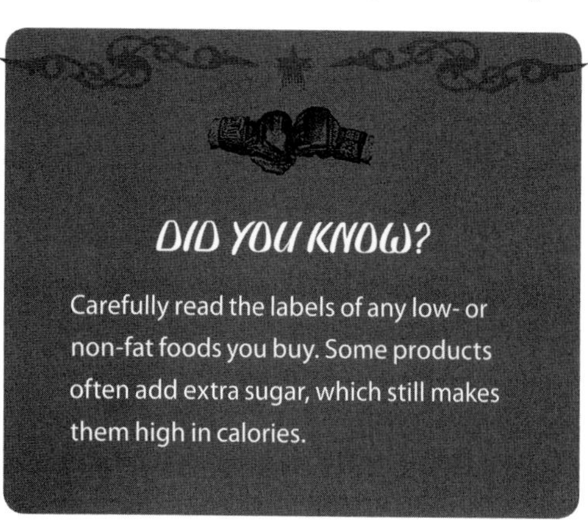

Overall, unsaturated and Omega-3 fats should make up no more than 25 percent of a fighter's diet during regular training. This will help give the body the good types of fat it needs to operate at peak levels. During preparation for a fight, however, some combat athletes choose to increase their healthy fat intake due to extended training sessions of four to six hours a day. Lastly, it is important not to eat fatty foods right before exercising. Fats can require three to five hours to digest, which reduces the physical output capacity of the body.

Vitamins and Minerals

Vitamins and minerals are very important to the human diet and an essential part of overall health. Vitamins are used by cells to perform metabolic functions and to help the body efficiently use the chemical energy provided in food. Minerals are used to promote nerve function and muscle contraction.

If a fighter is watching his food intake and ensuring that it is high in vitamins and minerals, additional nutritional supplements might not be important. This is because the body can only process so many vitamins and minerals and gets rid of any excess. However, many combat athletes choose to supplement their food with a multivitamin.

Before adding a multivitamin, it is important to correct your diet and follow the guidelines above for proper protein, carbohydrate, and fat intake. A multi-vitamin is really only a backup for a less than ideal diet. There are lots of differing opinions out there, but if you are going to take a multivitamin, we recommend selecting a natural, whole-food multivitamin over one that is synthetically manufactured in a lab.

Synthetic vitamins are often high dose, which, as we mentioned, are typically ineffective because the body excretes the excess. Whole-food vitamins, on the other hand, are made from natural ingredients and are designed to be taken in more frequent, but smaller doses. This complements the fighter's increased meal frequency and creates a steady supply of nutrients throughout the day.

Check out the following website for more information on whole-food vitamins: www.standardprocess.com/display/learnthebenefits.spi.

Fighters who eat fewer fruits and vegetables than they should often add a mixed-green vitamin supplement to their diets. This product essentially takes fruits and vegetables and grinds them into a powder. A popular mixed-green supplement among MMA warriors is LifeForce, created by UFC Champion Randy Couture (www.couturenutrition.com).

What to Avoid

The following suggestions are the nutritional no-no's of the MMA world. These are the things that fighters seek to avoid in their diet plans.

- Although a number of combat athletes drink their fair share of alcohol and caffeine, everyone recognizes their negative side effects on the body's productivity output. Think about it this way: A dog won't go anywhere near its food if you mix it with bourbon or Red Bull.

- Don't consume foods or liquids with high amounts of sugar, high-fructose corn syrup, and unsaturated fat. This stuff is no good for a high-performance athlete.
- Avoid combining significant amounts of fats and carbohydrates in the same meal. These are things like greasy pizza and cheeseburgers. Instead, stick to meals with protein and fat *or* protein and carbs.
- Stay away from mixing sweet dairy products with proteins and fats. These foods oppose one another and don't digest well together.
- Also avoid combining acidic foods (citrus fruits, berries, etc.) and sour dairy products (yogurt) with any other food groups. For an alternative, try to combine high-carbohydrate foods with sweet fruits or fresh (vs. aged) cheeses.
- Just like the rule your mom used to tell you about swimming, don't eat a large meal right before exercising. Make it a light meal, and allow at least one to two hours for digestion before your workout routine.

PRE-EXERCISE NUTRITION TIPS FROM THE PROS

Eating a specifically formulated light meal a couple hours before training can significantly enhance your performance. Fighters typically consume a low-fat, low-sugar, low-protein meal that is high in complex carbohydrates. This gives the body the chance to store up the energy it needs in the muscles necessary for a challenging session. Adding vegetables to this pre-exercise meal slows the entry rate of carbohydrates into the blood stream and aids in burning extra fat.

Right before beginning a workout, some mixed martial artists have a carb-protein shake. Typically in a three-to-one ratio of simple carbohydrates to protein, this shake boosts a warrior's energy level during his fitness conditioning. Fighters may also choose to have a cup of hot green tea, which has a small amount of caffeine that can provide an extra jolt during the workout.

POST-EXERCISE NUTRITION TIPS FROM THE PROS

After a tough conditioning session, the body needs to replenish the nutrients it has exhausted during training. Replacing those essential vitamins and minerals quickly is a key element of a fighter's nutritional plan. To accomplish this task, combat athletes often fuel back up by grabbing a post-exercise shake.

Similar to the pre-exercise shake, the post-workout shake is a carb-protein mixture with a four-to-one ratio. Ramping up the amount of simple carbohydrates helps to build back up the body's glycogen levels. To calculate the number of carbs in your shake, take your body weight and multiply it by 50 percent. For example, a fighter weighing 200 pounds will need 100 grams of carbs. Using a four-to-one ratio of carbs to protein means that the shake will have 25 grams of protein.

An excellent choice for the simple carbohydrates needed in a shake is maltodextrin powder. Although this stuff is often used to increase the flavor in beer, don't think that a beer makes a perfect post-exercise drink. Nice try, but you also need to replenish protein levels after a workout. A great choice is whey protein, which is quickly digested and absorbed by the body. On that note, avoid consuming vegetables after exercising because they contain fiber, and that slows down the absorption of nutrients. We want the body to recover as quickly as possible and a maltodextrin-whey protein shake does a fantastic job.

Another valuable post-exercise tip is to include antioxidant nutrients, such as vitamin C, vitamin E, and beta-carotene. Found in many fruits, these antioxidants help to protect the body from free-radical compounds that damage your cells. Consider adding blueberries or cranberries to your post-workout shake as a good source of antioxidant vitamins.

SUPPLEMENTS

Sports-supplement companies have found a lucrative new market in the MMA community. Two top supplement manufacturers, Xyience (www.xyience.com) and Bio-Engineered Supplements & Nutrition (www.bsnonline.com), are sponsors for the Ultimate Fighting Championship. Because of the explosion of the sport, there are a lot of companies hyping supplements purporting to help give fighters an edge in competition. Unfortunately, there are a lot of misconceptions out there regarding these products.

Supplements can be taken in a powder, liquid, or pill form. Again the concept to understand here is that supplements are not meant to be replacements for an unhealthy diet. If you follow the guidelines outlined in this chapter, you most likely won't need these kinds of products.

On average, the effects of these supplements are very short lived. Given the option between dropping $65 on a single supplement and buying a jiu-jitsu instructional DVD, we suggest the latter. If you're lucky, the first may only slightly improve your performance, but with the second you'll actually gain something that will help you win a fight.

All that being said, there are some good options out there if you really feel the need to take supplements. Make sure you do your homework and research any product before you spend your hard-earned cash. As we discussed earlier in this chapter in the pre- and post-exercise tips, a good carb-protein product is probably the best and most worthwhile supplement you can purchase. Your best bet is to mix the ingredients yourself, but you can also buy it pre-made in items like PowerBars (www.powerbar.com) and shakes from Optimum Nutrition (www.optimumnutrition.com) and Champion Nutrition (www.championnutrition.com).

Besides your carb-protein intake, here are a few of other supplements that you might find worth checking out:

- **Creatine monohydrate:** Although this supplement has received its fair share of negative press, the truth is that the controversy is overhyped. Creatine is found naturally in red meat, and taking it as a supplement can increase a fighter's strength and assist in workout recovery. Most combat athletes take an average of 5–10 grams per day during training and 3–5 grams per day on rest days. Consider adding it to a pre-workout cup of green tea, as well as your post-workout shake.

- **L-glutamine:** This supplement is an amino acid to aid in improved recovery and immune response before and after workouts. It also supports the immune system and prevents excess protein loss. Check out Power Glutamine from Champion Nutrition (www.championnutrition.com/power_glutamine).

- **Thermogenics:** These products are stimulants that often contain significant quantities of caffeine and are used to rapidly burn fat. Fat burners raise the body's core temperature and increase the metabolism. Although these supplements will boost your energy, they will also negatively affect the adrenal system. Thermogenics should only be used after a fighter has already reduced his body fat percentage through a long and strict fat-loss diet plan. For example, combat athletes use fat burners in preparation for a fight when they are trying to have as much lean muscle mass as possible for their weight division. If you decide to use thermogenics, we highly recommend taking an adrenal supplement to balance the adverse affects.

Although nutrition is a complex subject, you now have the necessary understanding of how and what a fighter eats in order to excel in MMA. If you keep your body supplied with several healthy nutritious meals during the day, you can expect better results in your training. In the next chapter, we're going to share with you the lost art of how the top combat athletes successfully and safely lose weight in preparation for a fight.

13 ★★★

WEIGHT CUTTING FOR THE WARRIOR

Since MMA now uses weight classes under the Unified Rules of Mixed Martial Arts, fighters typically want to be as big and strong as possible for their division. As we discussed in the last chapter, fighters follow specific nutritional guidelines to decrease their body fat levels. This increases their lean muscle mass and gives combat athletes an advantage over opponents who have a higher percentage of body fat.

Many MMA warriors also endeavor to lose several pounds just before a match. This is known as "cutting" or "dropping" weight. After weighing-in, they then try to put back on the pounds they shed in preparation for the bout. Combined together, these two strategies provide competitors the best chance to be the biggest overall fighter in their weight class.

A fighter who implements this method often looks much bigger and stronger than one who doesn't. Let's revisit our example from last chapter and add in the process of weight cutting to illustrate this point. A fighter who normally weighs 185 pounds and has 14 percent body fat has a lean muscle mass of 159 pounds. His opponent, the MMA warrior, normally weighs 197 pounds and has only 7 percent body fat due to a nutritious diet and excellent workout program.

In this scenario, the MMA warrior has a lean muscle mass of just over 183 pounds. He is almost at the maximum weight for his division in lean muscle mass alone. If he is able to temporarily cut 12 pounds (from 197 to 185) for the weigh-in, it means that the MMA warrior will be almost 25 pounds bigger than his opponent. This is a huge difference. The MMA warrior will essentially be more than an entire weight class heavier than the first fighter.

CAUTIONARY SUGGESTIONS

Cutting weight is something that should be done under medical supervision. The plan we describe in this chapter is designed to give you an outline of what is typically used in MMA. If you are planning on losing weight before a fight, we suggest you review this material with your physician. This aspect of MMA is an art form all its own that requires both knowledge and practice to be done safely.

A rapid drop in body weight can cause side effects and reduce overall performance. This is why it is important to use a well-thought-out plan. A fighter must lose the necessary weight safely while still maintaining optimal energy levels. Done incorrectly, this process can quickly fatigue a combat athlete, adding stress and depleting energy reserves. For this reason, it is best to have a doctor monitor your progress.

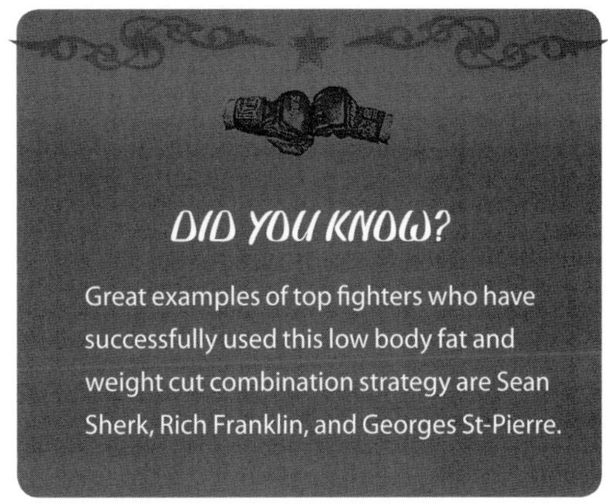

DID YOU KNOW?

Great examples of top fighters who have successfully used this low body fat and weight cut combination strategy are Sean Sherk, Rich Franklin, and Georges St-Pierre.

Practices to Avoid

Weight cutting has been a commonly used in both wrestling and boxing for many years. Unfortunately, some of the least effective weight loss methods have been carried over from these sports into MMA. Typically used the last few hours before weigh-ins, these practices can have an adverse effect on the performance output of the body.

One of these techniques that you'll want to stay away from is sweating off excess pounds through last-minute intensive exercise. This is usually done in heavy clothing, or even a plastic suit, in an effort to raise the core body temperature. While this often-used practice does work and can result in losing several pounds, it can also be detrimental to the body. This method expends vital energy that is needed for the fight. You want to save your stamina for the match, not waste it in a last-minute flurry of exercising to make weight.

Another method to avoid is extended dehydration. Never go more than twenty-four hours without water, especially right before the bout. The muscles in the body are approximately 70 percent water. Going without water for longer than twenty-four hours will not only dehydrate your muscles and sap your strength, it will also significantly reduce your speed.

Unfortunately, some athletes who lack common sense not only dehydrate themselves, but they even go without food for a few days before the fight. How can you expect to do well if your body is malnourished? If there is a sure formula for lousy performance, this is it. Do yourself a favor and avoid falling into these common weight-cutting traps.

There is one last technique used to drop weight that bears mentioning. Some athletes desperate to lose the last couple pounds have resorted to using diuretics. A diuretic is any drug that increases the rate of the excretion of urine from the body. These drugs force the expulsion of water from the body through urination. Although there are natural and synthetic diuretics, both can lead to electrolyte imbalances. Synthetic diuretics should only be used under the supervision of a doctor. If you follow the advice below, you should never need to use one.

WEIGHT-CUTTING BASICS

In the last chapter, we suggested that it is best to have a healthy diet plan before adding supplements. The same is true for dropping weight prior to a match. A healthy diet plan should be the core of this part of your training. If you are following a challenging MMA exercise routine and develop a disciplined meal program with nutritious foods, chances are good that you will be losing body fat. Having a low body fat percentage is the first key step in the overall weight-cutting process as covered in the beginning of the chapter.

In the last few weeks of training prior to a match, most combat athletes begin to decrease their daily calorie intake. This starts to get fighters closer to their target weight prior to our final weight-cutting process. What is an acceptable target weight? Most MMA warriors fighting above the 170-pound class try to be within ten to twelve pounds of the maximum allowable weight for their division.

For example, a fighter in the middleweight division at 185 pounds tries to weigh between 195 to 197 pounds seventy-two hours before the official weigh-in. Combat athletes competing below 170 pounds try to make their target weight within six to eight pounds of the maximum allowable weight. In other words, a fighter competing at 155 pounds will try to weigh 161 to 163 pounds seventy-two hours before the weigh-in.

Figuring out your target weight depends on a couple of variables. The first is how much heavier you currently are than your target weight. The second is how many calories you need to eliminate from your daily intake in order to lose one pound. If you are tracking your weight and monitoring your calorie intake during training, you should have a very good idea of this number. This is one of the best reasons to keep excellent records; the more information you have, the better you can calculate a weight loss plan.

For example, let's say that a fighter currently weighs 205 pounds and will be fighting in the middleweight division at 185 pounds. This means he needs to lose ten pounds to get to his target weight of 195 pounds. Let's also say that the fighter is currently consuming 3,075 calories per day to maintain his weight at 205 pounds. Through his records, he determines that reducing his calorie intake by 500 calories per day while maintaining his current training program results in a loss of one pound per day.

In order to be at his target weight, the fighter needs at least ten days of consuming only 2,575 calories daily to drop from 205 pounds to 195 pounds. Remember that the goal is to be at the target weight seventy-two hours before the actual weigh-in. So in this case, the fighter should begin his 500-calorie per day reduction no later than thirteen days prior to weigh-in to ensure he achieves this target weight goal of 195 pounds.

As we mentioned in the last chapter, some combat athletes take a thermogenic supplement as they prepare for a match. The draw down of weight illustrated above would be the ideal time for a fighter to utilize this type of supplement. In the scenario we've just covered, the MMA warrior could also take a thermogenic supplement over the ten-day calorie reduction period to help burn more body fat and make the target weight. Again, we highly recommend an adrenal supplement to balance any negative effects.

Continuing with this scenario, we recommend increasing your water intake to approximately one to two gallons per day during the last three to five days of your calorie-reduction period. The best strategy is often to drink one ounce of water for every pound of body weight. For example, a combat athlete who weighs 200 pounds will drink 200 ounces of water, which is just over a gallon and a half. If the climate is overly hot, we recommend drinking slightly more to compensate for the increased temperature.

While this process might not completely alleviate the slight hunger from your decreased calorie intake, it will ease your mind a bit to have something more to consume. It is also a critical part of the pre-weigh-in plan, so make sure you keep track of how much water you drink. Again, your goal is to drink one to two gallons per day for the last three to five days before your final pre-weigh-in cut.

The next step is to know the time of the actual weigh-in. Is it the same day of the fight or the day before? Under the Unified Rules of Mixed Martial Arts, weigh-ins take place no more than twenty-four hours before the actual event. Having a full day to replenish nutrients, re-hydrate, and put back on pounds is ideal.

Many amateur fight leagues, however, have weigh-ins just a couple of hours before the event. This means that the fighters will have less time to reload their bodies with nutrients and replace the weight they have lost. Knowing this information ahead of time is very important because it factors into a combat athlete's overall weight-cutting strategy. The more time there is between the weigh-in and the actual fight, the more weight a fighter can cut.

THE FINAL (PRE-WEIGH-IN) CUT

Let's say you successfully reached your target weight of 10 to 12 pounds greater than the maximum weight allowed in the division in which you will be competing. But don't throw a party yet because the hard part has just started. For our purposes, we are going to assume that the official weigh-in occurs exactly twenty-four hours before the actual event. Continuing with our example above, the combat athlete now weighs 195 pounds and has seventy-two hours to lose ten pounds to qualify in the 185-pound division.

Before we start into the final weight cut plan, it is important to make a couple of additional points. The first is that it is always best to have reviewed this plan with your doctor prior to implementing it. The second is that if the weigh-in occurs only a few hours before the actual fight, you will obviously have less time to replenish your body's nutrients. If this is the case, we recommend your target weight being within 5 to 8 pounds of the maximum for the division.

Fight night is set for Saturday at 8 P.M. The official weigh-in is set twenty-four hours earlier on Friday at 8 P.M. Today is Tuesday. It's crunch time, but the plan that follows is remarkably simple and reasonably painfree. It does require discipline and focus however, so this is no time to get lazy. Remember, the fighter has ten pounds to lose in only three days.

Seventy-Two Hours Before Weigh-In

Starting on Tuesday night at 8 P.M, the fighter begins to scale off his water intake much like he did his calorie intake. At this point, the MMA warrior has been consuming between one and two gallons of water per day for the last three to five days. This actually serves an important purpose in cutting weight because it speeds up the body's bladder functions and causes the need to urinate more often.

At 8 P.M., the fighter needs to reduce the amount of water he is consuming by half. At 195 pounds, he should decrease his water intake to approximately 97 ounces. This means that between 8 P.M. on Tuesday and 8 P.M.. on Wednesday, the fighter should only consume about three quarters of a gallon of water.

The combat athlete also ceases all training except for flexibility stretching and technique review. As food and water intake are restricted, this is to help the body rest up for the match and expend the least amount of energy. Speaking of rest, it is important for a fighter to get plenty of sleep, although that can sometimes be a challenge with an anxious mind. Review some of the warrior meditations from earlier in the book to help clear your thoughts.

Between Tuesday and Wednesday evening, the combat athlete will also modifies his food intake. The number of calories are reduced approximately 10 percent below the normal amount needed to maintain the fighter's target weight without any exercise. Lets say the fighter (without exercising) would normally consume 2,340 calories to maintain his target weight of 195 pounds. He should reduce his intake to roughly 2,100 calories starting Tuesday night. A simple way to calculate this is to take the MMA warrior's body weight and multiply it by 11.

What type of food should the fighter eat? Between Tuesday and Wednesday evening, the combat athlete makes sure his overall diet includes about 15 percent protein, which helps repair the muscle tissue. He also restricts his fat intake to about 15 percent. The remaining amount, about 70 percent, is complex carbohydrates. This is food like vegetables, brown rice, whole-grain pasta, oatmeal, and potatoes. Remember, complex carbs build the body's energy reserves, which will be important for the fight.

Forty-Eight Hours Before Weigh-In

It is now Wednesday night at 8 P.M. and two days out from the official weigh-in. Now the MMA warrior needs to again cut the amount of water he is drinking by half. This means that he will now be drinking approximately one fourth the amount from two days ago. Continuing our scenario, the fighter only drinks approximately forty-eight ounces of water between Wednesday night and Thursday night. Mostly, he drinks this water during meals.

Meals between Wednesday and Thursday night are also slightly modified. The combat athlete again decreases his calorie intake by about 10 percent. The fighter can simply take his body weight and multiply it by 10. For food, the combat athlete now restricts his protein and fat to 10 percent each, while consuming 80 percent of his calories in complex carbohydrates. Loading up on carbs helps to maximize the amount of energy the body retains.

Twenty-Four Hours Before Weigh-In

Only one day away from the weigh-in, it is now Thursday evening at 8 P.M. The next twenty-four hours are the toughest part of the weight-cutting process. From now until the actual weigh-in, the fighter is restricted to minimal water and food intake. Water should only be consumed to wash down a nutrition bar or a small piece of fruit.

Since the combat athlete has loaded up with complex carbohydrates, the body has plenty of energy in reserve for this one day fast. Also, since the fighter is resting, the risk of dehydration is minimal. We also recommend that the fighter dedicate some time to going through mental visual motor rehearsal drills and visualize seeing successfully making the weight.

Some fighters take gentle natural laxatives before going to bed on Thursday night. We recommend selecting one that is also used for a wellness or detoxification program. The intestines of the body are about twenty-five feet long and often hold more than five pounds of waste. Combat athletes who take a natural laxative at night are typically able to wake up the next morning and clear their bowels completely.

The Day of the Weigh-In

On Friday morning, the MMA warrior checks his weight to see how close he is to making weight. If you've followed this formula, you should already be at the proper weight for your division. At most, a fighter should only be a pound or two over. If this is the case, the best and most effective strategy is to go to a dry sauna to sweat off the remaining pounds. Most fitness facilities have one, and we always recommend taking a friend and your weight scale to monitor your progress.

Sweating off weight in the dry sauna beats expending vital energy trying to exercise it off. Using the dry sauna retains a greater percentage of the complex carbohydrates your body is storing for energy during the fight. Typically, a fighter can lose approximately one pound of sweat in a thirty-minute sauna session.

The best method for using the dry sauna is as follows: Go in for fifteen minutes, then step out to towel off and take a five-minute break. Remember, you are on water restriction so only have a small sip to keep your mouth wet. Then go back into the dry sauna for another fifteen-minute session.

Once you've done this, it is time to check your weight. If you still need to lose more, wait approximately twenty minutes and then repeat the process. It is important to give yourself this twenty-minute break for a couple of reasons. First, you want to avoid overheating the body. You won't be able to fight if you can't move.

Second, allowing the body's temperature to cool and then ramping it back up again increases the rate at which the body sweats. Losing a couple of last-minute pounds by having to use a dry sauna is no picnic. It makes the most sense to be as efficient as possible. Leave yourself as much time as possible to recuperate before the official weigh-in. Bottom line: You'll get better results by giving yourself a short break between sauna sessions.

THE OFFICIAL WEIGH-IN

Regulations generally allow fighters to have access to the official scale that is being used prior to the actual weigh-ins. Check with the fight promoter for details. Also ask the promoter how much time you'll be given if you fail to make weight on the first attempt. If you are allowed any time at all, it is typically only an hour or two at the most.

We highly recommend that you bring your own scale with you to the event. It is a good idea to compare the scale you are using against the official scale as soon as possible. This will let you know if there is any variance between the two scales. Most of the time there won't be, but it never hurts to check.

Although there is no reason you shouldn't be at the required weight, bringing your own scale also allows you to monitor your weight if you have to cut more at the last second.

Before heading out to the official scale to get weighed, go to the bathroom one last time. Some fighters, as they step on the scales, suggest looking upward and visualizing being light as a feather. Hey, whatever works.

If you are over the maximum allowable weight and are allowed more time, there is really only one thing left to do: Put on a bunch of heavy clothes and hope that you can sweat off the needed weight through exercise. Most combat athletes jump rope or go on a run in an effort to cut the last pound. Again, if you followed the plan above, there is absolutely no reason you shouldn't make weight.

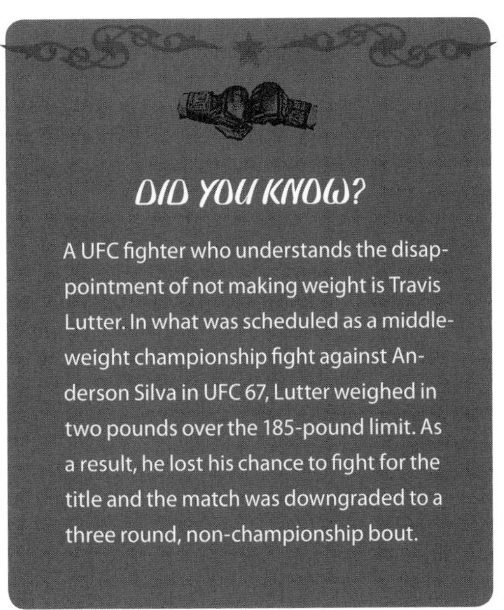

DID YOU KNOW?

A UFC fighter who understands the disappointment of not making weight is Travis Lutter. In what was scheduled as a middleweight championship fight against Anderson Silva in UFC 67, Lutter weighed in two pounds over the 185-pound limit. As a result, he lost his chance to fight for the title and the match was downgraded to a three round, non-championship bout.

AFTER THE OFFICIAL WEIGH-IN

So let's assume you made weight. Now it's time to replenish all the nutrients your body lost in preparation for the weigh-in. But this part of the weight-cutting process is as critical as what got you to this point. Don't assume you can just shove down a bunch of food and water and you'll be all set. If you do this, you're setting yourself up for less than optimal performance inside the cage.

As soon as you step off the scales, we recommend drinking a bottle of Pedialyte. This product is an electrolyte hydration solution that is an alternative to sports drinks. Most sports drinks have a high quantity of sugar, which can actually worsen your fatigue. Add a pinch of salt with the Pedialyte to help replace the sodium your body lost if you had to resort to sweating off the final pounds.

Once you've had the Pedialyte, start drinking regular amounts of water that are portioned out over a time period to avoid bloating. The goal is to consume 100 to 150 percent of your original water intake prior to the cut. Using our scenario, the fighter at 195 pounds was previously drinking approximately one and a half gallons of water per day. This means that he would drink between 195 and 292 ounces of water over the next twenty-four hours before the match.

Proportioned over twenty-four hours, the fighter should drink between eight and twelve ounces on average per hour. However, since he has already gone a day with minimal water, we recommend front-loading his water intake by tripling that amount for the first three hours. After that, it will probably be time for some rest.

Some professional fighters have a skilled medical professional administer an IV to maximize their return time to optimal nutrient levels. This is something we typically don't recommend unless approved by your physician. If you follow the guidelines in this section, you should be up to speed in no time.

Of course, the fighter also starts to rebuild his nutrient levels by eating as soon as he is finished with weigh-ins. For his meals, the combat athlete consumes small regular meals every forty-five minutes for the first three hours. Using this timetable, he can get in at least four meals before going to bed.

By far, the first small meal is the toughest because the MMA warrior is naturally very hungry after a full day without much food. Resist the temptation to eat more, because the body can only digest food at a certain rate. By consuming smaller meals, the body will process the food much faster and reach optimal nutrient levels more quickly.

As for the types of foods to eat, be sure to ramp up on complex carbohydrates to fuel up your muscles for the fight. The 80-10-10 principle of complex carbs, proteins, and good fats is the ideal formula. Avoid vegetables for your first two meals because they can slow the absorption of the carbohydrates into your body. Also, it is a good idea to take a few natural mineral supplements to restock the body's mineral deposits. We suggest taking some calcium, potassium, and magnesium, which also help in the prevention of muscle cramps.

THE DAY OF THE FIGHT

Upon waking in the morning, the MMA warrior approximately doubles his average water intake for the first couple of hours. Continuing our illustration, the 195-pound fighter would drink between sixteen and twenty-four ounces per hour. Afterwards, he can reduce his water consumption to an average of eight to twelve ounces per hour. This regulated water intake helps the fighter to be fully hydrated while avoiding any bloated feelings.

If possible, have smaller meals every hour until two hours before the fight. This is to give your final meal adequate time to digest prior to the match. We recommend alternating actual food meals with carb-protein shakes. It is also important not to change your food from what you normally eat. Stick to the types of food you are comfortable with and you'll be fine. Again, avoid consuming too much food at one time, which will leave you feeling sluggish.

Lastly, we recommend a power bar about twenty minutes prior to the fight. Since you have been loading up on complex carbohydrates, it is time to give your body that last-minute boost with some fast-acting simple carbs. Eating helps to calm your last-minute nerves and gives you a fast-acting boost of energy. You can also have some green tea, which will give you a final boost of caffeine.

PRACTICE, PRACTICE, PRACTICE!

Like with any other part of your training, weight cutting is something that takes practice. We highly recommend that you practice the entire process laid out in this chapter during the course of your MMA training. The best time to practice cutting weight is in conjunction with the taper-off period used to prevent overtraining. This simulates the preparation for a real fight.

Make sure you go through the whole process and make it as real as possible. Start from the beginning of the chapter and follow the procedure.

Decrease your calorie consumption to reach your target weight as you start increasing your water intake over the last several days. At seventy-two hours out, start decreasing your water intake and reduce your calorie consumption below your average weight maintenance level.

Forty-eight hours out, load up on carbs and cut your water intake even more. Get through the last twenty-four-hour fast and simulate your entire weigh-in process. After you successfully make weight in this practice run, go through the entire replenishing process, meals and all! Perform the whole fight-day routine, leading right up to a full practice fight against a sparring partner.

The goal is to make the whole situation as real as possible. Have your walk into the cage, even if you don't have one, with your entrance music. Even have your mock fight at the same time you expect to be competing. Have your corner men ready and somebody serving as the referee.

Set an agreement ahead of time to go about 40 to 50 percent speed and strength against your friendly sparring partner. Listen to your coaches, but we recommend wearing fight gear as close as possible to what you'll be wearing. Some fighters wear bigger grappling gloves in this practice fight to avoid really hurting their partners.

Make your mock fight go to the fifth round, even if your real fight will only have three rounds. This will test your conditioning level. Make sure the rounds are timed, and have your corner give you critiques during the rest period just like the real bout. If your sparring partner is a good sport, your coaches may ask him to give you an opportunity to win in the fifth round. He shouldn't give you anything, but winning a mock fight can really boost an MMA warrior's confidence. It is also a great idea to videotape the mock fight to further evaluate your skills.

Are you ready? Now that you understand the secrets of cutting weight like the pros, it's time to ask yourself if you want to test your newfound skills in an actual fight. Do you want to hear those famous words: "And now, standing in this corner ..."?

14

★★★

AND NOW, STANDING IN THIS CORNER ...

Having learned about all the major components of MMA, only one question really remains: Do you want to be a fighter? Chances are good that you already know the answer. MMA is an electrifying sport that is growing by the minute, but stepping into a cage to test your own skills isn't for everyone.

You certainly don't need to have a desire to actually fight in order to get the benefits of training. As we've already covered, the cardiovascular and strength exercises used by the athletes in this sport will take your fitness conditioning to a whole new level. The nutritional regiment followed by fighters will help keep you healthy and full of energy. And even if you never have to defend yourself, learning the striking, wrestling, and jiu-jitsu techniques in this book will give you an increased sense of confidence.

But if you're a natural athlete and competitive by nature, the intense and challenging training may have already peaked your interest in competing. If that is the case, and you've already decided you want to participate in an MMA match, then we have some additional things to cover before you are ready to step into the cage.

LOCATING A TRAINING FACILITY

In the past, mixed martial artists have had to find and train with separate, individual coaches for each discipline. In other words, a boxing coach, a Muay Thai coach, a wrestling coach, a jiu-jitsu instructor, and a personal trainer. While some fighters still use this approach, more and more training facilities dedicated to MMA are opening. These centers seek to consolidate a number of different coaches under one roof to provide all-in-one training.

So how do you find one in your area? The best way is to start with a phone book and call around to the local martial arts schools in your city. Ask them if they offer an MMA training program and if so, make arrangements to see the center. Depending on how many active MMA programs you find, you may have to check out several schools.

Generally speaking, the more coaches they have, the better the training will be at that particular school. This usually comes at a premium, however, so make sure you take the time to pick a program that fits your budget and parameters. In addition to the experience and types of coaches, you'll also have to determine if you feel comfortable with the other fighters training at that location.

During the writing of this book, we were able to catch up to Jason Appleton, the president of MMA Big Show (www.mmabigshow.com). Jason's promotion is one of the most successful Pro-Am MMA events in Ohio, Kentucky, and Indiana. He had some additional tips for fighters just starting out and looking for a training facility:

> Once you find a place, find out if it is a "hobby" gym or if it is a hardcore fighting center. One of the best ways is to ask if they have an active fight team. If so, ask one of the coaches how many active fighters train at the gym and inquire about their individual fight records. You can also ask how many titles the team holds to further gauge the caliber of the athletes training at that center. Remember, convenience is not always best. You may have to travel and pay premium fees to find a quality gym that meets all your training needs.

FINDING A LOCAL MMA LEAGUE

One of the next things you'll need to do is research the MMA events in your area. If you've joined an MMA program and are still unfamiliar with any local events, the best way is simply to ask the fighters at your training center. If you haven't found or signed on to a program yet, be sure to ask the fighters you do talk to about which organization they are affiliated with or what promotions are active locally. Once you are plugged into the local MMA scene, it can be pretty easy to find out where local shows are happening.

Another route is to contact your state athletic commission and inquire about what MMA organizations are licensed within your state. At the time of this writing, this won't apply to every state because some states don't currently regulate or allow MMA promotions. The majority of states, however, do support MMA, and you will probably be able to get the information you need by contacting the commissioners on your state board. These individuals can usually point you in the right direction for organizations near your area and even supply you with the promoter's contact information.

CHECKING OUT THE LOCAL MMA EVENTS

When you figure out when and where the local promotions are, it is time to take a field trip. If you've never seen an MMA event up close it can be an incredible experience. As you watch the event, keep an eye out for how the event seems to run and the competence of the officials, especially the referee.

If you are interested in being a fighter, ask to talk to the promoter or the president of the organization. Often the best way to get your foot in the door is to offer to volunteer at the promoter's next event. Organizers are notoriously short staffed, and having an extra helping hand can be a blessing. This approach can also get you behind the scenes where you'll have a chance to evaluate the event in a different way.

If you are considering fighting and your state regulates MMA, ask around and find the state athletic commission representative at the event. For your own protection, ask that person some questions to ensure the event is well run and detailed attention is paid to each fighter's safety. Chat with the referee and the trainers in a fighter's corner to get a feel for their perspectives on the quality of the promotion. Remember, if you are going to step inside a cage and square off against an opponent, it is in your best interest to make sure everything is on the up and up.

ASKING FOR A MATCH

Once you've attended a couple of events by the same promoter, it's time to talk to the matchmaker. This is the individual that sets up the matches between fighters. Ideally, the matchmaker is looking to create an exciting match between two fighters of the same caliber. Essentially, they should match you up with someone of the same experience level. For your first fight, this means that the matchmaker will be looking for another fighter in your weight class with no more than two fights under his belt.

This approach ensures that you don't get mismatched against a fighter who has an undefeated 5-0 record. Ideally, this would never happen, but unfortunately there are some shady promoters out there. If you are approached to take this type of fight, you should definitely decline. By pitting you against an experienced veteran for your first match, the promoter/matchmaker is just setting you up to be a highlight reel and advance his star fighter's record.

Amateur fights have a lot less lead-in time than professional matches, so it's a good idea to have been training for several months before asking the matchmaker to put you on a fight card. Often, amateur fighters are only given a few weeks notice before an event. Sometimes a fighter will have to drop out just before the event due to injury, sending the matchmaker scrambling to find a last-minute replacement. If you are a fighter on standby, the notice can be as short as forty-eight hours in these cases. Remember, you are never under any obligation to accept, so if you aren't ready, tell the coordinator you'll wait for the next event.

PREPARING FOR THE FIGHT

Once you've accepted an invitation to be on a fight card, it is time to really bear down on your training. Make sure you are developing your physical stamina, eating right, and refining your techniques. Your coaches and sparring partners should help keep you focused during your pre-fight training and help push you to your limits. Make sure you train hard, but stay smart to avoid injuries.

Ask your team to help you find out more about your opponent. Sometimes, you might be able to search your opponent's name on the Internet and find video clips of his fights. This research is exactly what the pros do, and if you can locate some footage on your opponent, it helps you and your team come up with a game plan.

It is also a great idea to utilize the ideas presented at the end of the last chapter and practice cutting weight and then doing a mock fight with one of your training partners. Simulating the entire day of the fight is invaluable and something that will really boost your confidence. When you actually step into the cage for real, this rehearsal will help eliminate fear of the unknown and allow you to feel comfortable because you've already experienced a similar situation in training.

When the week of the fight arrives, most combat athletes choose to rest up and recoup their strength from the intensive training they've just completed. It is a chance to focus their minds while they do some very light training and cut the final few pounds to make weight. If you follow the advice in the previous chapter, you'll be well rested and energized for your match.

THE DAY OF THE FIGHT

On the day of the fight, a lot of things are going to be going through your head. As strange as it may sound, making a checklist beforehand can really be helpful. Make sure that you check all your gear before packing. It can save you from the embarrassment of forgetting your gloves, groin protection, fight shorts, or mouthpiece. Trust us, we've been there when a fighter has forgotten an important piece of equipment. Having to borrow someone else's sweaty and bloody fight shorts is something you definitely want to avoid.

Although it's not something you'll probably want to think about, make sure your training partners who will be in your corner bring a cutman kit. It should contain several pairs of sterile nitrile surgical gloves, scissors, adhesive tape, petroleum jelly, gauze pads, and hand sanitizer. It is also wise to include clean towels, non-prescription pain medication for after the fight, and definitely ice packs or ziplock bags for improvised icepacks.

You can also purchase an enswell, a small piece of metal that looks like an iron. It is chilled in ice and used to reduce swelling. An enswell is used just like ice and is applied with moderate pressure directly to an injury. Make sure your corner knows not to press too hard or try to "iron out" any swelling, as this will only exacerbate the bruise and make things worse.

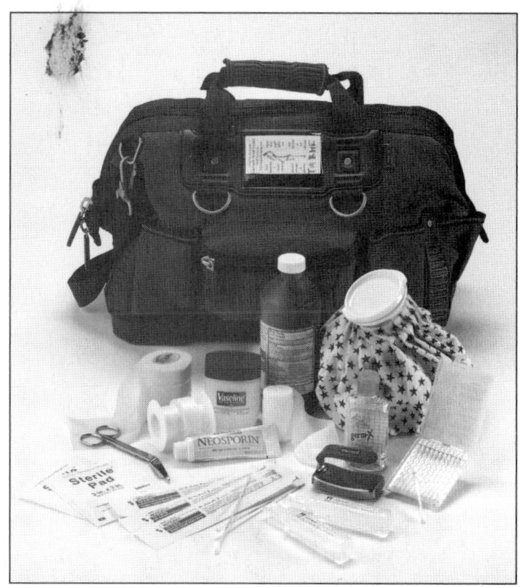

A standard cutman kit.

If your corner man is also serving as a cutman, we recommend also purchasing some hemostatic sponges. These gauze-like sponges have a chemical agent in the material that controls bleeding by speeding up the clotting process of the blood. Fighters sometimes receive cuts or lacerations on their face or head, and having a person in your corner who knows how to control bleeding could help you win a fight.

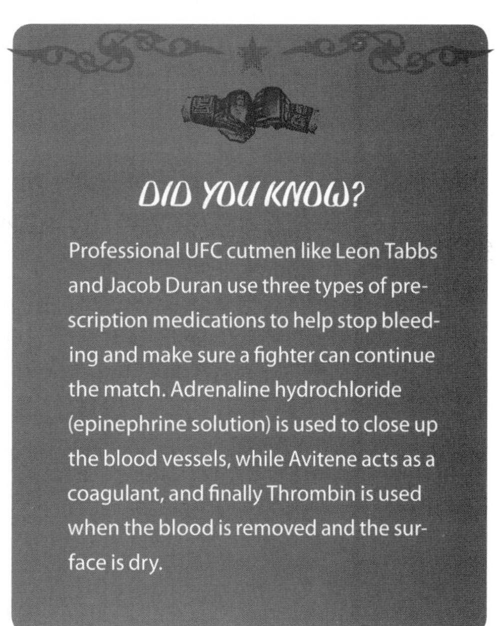
DID YOU KNOW?

Professional UFC cutmen like Leon Tabbs and Jacob Duran use three types of prescription medications to help stop bleeding and make sure a fighter can continue the match. Adrenaline hydrochloride (epinephrine solution) is used to close up the blood vessels, while Avitene acts as a coagulant, and finally Thrombin is used when the blood is removed and the surface is dry.

All right, fight gear accounted for? Check. Cutman kit? Check. Theme song music? Oh, yeah, definitely don't forget this critical item. Burn your entrance song on a CD to hand to the sound mixer when you arrive at the event. Make sure to find out where you fall in the lineup and put your full name on the label. If you've gotten this far, you might as well have your favorite song blaring as you walk to the cage.

Once you arrive, make sure you check in with the appropriate staff and find out where the staging or prep room is located. As the event gets under way, it is time to start getting ready for your match. Make sure you take plenty of time to stretch and do some light warm-up exercises. Even though you are probably pumped up, resist the urge to expend a lot of your energy hitting the pads. A lot of first-time fighters get geared up and then wail away at the pads for half an hour and waste their energy.

Your goal is to be stretched out, warmed up, and calm. Focus on some deep breathing exercises and try to keep your heart rate as normal as possible. If you ramp up too soon, your adrenaline will be tapering off by the time of your fight and you'll feel sluggish. You can also eat an energy bar, which will help to calm your body and give you some extra power for the match.

Typically the event coordinator will let you know when you have about fifteen to thirty minutes before your fight. Every fighter prepares differently in the final minutes. Some put on headphones with music that pumps them up while others put on music that calms them down. There is no right way or wrong way to be ready to fight. Just go with what feels natural for you because you know your body and mind best.

THE EXPERIENCE OF FIGHTING: REAL FIGHTERS TALK

At this point, we're going to pass the mike to some amateur fighters and let them share their tips. These athletes have been there, fought, and have the bad-ass t-shirt to go along with it. Their insights speak volumes about what it is actually like to compete in MMA. It is wisdom well worth paying attention to because it comes from experience.

What should a new fighter expect mentally, physically, and emotionally before his match?

I would spend the day trying to make yourself very confident, but at the same time you will have hundreds of doubts running through your mind. You should be training ten times harder then you think the actual fight is going to be. Before the fight, you are pretty tensed up. Your coaches should try to work on you and loosen you up. You are also overwhelmed with emotions. It is like being a kid, excited and waiting, before Christmas morning.

—Kevin Carroll, amateur record 3-1, Team Tarhe, thirty-one years old

You're always going to be nervous and have pre-fight jitters. You have a lot going through your mind with strategy and different techniques.

If you haven't prepared mentally, physically, and emotionally, you can get drained really quickly.

—Roger Bowling, pro record 5-0, Team Vision, MMA Big Show Professional Welterweight Champion, twenty-six years old

How do you overcome the fear factor of fighting?

I just told myself that I had trained long enough and hard enough that I was ready for anything. Everyone is going to be nervous before a fight. You never know how it is going to go. Over time, I have been able to put myself in a warrior mind-set before I get in the cage.

—Chris Bennett, amateur record 9-1, Team G-Force, MMA Big Show Amateur Lightweight Champion, nineteen years old

Well, it isn't necessarily a fear. The only way I would be scared and have fear is if I am not prepared for a fight. For example, if I did not do enough cardio or training in a certain aspect of the sport. I am always happy when I get into the cage. It is a relief. I train hard for the three to four months or whatever time it takes to train for a fight. I am not scared—I'm excited.

—Roger Bowling

How do you get in the zone to fight?

My teammates help pump me up, and they keep me focused. You just gotta know you're going to WIN and you have to know 100 percent. You've got to believe that you trained longer and harder than your competition.

—Chris Cummins, amateur record 1-0, Team Tarhe, twenty-six years old

It all starts the day before while you are cutting weight. It starts to show your dedication. You start getting ready then for the fight mentally. Make sure you stay around your coaches. They remind me why I am there, and what I have trained so hard for. The last few hours before the fight you are around the other fighters and feeling the energy. You calm your mind and focus on your game plan for the fight.

—Kevin Carroll

What I like to do is surround myself with good, positive people. Surround myself with people that help me feel good. My coaches and training partners help me get into the zone. I joke around and have fun with them. I don't even think about it before the fight. I just think of how many people want to do this and how I get to do what I love. There are so many people that want to be in the position I am in; I just take it in and enjoy the experience.

—Roger Bowling

How do you deal with the inevitable adrenaline rush?

Oh man, that is a good question. You can't really deal with it until after the first round. Listen to your coaches and concentrate on your game plan. My fights have only gone past the first round once. There is no controlling the adrenaline at the beginning. If you are not nervous and you don't feel that rush, then I think you're way too cocky. If you get too cocky, you get caught with something.

—Kevin Carroll

I take deep breaths before the fight starts. Usually the fighter will get the rush while entering the cage. So when you get in, you should take three to five deep breaths to calm down and try not to get overexcited when you start the fight.

—Chris Bennett

How do you stay calm?

Everyone is different. It is easy to get caught up in the experience. Breathing techniques help me get ready and control my heart rate. Deep breaths in and slow breaths out. For me, it is focusing more on my breathing.

—Roger Bowling

Through my training and dedication, I already know what to expect. I also keep my mind on the match and how I plan to put on a good fight for the fans.

—Ashley Brown, amateur record 0-1, Team Tarhe, twenty-five years old

What do you do whenever you step into the cage?

Take a deep breath to slow my heart rate. It's a fight, not a race. So I want to be calm and focus on what I'm trained to do and not get in a rush and lose my focus.

—Chris Cummins

Once I'm there, I like to meditate on what I plan on doing and tell myself "this is my fight." Doing this keeps me focused.

—Ashley Brown

When I first get into the cage, I like to circle around the cage and slap hands with my opponent to show respect. Then I see if they want to touch gloves before the fight. I always like to look for someone in the crowd that I know. It is usually my mom. I smile at her, and it makes me feel better. Whenever I am in the cage and they announce my name, I always get cold chills.

—Roger Bowling

As I walk into the cage, I stop and pray and then I bow to show respect. I stretch and look at the other guy with the intensity that I am about to bring on him. I look at him and nothing else. Most other guys don't want to look at their opponent. I don't take my eyes off him.

—Kevin Carroll

What is it like to actually fight in MMA?

It is an exhilarating feeling. You just feel on top of the world. You are center stage. Your heart will be tested. You have to have the heart to be in this sport. It's not for everyone. Win or lose, you need to know you wanted to be there and give your best.

—Chris Bennett

There is nothing like it! It is overwhelming, exciting, and intense. It is like stepping into a world that no one else can. It is a feeling of intense pride and glory. Win or lose, you have a chance to be there and do something you love and are passionate about.

—Kevin Carroll

It is almost unexplainable. To me, there are different stages of the fight. At first it is so fast paced. Then I settle down and settle into the fight. It is exciting, fun, and nerve-wracking all at the same time. It is a ball of mixed emotions. Every minute it is a different emotion in the cage.

—Roger Bowling

Does the crowd affect you during the fight?

Definitely. This is especially true if I am fighting in front of a hometown crowd. I feed off their energy. But remember, you don't want to feed off it too much because it will mess with your emotions and cause you to tire out.

—Roger Bowling

No, I don't really notice the crowd much once the fight starts. Coming out of your zone once the fight is over, you become more aware of the audience.

—Chris Bennett

What should a new fighter expect during the actual fight?

A huge adrenaline dump and sometimes your mind sort of locks up and goes into survival mode. I expected the worst, knowing that I was going to take some shots. You have to forget the pain, push through it, and remember that it is mind over matter.

—Chris Cummins

I'm thinking about how to counter my opponent and using my aggression against him. The emotions range from being pumped up to getting worn down.

—Ashley Brown

Expect to be overwhelmed with emotion. You have to struggle with the ups and downs of the rushes and learn how to use them to your advantage. Normally, when you get hit you don't really feel a lot. If your adrenaline has worn off, however, even the lightest punches will affect your body tremendously.

—Roger Bowling

Be ready to get hit. This is a sport just like any other. You know what to expect, so be prepared. Tell yourself between each round that you trained for this, so you're going to finish strong. But don't be a hero either. If you get caught in a submission and you know you're not getting out, don't let it break. Just take the loss and train harder next time.

—Chris Bennett

What about after the fight? What should a new fighter expect to feel mentally, physically, and emotionally?

Physically, your body will be bruised a bit and tense in certain places. To me, it is really no more damage that I get during training. The next couple nights, win or lose, you will be thinking about your performance. I don't show any emotions for a couple of days, then they hit me all at once. When you win, it is one of the best gifts and best highs you can ever have. When you lose, you'll be going over in your mind about what you did or didn't do and generally being hard on yourself. I still think about my last fight and get all tensed up thinking what I should have done. Finally, you take those emotions, good or band, turn it into determination and drive to prepare yourself for the next fight.

—Kevin Carroll

I get real emotional. All the hard training pays off and it feels like such a weight lifted off your shoulders. You'll want to celebrate with your family, friends, and team.

—Roger Bowling

Adrenaline will block the pain for a while and then you will find tenderness in spots you never knew you had. No matter what, you'll feel a sense of pride. Win or lose … unbridled pride.

—Chris Cummins

Some people say that MMA is just about beating people up. Having been there, what do you think?

MMA is a sport. It is no different from any other athletic event. I will hug my opponents before and after the fight. Yes, we beat each other up, but it is in a competitive way and not a hateful way. We are some of the hardest training guys around.

—Chris Bennett

This sport is all about testing myself as an athlete. It is much different than a street fight. After the weeks of training and knowing that I was physically and mentally able to do this, I look forward to going in there and putting on a show for the crowd and hearing them get into it.

—Ashley Brown

It is definitely about testing yourself as an athlete and the more time and effort you put into it, the better you become as a person. I think it is great especially for troubled kids. They won't want to beat people up out on the street once they get into the sport. When you put in all the time and effort, you definitely want to test your skills against another athlete.

—Roger Bowling

What is the most rewarding part of MMA for you?

Winning after a hard camp. When you know that you trained as hard as you could and you are completely ready for that fight and then you win, it is a great feeling. I also help to train youth in jiu-jitsu, so seeing them excel is a great feeling. It gives me the drive to train harder because they look up to me.

—Chris Bennett

> Having people congratulate me and tell me that I'm out there doing what they don't have the balls to do. I love knowing what I'm doing inspires people to do better in their own lives.
>
> —Ashley Brown

> Pride! Knowing you've done something that a thousand people want to do but only a handful actually have the will and the guts to do.
>
> —Chris Cummins

> The most rewarding part is bettering myself as a well-rounded person. It helps me so much to be on a fight team with very humble and great fighters who work with kids. To be able to be a hero—someone the kids in the community can look up to. To show the kids that there is something better to do than get into trouble.
>
> —Kevin Carroll

ADDITIONAL RESOURCES

This book was created to help educate people about MMA and introduce the sport to a new audience. We have endeavored to walk you through the numerous factors that go into training an MMA athlete, and we're honored that you've been a part of the journey. If you have already successfully competed in numerous amateur bouts and want to take your training to the next level, we have included some additional resources below.

Fight Promotion Websites

- UFC: www.ufc.com
- WEC: www.wec.tv
- Strikeforce: www.strikeforce.com
- KOTC: www.kingofthecage.com
- MMA Big Show: www.mmabigshow.com

Fan Websites

- MMA Weekly: www.mmaweekly.com
- Sherdog: www.sherdog.com
- MMA Fighting: www.mmafighting.com
- Full Contact Fighter: www.fcfighter.com

- Yahoo! Sports: http://sports.yahoo.com/mma
- Mixed Martial Arts: www.mixedmartialarts.com
- MMA Universe: www.mmauniverse.com

PROFESSIONAL MMA TRAINING CAMPS

These are some of the top camps in North America. Attending any one of them will help advance your skills by putting you alongside some of the best coaches and fighters in the world.

- American Kickboxing Academy: www.akakickbox.com
- American Top Team: www.americantopteam.com
- Extreme Couture: www.xtremecouture.tv
- Greg Jackson's Mixed Martial Arts: www.jacksonsmma.com
- Miletich Fighting Systems: www.mfselite.com
- Minnesota Martial Arts Academy: www.mmaacombatzone.com
- Team Sityodtong: www.sityodtong.com

INDEX ★★★

Acknowledgments

CHAD SEIBERT. Through the course of our lives there are many influences that shape the people we become. I feel very fortunate to have had so many positive individuals who have taken the time to share their wisdom and experience in an effort to help me grow. Though I know I won't be able to thank everyone, the acknowledgments that follow represent my best attempt to express my gratitude to those who have helped shaped this book.

First and foremost, to my family, Mom, Dad, and L: I love you and owe you everything.

This book simply wouldn't exist without the insight and guidance of the very best editor in the publishing business, Kelly Nickell. Her dedication to this project never wavered, and her incredible expertise, seemingly endless knowledge of writing, and spectacular advice were invaluable. Any success this book receives is due in large part to her vision and amazing talents. When it comes to the art of communication, Kelly is one of the leading experts in the field and I feel honored to have had someone of her caliber directing this book. In my humble opinion, she is one of the most talented individuals I've ever met. Thank you for being a beacon of light in my life.

Thanks to all of those at the F+W team who believed in this project and helped make it a reality. I'm indebted to Terri Woesner for her brilliant design work and for her patience and understanding. Terri is simply amazing and an extraordinarily gifted designer. Her artistic talents will be one of the reasons that readers will truly be able to enjoy this book. Special thanks also go to Ric Delantoni, our incredible photographer, without whom this book would be half empty! Ric's patience, ideas, and expertise helped the photo shoot go smoother than I could have ever anticipated. Thank you both for your extra effort and dedication!

My cousins Ryan Shaw and Joel Seibert deserve special recognition for their willingness to adjust their schedules and lend their incredible wealth of martial arts expertise to this book. Thank you from the bottom of my heart for your help with our photo shoot. It meant more than you can imagine. Thank you for being the warriors who help protect our family, as well as the families of others.

Thank you to Chris Cummins, Kevin Carroll, and Eric Covey for driving through all the snow to be there for the photo shoot. You guys were awesome, and your dedication was greatly appreciated!

I would have never been able to write this book if it weren't for my martial arts mentors. Jason Patten, my original instructor, started me on my martial arts path when I was only fifteen and literally changed my life. His mentorship has been such a positive influence, and I feel truly blessed to have been his student. Gary Rooks, a friend of Mr. Patten's, helped take my martial arts skills to new levels. A world-renowned instructor, Mr. Rooks has been a huge mentor and cherished friend for the better part of my life. Mr. Rooks has introduced me to countless incredible martial artists, and I am truly honored to call him my teacher. Lastly, I would like to thank a more recent mentor in the martial arts field, Emmanuel Manolakakis. Quite simply, he is one of the most amazing instructors I've ever had the privilege of knowing. Emmanuel's calm demeanor, martial finesse, and profound wisdom are a constant source of inspiration in my life. (Deep bow to all my teachers.)

Of course, I would be remiss if I didn't say thank you to a few more of the numerous teachers, training partners, colleagues, and friends that have been a part of my martial art journey: Wally Jay, George Dillman, Leon Jay, Jim Corn, Evan Pantazi, Mark Kline, Mikhail Ryabko, Vladimir Vasiliev, Sonny Puzikas, Fred Mastison, Asa Seeley, Shawn Steiner, Gary Boaz, Evin Hunt, Jim Greenwood, Alejandro Del Toro, Matt Tracey, Tony Saad, Steve Osha, Matt McCormick, Aaron Coover, Bill Parravano, Jonah Lucas, and, of course, Danny Plyler.

A final thanks to Mr. Patten for letting us use his mats for the photo shoot, and to Mr. Rooks for providing some of the pads and equipment.

Lastly, I would like to thank all of the warriors out there who serve and protect others. Your strength, sacrifice, and valor will never be forgotten.

DANNY PLYLER. Chad Seibert, co-author, friend, and training partner: You were the reason this book happened! Thank you!

Gary Rooks, master, mentor, friend: There are few people in history with your knowledge and skill of the combat arts. I am blessed to be your student.

Gatewood Galbraith, friend and mentor: You have been a major influence in my success. Keep up the fight! "Last Free Man in America!"

Gene Dale and Sue Moore, my in-laws: I could not have picked better in-laws! Thank you for your support!

Jason Appleton, owner of MMA BigShow, LLC, and friend: You gave me my first shot at the "Cage." Now look where it has gone!

Kevin Carroll, friend, student, and Team Tarhe coach: Thank you for your dedication!

Levi Adams, friend and Team Tarhe coach: The hours on the mat with you were priceless! Thank you.

Chris Cummins, friend and Team Tarhe fighter: You have a huge future!

Eric Covey, friend and student: You were one of my first students! Thanks for all the years of dedication!

Josh Souder, jiu-jitsu coach and friend: You took our ground game to another level!

Chris Bennett: You are a beast! I am a lucky man to be the first to put you in an MMA book!

Roger Bowling: You are a role model for the MMA! Thanks for stepping up!

About the Authors

CHAD SEIBERT

Chad Seibert has been training in the Martial Arts since 1996 and holds a 4th degree black belt in RyuKyu Kempo and is a senior instructor under United States Martial Arts Hall of Fame inductee Grandmaster Gary Rooks. Chad also holds a 2nd degree black belt in Maududo and has trained extensively in Kyusho since 1997, studying with some of the world's top martial artists. In 2004, he also began studying the Russian martial art of Systema, and has trained in tactical shooting. He gives seminars throughout the United States and offers private training and coaching sessions in Cincinnati, Ohio.

DANNY PLYLER

Known as the "Hyper Bald Guy," Danny Plyler is a former United States Marine and founder of the Tarhe Martial Arts Institute. A seasoned Instructor, Danny holds a black belt in Okinawan RyuKyu Kempo under United States Martial Arts Hall of Fame inductee Grandmaster Gary Rooks. With a background in wrestling and security work, Danny excels as a personal-training coach helping others to reach their martial arts and fitness goals. He owns and operates his school in Kentucky, where he offers group classes and private instruction in Okinawan Karate, mixed martial arts, and intensive cardio and strength fitness conditioning. Featured in numerous newspaper articles and TV news spotlights, he is a local hero in his community. His website is www.hyperbaldguy.com.

About the Fighters

CHRIS CUMMINS: Chris has participated in amateur MMA matches and trains under the direction of Danny Plyler and Kevin Carroll.

KEVIN CARROLL: Kevin is a coach for Team Tarhe and has fought in numerous MMA matches. He instructs the MMA training program at Danny Plyler's school, the Tarhe Martial Arts Institute.

RYAN SHAW: Ryan started wrestling at the age of ten and continued through high school. His martial art training includes Jeet Kune Do, Bando, and submission grappling.

ERIC COVEY: Eric is one of Danny's first students and an assistant instructor at the Tarhe Martial Arts Institute.

JOEL SEIBERT: Joel has been involved in martial arts for most of his life. He has trained in Muay Thai Kickboxing, Jeet Kune Do, and currently holds a purple belt in Brazilian Jiu-Jitsu under Master Jean Jacques Machado.